Volume 14

THE CONTRIBUTIONS OF ALEXANDER HAMILTON CHURCH TO ACCOUNTING AND MANAGEMENT

THE CONTRIBUTIONS OF ALEXANDER HAMILTON CHURCH TO ACCOUNTING AND MANAGEMENT

Edited by
RICHARD VANGERMEERSCH

Routledge
Taylor & Francis Group

LONDON AND NEW YORK

First published in 1986 by Garland Publishing, Inc.

This edition first published in 2021
by Routledge
2 Park Square, Milton Park, Abingdon, Oxon OX14 4RN

and by Routledge
52 Vanderbilt Avenue, New York, NY 10017

Routledge is an imprint of the Taylor & Francis Group, an informa business

British Library Cataloguing in Publication Data
A catalogue record for this book is available from the British Library

ISBN: 978-0-367-33564-9 (Set)
ISBN: 978-1-00-304636-3 (Set) (ebk)
ISBN: 978-0-367-52110-3 (Volume 14) (hbk)
ISBN: 978-0-367-52111-0 (Volume 14) (pbk)
ISBN: 978-1-00-305658-4 (Volume 14) (ebk)

Publisher's Note
The publisher has gone to great lengths to ensure the quality of this reprint but
points out that some imperfections in the original copies may be apparent.

Disclaimer
The publisher has made every effort to trace copyright holders and would welcome
correspondence from those they have been unable to trace.

THE CONTRIBUTIONS OF ALEXANDER HAMILTON CHURCH TO ACCOUNTING AND MANAGEMENT

Richard Vangermeersch, editor

Garland Publishing, Inc.
New York and London
1986

For a complete list of Garland's publications in accounting,
please see the final pages of this volume.

Library of Congress Cataloging-in-Publication Data

Church, A. Hamilton (Alexander Hamilton), 1866–
The contributions of Alexander Hamilton Church to
accounting and management.

(Accounting theory and practice through the years)
"List of publications, A. H. Church": p.
Includes index.
1. Accounting. 2. Cost accounting. 3. Industrial
management. I. Vangermeersch, Richard G. J. II. Title.
III. Series.
HF5635.C56 1986 657 86-9940
ISBN 0-8240-7873-X

Design by Bonnie Goldsmith

The volumes in this series are printed on acid-free, 250-year-life paper.

Printed in the United States of America

CONTENTS

Preface

Introduction

A. H. Church, "The Meaning of Commercial Organisation,"   3
The Engineering Magazine, December 1900.

A. H. Church, "British Industrial Welfare: The Erring Policy   12
of the British Workingman," *Cassier's Magazine*, March 1901.

A. H. Church, "The Meaning of Scientific Management,"   17
The Engineering Magazine, April 1911.

A. H. Church, "Intensive Production and the Foreman,"   22
American Machinist, May 4, 1911.

A. H. Church, "Distribution of the Expense Burden,"   25
American Machinist, May 25, 1911.

A. H. Church, "Has 'Scientific Management' Science?"   28
American Machinist, July 20, 1911.

J. Edtterson, "Direct and Indirect Costs," *American Machinist*,   33
March 7, 1912.

A. H. Church, "Direct and Indirect Costs," *American*   35
Machinist, May 9, 1912.

A. H. Church and L. P. Alford, "The Principles of   37
Management," *American Machinist*, May 30, 1912.

Dexter S. Kimball, "The 'Principles of Management,'"   43
American Machinist, June 13, 1912.

John Calder, "The 'Principles of Management,'"   43
American Machinist, June 13, 1912.

A. H. Church, "Comments," *Transactions of the American Society of Mechanical Engineers, 1912*, New York: American Society of Mechanical Engineers, 1913. 46

Carl G. Barth, "Comments," *Transactions of the American Society of Mechanical Engineering, 1912*, New York: American Society of Mechanical Engineers, 1913. 51

Editor, "The Treatment of Interest on Manufacturing Investment," *The Journal of Accountancy*, April 1913. 55

William Morse Cole, "Interest on Investment in Equipment," *The Journal of Accountancy*, April 1913. 56

A. H. Church, "On the Inclusion of Interest in Manufacturing Costs," *The Journal of Accountancy*, April 1913. 60

W. B. Richards, "Interest Not a Charge Against Costs," *The Journal of Accountancy*, April 1913. 64

J. E. Sterrett, "Interest Not a Part of the Cost of Production," *The Journal of Accountancy*, April 1913. 65

A. H. Church, "Premium, Piece Work, and the Expense Burden," *The Engineering Magazine*, October 1913. 69

A. H. Church, "Bonus Systems and the Expense Burden," *The Engineering Magazine*, November 1913. 81

A. H. Church, "The Scientific Basis of Manufacturing Management," *Efficiency Society Journal*, February 1914. 92

A. H. Church, "The Evolution of Design," *American Machinist*, June 10, 1915. 100

A. H. Church, "Machine Design and the Design of Systems," *American Machinist*, July 8, 1915. 101

H. L. Gantt, "The Relation Between Production and Costs," *American Machinist*, June 17, 1915. 103

A. H. Church, "Mr. Gantt's Theory of the Expense Burden," *American Machinist*, July 29, 1915. 107

H. L. Gantt, "Relation Between Production and Cost," *American Machinist*, August 26, 1915. 109

A. H. Church, "Relation Between Production and Cost,"   111
American Machinist, September 2, 1915.

William E. M. McHenry, "Relation Between Production and   112
Cost," *American Machinist*, September 23, 1915.

H. L. Gantt, "Relation Between Production and Cost,"   113
American Machinist, October 21, 1915.

A. H. Church, "What Is a Cost System?" *American Machinist*,   115
September 9, 1915.

A. H. Church, "What a Foreman Should Know About   119
Costs," *American Machinist*, September 23, 1915.

A. H. Church, "What the Superintendent Should Know,"   123
American Machinist, October 14, 1915.

A. H. Church, "What the Executive Wants to Know About   127
Costs," *American Machinist*, October 28, 1915.

A. H. Church, "Industrial Management," *Transactions of the*   132
International Engineering Congress, Paper 238, San Francisco,
1915.

A. H. Church, "The Future of Industry," *The Unpopular*   159
Review, June 1917.

A. H. Church, "Overhead: The Cost of Production Prepared-   182
ness," *Factory and Industrial Management*, January 1931.

PREFACE

My interest in A. H. Church began when I was involved in a project to redesign a cost accounting system for a highly capital-intensive firm and discovered Church's concept of the "machine-hour rate" method. An article discussing this was published in *Management Accounting* in July 1983 and was awarded the NAA Certificate of Merit. After presenting a paper on Church at the 1983 American Accounting Association meetings, which was commented on by Robert Kaplan in his plenary session address at the 1983 meetings and in his 1984 article "The Evolution of Management Accounting," I continued my research on Church. One aspect of this research dealt with an innovative accounting flowchart prepared by Hans Renold in apparent collaboration with Church that was used to illustrate the redesign of cost accounts for the robotics age at Robots 9, a conference in Detroit in June 1985. I believe that Church has much to say about accounting and management for today and the future and hope that this anthology spurs the reader to review more of Church's work.

INTRODUCTION

Alexander Hamilton Church was a renowned expert in the fields of cost accounting and management.[1] He introduced the "machine-hour rate" method,[2] the production-center concept,[3] the "regulative principles of management" (with L. P. Alford),[4] and distribution cost-analysis.[5] Church was selected as one of the pioneers of management by Urwick, who said that his contribution to management "was as great as or greater than that of many whose names are famous in the movement."[6]

Church was born on October 11, 1866,[7] near London of American parentage.[8] All we know about his early history was that he had a liberal education, after which he worked for the National Telephone Company.[9] He was then employed as either an electrical engineer[10] or a technical expert and works manager[11] for an electrical manufacturing business, where he was an associate of J. Slater Lewis for a few years.[12] (Lewis was another pioneer of management chosen by Urwick.[13]) Church then went to B. & S. Massey in Manchester, England, from 1898 to 1900[14] and then to Hans Renold Ltd. for three[15] or five[16] years. After this, he became European editor[17] or manager[18] of *The Engineering Magazine*, which had its main office in New York and was founded by John R. Dunlap.[19] Church went to the United States in 1909.[20] Until the early 1920s, he was, apparently, self-employed as a consulting industrial engineer,[21] except for short periods with C. H. Scovell and Co. in 1911[22] and Patterson, Teele, and Dennis in 1913.[23] From the early 1920s to his death in 1936, he had a long-standing relationship with the Mount Hope Finishing Company of North Dighton, Massachusetts.[24]

Church was a prolific writer who wrote mainly on the areas of cost accounting and management, but also published papers on business and society and industrial engineering. A list of his published work is presented chronologically at the end of this Introduction. If a reference to the publication is cited elsewhere, the source is noted, and each work is classified under accounting, management, business and society or industrial engineering.

This collection includes primarily articles written by Church not reprinted in his books. For instance, the series of articles written in 1901 and 1909 were published in the 1908 and 1910 books and are not included in this collection. However, since the 1913 articles in industrial engineering were reprinted as awkwardly placed appendices to the 1914 book, they are reprinted here. For this reason, the four-part series on reporting from the *American Machinist*, which was reprinted as the third part of Church's 1917 book, are also included. This anthology contains some related work by Cole, Richards, and Sterrett on the inclusion of interest as a manufacturing cost; the exchanges with Gantt and support by McHenry; an article written by Edtterson on which Church commented; the comments by Barth, which included a reference to Church; and two reviews of Church and Alford's 1912 article.

This collection demonstrates the breadth of Church's work and proves him a holistic writer. Church himself never put his ideas together even though there were central themes in his writings, as evidenced by the following brief review of each of the selections in this volume.

"The Meaning of Commercial Organisation" (1900) identified Church as an associate of J. Slater Lewis. The article was, most likely, a continuation of a series of articles written by Lewis, who was quite ill at the time[25] and died shortly thereafter in July of 1901.[26] Church stressed that a new world had been entered and that coordination between independent operations was needed. He considered administrative control to be the key, with accounting included as an important factor. Prime cost was not the only cost with which to be concerned: there were also work expenses and general establishment expenses. He used an interesting analogy of the master's eye and brain for the collection of necessary detail in this more complex world. Church demanded monthly statements and amount of profit on every order.

"British Industrial Welfare" (1901) was concerned with the declining status of British production in comparison to that of the United States and Germany. Church was concerned that British workers were not being informed about management concerns. Church expressed a recurrent theme that low wages with good productivity is less desirable than high wages with high productivity. He was worried about a fear of new machinery by the workers.

"The Meaning of Scientific Management" (1911) was a continuation of Church's attacks on what had become known as "scientific management." Church was concerned with the claim that "scientific management" was going to settle magically the warring claims of capital and labor. He here presented his first version of principles of management. His first principle was the planning of industrial activity from a consideration of its simplest units; the second was the comparison of actual results with the forecasted results. Church felt this quest for accuracy would lead to a larger surplus to distribute to capital and labor and, therefore, decrease labor's attraction to socialism, which Church feared. He also brought into this article his notion of the machine-hour rate method. Church was quite optimistic about the evolution of the science of management.

"Intensive Production and the Foreman" (1911) showed Church's concern for the foreman in relationship to outside experts (systematizers) brought in to increase production. Church expressed a central theme, that evolutionary change was to be preferred to revolutionary methods. The foreman should be given a new role in the maintenance of a certain elasticity that would allow adaptation to the rigidities of planning. This article also illustrates Church's concern for the individual, another theme in his writings.

"Distribution of the Expense Burden" (1911) was presented as a paper at the convention of the National Machine Tool Builders Association. In it Church stressed his machine-hour rate method. Increased competition had made cost analysis quite important. He attacked the "jumbled" nature of allocating overhead on direct labor dollars. He argued that overhead was in reality a series of charges for factors of production and was the cost of capacity to produce. He also discussed his philosophy of idle time charges, which were to be charged via a supplementary rate to all jobs.

"Has 'Scientific Management' Science?" (1911) marked Church's shift of interest from accounting to management. In this article he began his attack on the claims of Frederick Taylor and his disciples that they had founded a science of management. Church felt that Taylor had done a fine job in rediscovering certain management mechanisms like time study, but these mechanisms were not a science of management. Since this article led to a "war" between Church and L. P. Alford on one side and Carl Barth and H. L. Gantt on the other, it is an important one.

"Direct and Indirect Costs" (1912) was written by J. Edtterson, and a comment on that article by Church showed that while the "direct costing" school had not yet evolved, Church's response would have been right on target as an attack on that school of thought in accounting.

"The Principles of Management" (1912), coauthored with L. P. Alford, is a classic in management and was chosen by Harwood F. Merrill for the American Management Association's *Classics in Management*.[27] Church and Alford here projected their three principles of management: (1) the systematic use of experience; (2) the economic control of effort; and (3) the promotion of personal effectiveness, in which they made use of the field of psychology. The authors stepped up their attack on Taylor, whose work was labeled a collection of axioms and arbitrary combination of specific mechanisms rather than a body of principles. The comments by Kimball and Calder were very favorable.

"Comments" (1912) by Church and by Barth were written for the 1912 discussion at the American Society of Mechanical Engineer's (ASME) Subcommittee on Administration, whose secretary was Alford.[28] The report of the subcommittee had endorsed the three principles of Church and Alford[29] and added a fourth one of transfer of skills.[30] Church continued his attack on the emphasis on mechanisms by the schools of scientific efficiency; he felt that the study of machines would yield the true line of progress and also stressed the importance of habit. Church was mildly rebuked by Barth in his comments to the subcommittee's report. Barth, also chosen as an early pioneer in *The Golden Book of Management*,[31] gave an interesting and a spirited defense for Frederick W. Taylor. The comments by Barth are illustrative of the split that Church and Alford must have had with the "Taylorites."

"The Treatment of Interest on Manufacturing Investment" (1913) was a debate on the inclusion of interest on manufacturing investment as a manufacturing cost. Cole argued for the affirmative in that interest computed on capital was crucial for determining prices, eliminating wastes, and determining what is to be undertaken. Church also argued for the affirmative and stressed that interest charges were related to various production factors. Richards and Sterrett argued the negative side and stressed that (1) taking depreciation results in a double charge if one computes interest; (2) it is important to keep interest as a financing cost; and (3) interest should not be charged to inventory. This debate does show that the current concerns about imputed interest are not new.

"Premium, Piece Work, and the Expense Burden" and "Bonus Systems and the Expense Burden" (1913) tried to make readers aware of how important burden was when a wage incentive system was chosen. Church gave excellent discussions of four such plans: (1) Piecework 100% premium; (2) Halsey 50% premium; (3) Halsey 33⅓% premium; and (4) Rowan premium. He was very fearful of the controversies inherent in the 100% piecework system. The Gantt Bonus Method and the Emerson Efficiency Method offered great hope as they were based on a minute survey of the maximum possible production, and they caused workers to strive for an attainable ideal.

"The Scientific Basis of Manufacturing Management" (1914) was a preview of Church's 1914 book. It was not to be a book of recipes or plans but of principles. He added the five organic manufacturing functions of design, equipment, control, comparison, and operations and retained his and Alford's three principles.

"The Evolution of Design" (1915) included a comment by Church that the sight of a collection of chemical apparatus may be just as intellectually appealing as the Sistine Madonna. "Machine Design and the Design of Systems" (1915) was much more rigorous and raised the key point that while a poorly designed machine and its effects can be easily spotted, a poorly designed control system is much more difficult to spot. One does not throw away a machine that is working until a new model is made and tested, but control systems are easy to tinker with.

"The Relation Between Production and Costs" (1915) was written by H. L. Gantt, who stated that idle time costs should not be charged to production. It led to the most colorful and interesting exchanges in this collection of readings. He made no reference to any of Church's works, which set Church ablaze. In "Mr. Gantt's Theory of the Expense Burden" Church reminded Gantt that he (Church) had already dealt with burden distribution and that Gantt had been careless in assuming that there were no other burden methods but the general burden approach. Gantt soon responded with "Relation Between Production and Cost," a vituperative attack on Church, who was, he claimed, preempted by Taylor on the machine-hour rate approach. Gantt also felt Church had slurred him as an engineer. It was Church's turn to rebut in a mild letter headed "Relation Between Production and Cost," where he wrote he had no knowledge of Taylor's machine-hour rate method. In this letter Church, for the first and last time, referred to himself as an accountant and also called cost accounting the field where accounting and engineering meet. William McHenry entered the fray and took Church's side, befitting one who called Church his "master." Gantt then ended this exchange by concluding that he and Church were not very far apart, although he had some harsh things to say about accountants. Since this exchange has apparently not been noted by other sources, these articles are important.

"What Is a Cost System?" (1915) was an overview, and a very thorough one, of a good reporting system. Church stressed reporting on management by exception. At the foreman level, that level would be the job. Church advocated quick reporting for immediate action. Spoiled work would be analyzed by workmen as the superintendent was more interested in the control of orders than in a specific job, the executive was most interested in the budget/actual comparison, and the proprietor was most interested in profits. "What a Foreman Should Know About Costs" gave illustrations of very specific forms for such control documents as the time card, the shop album, and the daily payroll report. "What the Superintendent Should Know" focused on forms of a broader nature, such as a finished-order stub, finished-order list, spoiled-work register, list of machine earnings, and burden schedule. "What the Executive Wants to Know About Costs" gave illustrations of even broader reports. There is no doubt that Church emphasized the need for accuracy, accuracy, and more accuracy with detail, detail, and more detail. Church was, therefore, concerned not only with broad managerial principles and organic functions but also with the most minute details.

"Industrial Management" (1915), presented at the International Engineering Congress in San Francisco during the Pan Pacific Exposition, was a synopsis of Church's 1914 book. Church summarized it as a movement away from rule-of-thumb management to quantitative treatment of management problems. He placed management into an evolutionary model and contrasted analysis and synthesis. Increased competition was again stressed as a key reason for more detailed accounting. This paper is a good preparation for reading Church's 1914 book.

"The Future of Industry" (1917), by far the most offbeat work done by Church, was published in *The Unpopular Review*, a "progressive" quarterly journal published by Henry Holt and Company. The themes of the science of management, of the importance of coordination, and of America as the chief hope for the future of the world were old refrains for Church, but his views on competition and cooperatives were surprising. Ultimately, Church was an optimist rather than an utopian. He was also a humanist with a global viewpoint.

"Overhead: The Cost of Production Preparedness" (1931) previewed Church's 1930 book on overhead. His ideas on overhead burden rates were consistent, and he introduced some very interesting figures to portray the effects of idle time. This article represents the last work published by Church and showed that he was still innovative and sharp in his mid sixties.

Since Church was an engineer, an accountant, an editor, a consultant in factory administration, a consulting engineer, and an industrial engineer, his writings would be expected to cover a wide area. In fact, they spanned the fields of accounting, management, business and society, and industrial engineering. While Church wrote many books, not one of them captured the essence of his work and his central themes. This anthology attempts to do just that.

NOTES

1. Lyndall Urwick, ed. Part One, and William B. Wolf, ed. Part Two, *The Golden Book of Management*, new expanded edition (New York: American Management Association, 1984), p. 13.

2. *Ibid.*

3. S. Paul Garner, *Evolution of Cost Accounting to 1925*, Accounting History Classic Series (University of Alabama, 1954, 1976), p. 249.

4. Urwick and Wolf, *op. cit.*, p. 114.

5. Garner, *op. cit.*, p. 142.

6. Urwick and Wolf, *op. cit.*, p. 115.

7. Urwick and Wolf, *op. cit.*, p. 116.

8. F. G. Colley, reviewer of *The Science and Practice of Management*, *The Journal of Accountancy*, December 1914, p. 484.

9. *Ibid.*

10. Urwick and Wolf, *op. cit.*, p. 116.

11. Colley, *op. cit.*, p. 484.

12. Urwick and Wolf, *op. cit.*, p. 116.

13. *Ibid.*, pp. 55–57.

14. *Ibid.*, p. 116.

15. Colley, *op. cit.*, p. 19.

16. Urwick and Wolf, *op. cit.*, p. 116.

17. Editor, *Management Engineering*, in an April 1922 note to Church's "Internal Transportation in a Large Textile Finishing Plant—I," p. 197.

18. Colley, *op. cit.*, pp. 484–485.

19. Editor, "Inspiring Growth of the New Science of Industrial Management," *Industrial Management: The Engineering Magazine*, November 1916, p. 148.

20. Editor, *Management Engineering*, *op. cit.*, p. 197.

21. A. Hamilton Church, "Industrial Management," *Transactions of the International Engineering Congress*, Paper 238 (San Francisco: Neal Publishing Company, 1916), p. 446.

22. A. Hamilton Church, "Intensive Production and the Foreman," *American Machinist*, May 4, 1911, p. 830.

23. A. Hamilton Church, "On the Inclusion of Interest in Manufacturing Costs," *The Journal of Accountancy*, April 1913, p. 236.

24. Urwick and Wolf, *op. cit.*, p. 117, and A. Hamilton Church, "Internal Transportation in a Large Textile Finishing Plant—I," *Management Engineering*, April 1922, p. 197.

25. J. Slater Lewis, "Works Management for Maximum Production," *Management Engineering*, Vol. 19, May 1900, p. 211.

26. Urwick and Wolf, *op. cit.*, p. 57.

27. Harwood F. Merrill, ed., *Classics in Management* (New York: American Management Association, 1960), p. 196.

28. Subcommittee on Administration, "The Present State of the Art of Industrial Management," *Transactions of The American Society of Mechanical Engineers, 1912* (New York: ASME, 1913), p. 1147.

29. *Ibid.*, p. 1142.

30. *Ibid.*

31. Urwick and Wolf, *op. cit.*, pp. 86–90.

LIST OF PUBLICATIONS BY A. H. CHURCH

1900 "The Meaning of Commercial Organisation," *The Engineering Magazine*, December, Vol. 20, pp. 391–398.
Source: Urwick and Wolf, *The Golden Book of Management* (1984)
MANAGEMENT

1901 "British Industrial Welfare: The Erring Policy of the British Workingman," *Cassier's Magazine*, March, Vol. 19, pp. 404–408.
Source: Urwick and Wolf
BUSINESS AND SOCIETY

1901 "The Proper Distribution of Establishment Charges," *The Engineering Magazine*, Vols. 21 and 22 (three articles in each volume).
Source: Urwick and Wolf
ACCOUNTING
(These articles were basically reprinted in Church's 1908 book and, hence, are not included in this collection of readings.)

1908 *The Proper Distribution of Expense Burden*, Works Management Library, London: *The Engineering Magazine*, 116 pages.
Source: *The Accountants' Index, 1920*
ACCOUNTING

1909 "Organization by Production Factors," *The Engineering Magazine*, Vol. 38 (in six parts).
Source: Urwick and Wolf

ACCOUNTING
(These articles were basically reprinted in Church's 1910 book and, hence, are not included in this collection of readings.)

1910   *Production Factors in Cost Accounting and Works Management*, Industrial Management Library, New York: The Engineering Magazine Company, 187 pages.
Source: *The Accountants' Index, 1920*
ACCOUNTING

1911   "The Meaning of Scientific Management," *The Engineering Magazine*, April, Vol. 41, pp. 97–101.
Source: Urwick and Wolf
MANAGEMENT

1911   "Intensive Production and the Foreman," *American Machinist*, May 4, Vol. 34, pp. 830–831.
Source: Urwick and Wolf
MANAGEMENT

1911   "Distribution of the Expense Burden," *American Machinist*, May 25, Vol. 34, pp. 991–992, 999.
Source: Urwick and Wolf
ACCOUNTING

1911   "Distributing Expense Burden," *The Iron Age*, June 1, pp. 1325–1326.
Source: *The Accountants' Index, 1920*.
ACCOUNTING
(This was basically the same article as the preceding item and, hence, is not included in this collection of readings.)

1911   "Has 'Scientific Management' Science?" *American Machinist*, July 20, Vol. 35, pp. 108–112.
Source: Urwick and Wolf
MANAGEMENT

1912   "Direct and Indirect Costs," *American Machinist*, May 9, Vol. 36, p. 763.
Source: not previously cited
ACCOUNTING

1912   "The Principles of Management," (with L. P. Alford), *American Machinist*, May 30, Vol. 36, pp. 857–861.

Source: Urwick and Wolf
MANAGEMENT

1912 *The Proper Distribution of Burden*, 2nd edition, New York: The Engineering Magazine Co., 144 pages.
Source: Urwick and Wolf
ACCOUNTING
(This was a word-for-word republication of the 1908 book; only the format was changed.)

1913 "Comments" on "The Present State of the Art of Industrial Management," Report of the Subcommittee on Administration, *Transactions of the American Society of Mechanical Engineers*, 1912, pp. 1156–1159.
Source: not previously cited
MANAGEMENT

1913 "Practical Principles of Rational Management," *The Engineering Magazine*, Vols. 44 and 45, (three parts in each volume).
Source: Urwick and Wolf
MANAGEMENT
(These articles were basically reprinted in Church's 1914 book.)

1913 "On the Inclusion of Interest in Manufacturing Costs," *The Journal of Accountancy*, April, pp. 236–240.
Source: *The Accountants' Index*, 1920
ACCOUNTING

1913 "Premium, Piece Work, and the Expense Burden," *The Engineering Magazine*, October, Vol. 46, pp. 7–18.
Source: Urwick and Wolf
INDUSTRIAL ENGINEERING

1913 "Bonus Systems and the Expense Burden," *The Engineering Magazine*, November, Vol. 46, pp. 207–216.
Source: Urwick and Wolf
INDUSTRIAL ENGINEERING

1914 *The Science and Practice of Management*, New York: The Engineering Magazine Co., 535 pages.
Source: Urwick and Wolf
MANAGEMENT

1914 "The Scientific Basis of Manufacturing Management," *Efficiency*

Society Journal, February, Vol. 3, pp. 8–15.
Source: Urwick and Wolf
MANAGEMENT

1914 "What are the Principles of Management?" *Efficiency Society Journal*, February, Vol. 3, pp. 16–18.
Source: Urwick and Wolf
MANAGEMENT
(This article was basically a reprint of part of Church's and Alford's 1912 article and, hence, is not included in this collection of readings.)

1915 "The Evolution of Design," *American Machinist*, June 10, Vol. 42, p. 1008.
Source: not previously cited
INDUSTRIAL ENGINEERING

1915 "Machine Design and the Design of Systems," *American Machinist*, July 8, Vol. 43, pp. 61–62.
Source: not previously cited
MANAGEMENT

1915 "Mr. Gantt's Theory of the Expense Burden," *American Machinist*, July 29, Vol. 43, pp. 209–210.
Source: not previously cited
ACCOUNTING

1915 "Relation Between Production and Cost," *American Machinist*, September 2, Vol. 43, p. 431.
Source: not previously cited
ACCOUNTING

1915 "What Is a Cost System?" *American Machinist*, September 9, Vol. 43, pp. 455–457.
Source: not previously cited
MANAGEMENT

1915 "What a Foreman Should Know About Costs," *American Machinist*, September 23, Vol. 43, pp. 553–556.
Source: not previously cited
MANAGEMENT

1915 "What the Superintendent Should Know," *American Machinist*, October 14, Vol. 43, pp. 675–678.

Source: not previously cited
MANAGEMENT

1915   "What the Executive Wants to Know About Costs," *American Machinist*, October 28, Vol. 43, pp. 763–766.
Source: not previously cited
MANAGEMENT

1916   "Industrial Management," Paper 238, *Transactions of the International Engineering Congress, San Francisco, 1915*, pp. 446–472.
Source: Urwick and Wolf
MANAGEMENT

1917   *Manufacturing Costs and Accounts*, New York: McGraw-Hill, 452 pages.
Source: *The Accountants' Index, 1920*
ACCOUNTING

1917   "The Future of Industry," *The Unpopular Review*, June, pp. 251–272.
Source: *Reader's Guide To Periodical Literature, 1915–1918*
BUSINESS AND SOCIETY

1922   "Internal Transportation in a Large Textile Finishing Plant—I," *Management Engineering*, April, Vol. II, pp. 197–202.
Source: not previously cited
INDUSTRIAL ENGINEERING
(This article and the next one were not included in this collection of readings because of their limited scope.)

1922   "Internal Transportation in a Large Textile Finishing Plant—II," *Manufacturing Engineering*, May, Vol. II, pp. 293–296.
Source: not previously cited
INDUSTRIAL ENGINEERING

1923   *The Making of An Executive*, New York: D. Appleton & Co., 457 pages.
Source: Urwick and Wolf
MANAGEMENT
(This book was reprinted in 1972 by Hive Publishing Company as Part 3 of its Management History Series.)

1927   "Selecting a Plant Transport System," *Industrial Management*, December, Vol. LXXIV, pp. 368–371.

Source: *Reader's Guide to Periodical Literature, 1925–1928.*
INDUSTRIAL ENGINEERING
(This article was not included in this collection of readings because of its limited scope.)

1929 *Manufacturing Costs and Accounts*, 2nd Edition, New York: McGraw-Hill, 507 pages.
Source: *The Accountants' Index 1928–1931*
ACCOUNTING

1930 *Overhead Expenses in Relation to Costs, Sales, and Profits*, New York: McGraw-Hill, 516 pages.
Source: *The Accountants' Index 1928–1931*
ACCOUNTING

1931 "Overhead: The Cost of Production Preparedness," *Factory and Industrial Management*, January, Vol. 81, pp. 38–41.
Source: *The Accountants' Index, 1928–1931*
ACCOUNTING

THE
CONTRIBUTIONS OF
ALEXANDER
HAMILTON CHURCH
TO ACCOUNTING
AND MANAGEMENT

THE MEANING OF COMMERCIAL ORGANISATION.

By A. Hamilton Church.

THE development of industrial and particularly of manufacturing operations has been so rapid in the latter half of this century that it is not surprising to find some portions in a state of relative backwardness. This is particularly the case, as indeed might be expected, in those departments in which the actual productive factor does not come into active play, but which are rather concerned with methods of working and with the effecting of adaptations from the old order of things to the new. We have progressed indeed, almost without realising it, from an era in which all mechanical operations were of the simplest character, demanding no very high order of intelligence but merely a certain manipulative skill and craftsmanship, to the present time in which the actual mechanical problems are almost subordinated to questions of co-ordination and of simultaneous production under conditions of imperative exactness and accuracy.

The spectacle afforded by a modern works of the first grade is one of a great series of independent operations, carried on out of sight and for the most part out of knowledge of one another, but so carefully and cunningly devised that their products are in perfect co-ordination. When we contrast this with the machine works of a hundred years ago, in which a "mechanic" was one who exercised all branches of a craft, to-day split up into almost numberless separate pursuits or callings, the truth is realised that this ancient condition of things not only no longer exists but has no possible parallel in our day.

To the toilsome and uncertain progress of the "base mechanic" of our polite forefathers came the enlightening spark of genius from the brains of a host of great mechanicians, transferring the area of possible triumphs from the merely manipulative to the mental field. It became no longer a question of a single device painfully wrought into shape by almost unassisted hand labour, but of the coming of machines which were of themselves producers, and far more accurate producers than the most skilful craftsman ever was.

The advent of the machine tool, with its endless reproductive powers, with its yet unexhausted possibilities in the way of division of

3

Mr. Church, the associate of Mr. J. Slater Lewis, is one of the leaders of the new science of modern manufacturing. The strong feature of his article is his demonstration that organisation is an integral and even basal part of successful works management—not merely an auxiliary to it.—THE EDITORS.

labour, and its infinitely greater accuracy and power, was bound to revolutionise and transform the operations on which it could be directed. But this of itself is perhaps the least important of the changes differentiating the old from the new order. Close on the heels of the machine tool came the necessity for an altogether higher type of intelligence to control the increasing complexity of industrial operations. The "mechanic" disappears; in his place we have the "captain of industry," with his keen intelligence fully awake to the interaction of complex forces whose field is the whole world; he requires the capacity not merely to manipulate iron and steel, but—a much rarer gift—to understand men of many capacities and of a number of different social grades. To-day, indeed, the manufacturer might be said without much exaggeration to be the pivot on which society at large revolves. On his training, his intelligence, and his fitness for his life-work depend the future and destiny of nations. So true is this that it is almost a truism, recognised publicly by the frantic rush for technical education or whatever other panacea is fashionable at the moment for spreading the glamour of hope over the cruel statistics of diminishing or non-progressive trade.

The most progressive manufacturer is bound and limited, however, by the environment in which he finds himself. If it is true that industry is undergoing a process of change which is as yet far from finality, it is still more true that the process has many currents, and that it is impossible to master and turn all of them to account by a sudden effort, or by partial measures of reform. The older and the larger the undertaking, the more cautious we must be in making changes and the more resolute not to be satisfied with a fractional success. In an old organism the roots are deep, and their ramifications are not at all on the surface. Even in the interior arrangements of great factories there are vested interests that the most despotic reformer will hesitate to disturb, preferring to undermine than to carry by assault. What a writer in THE ENGINEERING MAGAZINE has well termed the "departmental ogre" has to be reckoned with, and it is a matter of intelligence rather than strength to do so.

All these considerations tend, as it happens, to one and the same result. Reform begins and generally ends with the modernising of machinery and non-productive appliances in that department, such as cranes, shop-transport, tool-rooms, and the like, leaving untouched the system of nerves, by which the whole is directed, and the importance of which has been recently brought into the light of day by the appearance of Mr. Slater Lewis's great work, under the title of Commercial

Organisation. The general effect of leaving this important section out of account is much the same as that of trying to restore life to a dying man by mounting him on a bicycle, instead of by building up the decaying tissues first.

Small wonder it is that drastic re-organisations often fail to give relief. Co-ordination is the keynote of modern industry, but it is a word of which the meaning is too often ignored by would-be reformers. Add that co-ordination is the very antithesis, the irreconcilable opposite, of rule of thumb, and we see the reason why the introduction of modern appliances does not always spell commercial salvation, but may even hasten the day of disaster. Congestion of work, dislocating the even flow of output, is no rare phenomenon; but it is getting to be a more and more inexcusable one, in so far as it does not arise from a sudden and unforeseen press of business.

5

Nothing is less elastic than the commercial organisation of a large place of business. Nothing clings more closely to tradition. The lines by which communication between the various departments is effected tend to wear ruts, out of which it is not permissible to jump. There is no remedy for this. The system will never be devised that will change with new conditions of the work it has to perform. The case of our government departments is a notorious example of systems once and temporarily good which have been left to harden and petrify. Most old businesses show on examination a similar state of results. As it is in the nature of things that this should be so, we can only look to the remedy, and no deeper. The remedy is to be continually on guard, and to bring the whole question under review when it is known that new factors have entered into actual practice. That this condition exists in most engineering concerns is evident enough.

From a practical point of view it may be said that as co-ordination is the imperative need of to-day, the nerve system must be re-arranged with that end kept steadily in view. The object of the commercial, or, as it might also be termed, the administrative organisation scheme, should be to collect knowledge of what is going forward, not merely qualitatively, but quantitatively; it should also provide the means of regulating as well as the means of recording. It is no mere matter of accountancy, although the element of cost is an important factor. Nor is the matter merely a technical one. It is essentially a matter of administrative control that is in question, stretching through every department and regulating the healthy life of the whole.

Having thus generally outlined the meaning of commercial or administrative organisation, a definition of its closer application to practical affairs may be attempted. A common mistake is to assume that there exists any cut-and-dried scheme applicable without thought or trouble to various types of business. The fallacy has arisen in the confounding of book-keeping with organisation. Epigrammatically it may be said that there is some book-keeping in organisation, but that there is no organisation in book-keeping.

Local conditions will always demand the first consideration. With a good system as a basis, modifications may be arranged to suit these; but the operation is a dangerous one for amateur exercise. The reason is obvious. In a well-ordered system there are far-reaching tentacles, complex interlockings, disturbance of which may vitiate a good deal of the value of the new results. But the greatest danger is that a partial solution only is reached where a complete one lies within grasp. More especially must it be emphasised that a knowledge of what is termed prime cost is no evidence of an intelligent control of the commercial side of a manufacturing business. It is true that some small businesses manage to rub along without even this elementary attempt at systemising, but the majority of firms of any size have some sort of cost method, however rough and home-made, which enables them to tell how much labour and what value of material have been expended on any particular job. Between this elementary stage and the next there is a very wide gap, which is bridged over by comparatively few firms, even in the go-ahead United States. The analysis of the working indirect expenses of the business, and in particular the discrimination between "works expense"—that is, the expenditure on productive departments—and "general establishment expenditure"— representing the expenses of the selling organisation—is a principle the fundamental importance of which had only dimly been realised by the book-keeping mind, and was first given the prominence due to its importance in the Slater Lewis system.

There is yet another stage before finality is reached. When once the distinction has been pointed out, it is obviously not enough to know the mere prime cost of work, without taking into account the indirect expenditure of the particular shop or department in which such work is carried out. One job may cost exactly the same in labour and materials as another job, and yet be quite unremunerative if taken at the same price; for one may be made under totally different conditions, and in itself may be an entirely different class of product from the other; yet this difference is in no-wise reflected in the prime-cost accounts. The item "labour," for instance, may be representative of a large amount of cheap labour or a small amount of highly-skilled labour, with a totally different incidence of indirect expense in either case. This is, to a large extent, set right by the above-mentioned analysis of works expenditure by departments, so that work done in one shop may be burdened more heavily with such indirect expenses than work done in another shop. But even when this is done, and when the local conditions peculiar to each department have been fully ascertained and means for the due reflection of this factor in the costs have been arranged, there still remains the problem of the department which, as a matter of practical convenience, cannot be divided up, but in which several diverse kinds of work are habitually done. To discriminate between these different classes of work when in the same shop is the third and final stage in the analysis of the statistical information called "costs," and it is the most difficult as it is the most important of all. It is not possible here to do more than refer to the existence of the problem; the discussion of the methods to be adopted for its solution requires separate and very detailed treatment.

7

The necessity for co-ordination already referred to is an inevitable result of the evolution of the factory. No one mind can grasp and hold all the details. The object of modern administrative organisation is to readjust the balance of responsibilities disturbed by the expansion of industrial operations, and to enable the central control to be restored in its essential features. If we seize this truth firmly we shall be able to criticise intelligently any proposals which may come under discussion, because this and this only is the proper perspective from which to regard all systems of organisation. Hence it will be readily seen that no method fulfills its purpose in which the operations are not immediately known, and their digestion and analysis subject to no delay. It is difficult, unfortunately, to realise the money value of absolute smartness in the presentation of results, until we remember that these results are our only substitute for that keen and active participation of the master's eye and brain in the daily progress of his work which is the life-blood of the small business, and which in the fortunes of industrial progress chiefly assists in its expansion into a large business. How many concerns languish when the care of their founder is withdrawn—and why? Simply because he cannot transfer the multitudinous details of organisation from his memory to that of a successor. It is these details that are essential, and it is their absence that must be fatal unless their place is supplied anew.

Nor must it be forgotten that the introduction of modern organisation is not in any sense the reduction of the subordinate to the *rôle* of an automatic machine. If it is true that mechanical devices—such as the comptometer, the slide rule, and the card system—loom very large in the programme, this is because they are labour savers. Now it is not cheap labour that is the chief thing to be saved, but expensive labour. The clerkly drudge with his everlasting copying tends to disappear. But the necessity for intelligence does not tend to disappear. If anything, the trend is in the opposite direction. Fewer people. perhaps, or at least not more people, but people of a higher grade of intelligence. A well-known engineer said to the writer not long since "one of the chief things that hinders British manufacturing enterprise is that they do not get the right grade of people in positions of responsibility. They try to work the thing on a cheap scale. In America the highest types of intelligence find their life work in industrial operations, and—the result is getting pretty evident."

8

This indictment is no doubt true. The vast scale of Transatlantic enterprise renders it possible to use higher intelligence, which in Great Britain would be frittered away in so-called "learned professions," or, still more uselessly, in an amateur political career. And the converse is also true; the vast scale of enterprise is a result of the mental power engaged in industrial operations. In more precise language, the Americans are creating in the industrial arena an environment superior in intelligence and enterprise to that existing elsewhere in the world. Their consequent supremacy is inevitable unless other nations are prepared to tread the same path of reform.

In any system there will remain always a mass of work which is pure mechanical routine. Of this class is computation, and generally all those arithmetical processes which occur in the digestion of each day's operations. Amongst these may be cited: the extension of wages, of material, the computation of establishment charges, aggregation of costs, and all the additions of financial books, such as the sales journals, purchases journals, with their cross-classification totals, and the checking of all classes of returns involving the addition or multiplication of figures. All these operations are much better carried out by an accounting room fitted up with mechanical appliances for the work than by a number of men scattered about the offices and works, each painfully toiling to attain accuracy, and in most cases frequently failing to do so, thereby causing annoyance and confusion at a later date, probably at a most inconvenient moment.

To this extent it may be said that it is proposed to substitute mechanical methods for older ones requiring intelligence. Yet even here the substitution is more apparent than real. The operator of a calculating machine can find plenty of use for an even considerable quantity of brains, whilst on the other hand the work of say, addition of long columns of figures, or the calculation of numbers of percentages, is drudgery pure and simple, and is usually paid at a low rate.

The most costly thing about a factory is an incomplete organisation. Yet the cost of establishing a good one is often shrunk from like the plague. The reason is particularly obvious where the principals are not their own managers, as in the case of almost all companies. The cost of establishing a new and better system is seen at once in the pay-roll; an additional clerk or a higher salary makes itself clear to the most obtuse board. "Expenses must be kept down," and so the proposal is vetoed. This may, nevertheless, be very far from clever business. The addition of £100 a year is seen, but what is not so clearly seen is the cost of mistakes due to an organisation outgrown. These are smothered. The shops can easily keep their own counsel. The ultimate result of such mistakes, failures of co-ordination, shows, of course, at the year-end in diminished profit in the "Trade a/c." But nobody knows why or wherefore. In the course of a year, several times the cost of a highly-paid staff may easily be muddled away in a large concern, and nobody be a penny the wiser. An incompetent foreman in one single shop, in the absence of proper control, may waste the firm's resources to a perilous extent, and yet the management may be only vaguely conscious that "So-and-So is not as sharp as he might be." The money value of his want of sharpness is an unknown quantity. It ought not to be.

With the growth of competition the necessity for co-ordination and of an accurate and swift presentation of results is more and more imperative. The margin for waste is less, the necessity for detail greater. Everything should be the subject of forecast as to financial results, and of prearrangements as to the actual carrying out. And when it is completed, the records of what did actually take place should be capable of comparison with what was intended to take place. Control then becomes a living reality. Co-ordination implies prevision, of necessity. The place where it pays to spend time and money on work is before it has begun the serious and irrecoverable expenses of production. It is the place, too, where it is most efficiently applied to produce a maximum of smooth working.

To sum up the principles on which a good system should be based and to enumerate the points that it should embrace is not as easy as it may appear, on account of the diversity of the local needs of each special business. With this reservation in view, it may be said that no system is satisfactory and complete in the fullest sense that does not provide for the immediate serving up of its results, day by day, as they occur, that does not provide in advance for the progress of every piece of work, and that does not present its cost details interlocked with its general and shop establishment charges in such a way as to discriminate: (1), between incidence of indirect shop expenditure and incidence of office and sale-organisation expenditure; (2), between the incidence of shop expenditure in one shop and in another, and (3), between different classes of work in the same shop.

There should also be so close a control over the stores and shops that the present value of assets may be known at least once a month. This implies, as will be obvious to an accountant, that monthly balance-sheets must be furnished, with the advantages which a continuous audit gives. There will also be—what is no less important—a continuous stock-taking. The present state and cost of any order should also be known at any moment, without calculation or more than two references at the most.

With these arrangements should be coupled—in all businesses in which orders have an individuality, *e. g.*, machinery—a method of finding not only the total works cost, including charges, but also the expenses incurred by the individual order after sale, such as commissions, freight, customs duty, workman's out-time and travelling expenses, and the like. The difference between the aggregate of these sums and the sale price is the net profit on that transaction. The sum of all such profits in any period should agree with the profit as declared by the financial books. *Every item of profit, as well as every item of loss, should be traceable by the management, and no covering up allowed.* If these elements are established and intelligently made use of, we have as near approach to the restoration of personal control over the details of a large business as the situation permits.

The catalogue may seem formidable. No doubt a newly commencing business has the advantage in establishing a system of administrative organisation, as it has the advantage of being able to base its productive arrangements on the latest available experience. But if one were to hazard the crystallising of a suitable exhortation to the older type of manufacturer into one sententious phrase, it would run something like this: "Don't be afraid of 'system.' Your present method is a system of some sort, probably an incomplete and bad sort. If it were detailed and described in all its workings it would read quite as formidably as any modern one. Every method requires expenditure to keep it up. A modern system costs less in proportion than an old one, because its results are significant and indispensable."

12

BRITISH INDUSTRIAL WELFARE

THE ERRING POLICY OF THE BRITISH WORKINGMAN

By A. Hamilton Church

HE British work-man finds himself to-day in the pres-ence of wide changes and developments in the meth-ods and organisation of production. He is, as a body, strong and well or-ganised, and, therefore, in a position not only to form a corporate opinion, but to give that opinion practical expression. Upon the correctness of his attitude towards these changes depends the welfare not merely of a few individual firms, nor of a few particular trades, but of the entire body politic.

In one sense, the apparent conflict between the interests of employer and employee will never admit of a final and satisfactory solution of the labour problem. It is in the nature of things that the one should cry continu-ally,—"I want more return for the wages I pay. Competition becomes keener day by day." The other as promptly replies,—"The tendency of the times is towards easier life. We must share in that tendency. We want shorter hours, but the same, or higher, wages."

The amount of a day's work cannot be measured in foot-pounds of energy. There is no standard applicable, except the quantity of any particular output. And the overwhelming tendency, far beyond control either of employer or workman, is for the value of output, as measured in labour-hours, to fall. But the absence of any natural standard, any positive connection between a fair day's wage and its outcome in a fair day's work, makes the problem a hardy perennial, surviving all possible changes, and ready to break out amidst the newest of circumstances at a mo-ment's notice.

This must not be considered a dis-couraging circumstance. It merely in-dicates that no shibboleth, no conven-ient, all-resolving formula will ever be found to reconcile, once and for all, the conflicting interests of the two factors in productive work. It means, further, that we must be suspicious of any prin-ciple, except mutual respect and fair dealing, that professes to offer such a solution.

There is also something that it does not, and should not, mean. It does not mean that there is no real mutual interest between employer and workman. On the contrary, nothing is clearer than that their mutual interests are a very much larger item than their mutual differences. Looking at a nation as a whole, we think of what binds it together,—we do not think of the little jealousies and party differences by which its units are divided. So with the industrial section, we see that it is a single or organic whole, with only one life, and that its life is threatened if the smaller antagonisms contained in it become prominent features.

Thus by another route we come to a realisation of the vast importance of the correctness of the British artisan's attitude towards the tendencies of the day. We see that he must distinguish between output and rate of labour,—two things which had a very close relation when every man laboured solely for himself, but the interrelation of which under latter-day conditions has practically vanished. From that day on which intelligence came to the rescue of muscle, output began to be independent of rate of labour.

The workingman must grasp the simple truth that as long as man's daily work does not take him near the limit of physical or mental endurance, the amount of his output is, in reality, a matter of indifference to him in the personal sense. If, physically and mentally, his work is well within his powers; if, in the pecuniary sense, he is well up to the standard of comfort he is used to, any increased productiveness which improved methods have enabled his employer to arrange are so much clear gain, not to him personally, nor very often to his employer personally, but to the national industry in its power of competing successfully in the markets of the world. This truth is surely not so deep nor so vague that it should require much illustration. It may be well, however, to restate it in other terms.

The demand for any article is not a fixed quantity at any one time. The capacity of the world to give orders for steel rails, or locomotives, or even for door-knobs and fire-irons, does not depend upon the desire of this or that person for these articles. It depends upon the intensity of the demand in relation to the market price of the things. A foreign or colonial railway company, for example, thinks of new equipment. Its engines are the worse for wear, need replacing, will not, in fact, do their work as efficiently and economically as new ones would. But the railway company does not, therefore, rush into the market and give orders right and left for new locomotives. Not at all. It has first to consider the market price. Will it do better to wait? Again, shall it inquire in the Belgian, or the American, or the German, or the British market? If, on inquiry, it finds all these markets unfavourable, it will not purchase engines at all. It will simply wait for more favourable times.

But, it will be objected, the order will have to be given out some day. Quite true. But the point is that here, by a single, though typical, instance, has been demonstrated the principle of " elasticity of markets,"—the tendency they have to expand into " orders " under favourable conditions, or to remain in the unsatisfactory stage of simply " inquiries " when conditions are not favourable. The fallacy of the popular idea of there being " so much work in the world " at any one time and no more, follows as an inevitable deduction.

To resume the history of this particular order! The day comes when the railway company hears of a downward tendency in the producing centres. Orders are " slacking off." Shops are getting empty. Directors are walking about with long faces. Overtime is " knocked off." Reductions in the working strength are heard of amongst the men. General gloom sets in. But the railway does not share in this gloom. It smiles broadly, disinters its plans and specifications, and posts them, as before, to Liége and Manchester, Pittsburgh and Essen.

We come here to the question which,

13

above all others, the British artisan must understand. He knows well enough that the order will go to the manufacturer who can quote the lowest price; for quality here is not in question; that is guarded by the specifications. Who will stand the best chance of getting that order? Will it go to the country where the typical employer is he who pays the lowest wages, who has the least consideration for his men, who looks upon his business as a mill to grind out profits and dividends, and nothing else?

It will not. It will go to that country, and no other, which has organised its business so that it has the largest output for the smallest expenditure. But this does not mean that the smallest rate of wages will be paid there. On the contrary, we have the example of America to show us that a high ratio of output to expenditure is always connected with a high wages-rate. The order will go to that country in which the artisans, as a body, not only " work new methods for all they are worth," but are eager to find out and adopt such methods. It will go to that country in which the artisans do not seek to handicap their employers by trying to make rates of wages independent of output, but base their claims for higher wages and more consideration on the only intelligible, and, in the long run, successful, basis,—higher efficiency in production per working day.

Finally, it will go to that country in which the highest intelligence is displayed by the industrial body, both employer and employee, as a whole, in which the entire industry, in its every member, is animated by a determination to be in the front rank in means and methods, and to allow no conflict of interests, however difficult of adjustment, to stand in the way of " working better methods for all they are worth."

Putting aside the baseless theory of a fixed amount of work existing in the world, what possible and reasonable excuse is there for the artisan to put his own industry at a disadvantage? He puts no more money in his own pocket. On the other hand, by basing his earn-ing powers on something unreal (and what else can that practice be called which insists on two men being employed to do what one alone is fully capable of doing?) he is running a risk of an unpleasant awakening in these days of sensitive markets and swift communication between producer and consumer.

It is easy to say that one man has been displaced by the adoption of a new method. Let us examine this proposition somewhat more closely! It may be a busy time, or a slack time. We will picture both these conditions. If a busy time, with orders rushing into the world's markets beyond the productive capacity to turn them out, then it is clear that the displaced man is not made idle. It simply means that the productive capacity of the world is increased, and that it can better cope with the work. One man does what required two a short time since. Hence, we have a clear addition to the wealth of the world, and to the strength and importance of that particular industry.

With slack times, there is a keen competition for orders. Few workmen understand this part of the industrial process. They frequently, if not generally, fail to grasp the simple truth that employers have to struggle for their orders. It is not a case of simply turning on a tap to enable the employment of workmen, the running of machines, and the making of profits. In these days the arena of the struggle is the whole world. The consumer in South Africa or South America knows quickly where his advantage lies in purchasing. If it be a slack time, he can, at leisure, turn over in his mind the comparative merits of the Belgian, the German, the British, the American, and, in some cases, even the French, producing areas.

But though the times be slack, some one will benefit by an order to be given out. Work will be provided for some artisan, profit for some manufacturer. But which? Will it be that artisan who insists on continuing to give the whole of his time to work which in more enterprising places is done in half that time? Will it be that employer who has to charge prices to cover unreal services performed by his workmen? Is it not clear that that employer will be out of the race, and that, so far from that artisan benefiting from his peculiar attitude towards modern progress, he will equally be out of the race? Instead of maintaining the ratio of wages to output he intended, there will be, in the case of this particular order, no output, and consequently no wages. The order will go, other things being equal, to that market in which the work can be most cheaply produced. It will be divided amongst those artisans who, by freely entering into the modern spirit of productive organisation, helping and not hampering it, have put their employers into a position to successfully compete in the world's markets.

Neither trades unions, nor employers' federations, nor acts of Parliament can prevent the trade of the world from flowing into the channels wherein it is best served. In the five years ending 1898 the rate of increase in exports from Germany was more than double, and that from the United States more than quadruple the increase in British exports in the same time. Do these figures favour the policy of restriction? Is not every workman, quite as much as every employer, interested in trying to realise their full significance?

That they are not so realised is, however, perfectly plain. A Yorkshire engineer told the writer recently that amongst his employees, there is not only the bitterest antipathy exhibited towards new machines and new processes tending to increase output, but that this attitude is backed up by a selfish cynicism that is the most saddening feature of the situation. "My men say that they will not do anything to increase output. It is nothing to them that business is lost. They tell me openly that when it goes elsewhere they will follow it."

This may be, and probably is, an extreme and exceptional case; but that it is becoming typical, more and more, of the British artisan's attitude cannot be doubted. That, if not combated and

dispelled, it will lead to disaster, no less to men than to masters, requires no profound thought. But that it will be in the power of the men, having ruined their trade at home, to follow it abroad, is one of those reckless propositions that can be believed only by those who dare not face the facts.

Where is the British artisan of this type likely to be welcomed? In Germany, or in America? It is possible, but not, by any means, probable. In any case, he can obtain a footing in either country only by abandoning his old policy, his cherished convictions, and by remodelling himself on lines in harmony with his new surroundings. This might, with better grace, have been done at first, without the sharp spur of distress due to closed works and moneyless Friday nights to drive him forward into proper enterprise and activity.

What, too, can be said of another case, typical of another kind of policy, which cannot be regarded as remarkably helpful either to master or man? Some time ago a man started business as an engineer, not in a large way, but on a sound footing. A few months later he put in a new machine, in order to do some particular piece of work. That was the beginning of the end. Over the work done on this unlucky machine a tremendous dispute arose. Not with the employer, be it noted. He was not concerned in it. No one said, or wished to say, a word against his right to put in the machine, or to do that particular work on it. It was simply a dispute between rival trades unions, each claiming the sole right of its members to do the work. One body claimed it because it was part of a certain mechanism; the other claimed the work because it was being executed by a machine process. A strike ensued. It lasted several months. In fact, as far as that particular employer was concerned, it lasted for all time, for the works were soon after closed, and the owner went to the wall.

If the "man can follow the work," then to a far greater extent can those who organise and direct enterprise afford to ignore Great Britain as a field

15

for that enterprise. They, too, can go abroad, and, what is more, they are going abroad. It is as easy to build a works in Ohio as in Lancashire, and with very little difference, as far as selling facilities on the British market are concerned.

How far is this process of disintegration, due to cross purposes, to go? Is it unreasonable to ask for, and to expect, a more generous and more enlightened attitude of organised labour towards the industry, as a whole, by which it lives? Will no one undertake a campaign to convert the British artisan to a proper appreciation of the true principles of progress? Millions are spent in the course of a few years in the strife of political parties to decide whether A or B shall occupy a certain office; but the far more vital question of bringing the interests of masters and men to one focus, uniting them in defense of their own industry, permeating them with a desire to increase the efficiency of their powers, mental, physical, and mechanical, so that they may keep to the front, in spite of all opposition and competition, is wholly neglected.

No sensible person will question the usefulness of trades unions. The trades union is the turning point on which British industry has to revolve, but it is an essential and vital matter that it shall not be a turning point of high resistance. In the British engineering trades alone 390,000 working days were lost by strikes in 1899. And, in addition to this, what figure must be put down to the silent and passive hostility of unions and their members towards improvements and economies in productive processes? Such items of loss do not appear in any official returns, but they are none the less formidable.

So far as the effect of machine improvements on the welfare of the workingman is concerned, it may be mentioned that when the machine welding of gun barrels came into operation, and, in its turn, gave rise to the infinitely larger industry of tube making, the workmen engaged on the older hand process lost their work. A similar fate

overtook those who made "skelps" for muskets. Instances might be multiplied to any desired extent of similar happenings. It is on these that the militant unionist takes his stand.

The mistake is to contrast an early stage in the evolution of manufacturing industry with the present advanced stage. Fifty years ago, and from that time backwards, hand skill dominated industry. Every improvement destroyed some old trade, some ancient handicraft, learned with laborious training, and commanding exceptional terms in proportion. The hand loom had to go. The hand-wrought man had to go. A hundred separate trades had to go, and were merged in new and wider groupings. How many former separate trades are to be traced within the field of the modern engineer?

What possible improvements can be made to-day that are likely to have similar uprooting and destructive effects? Surely very few. In former days, with their subdivision of crafts, the introduction of the machine meant, perhaps, ruin to the hand craftsman. He had but that one narrow skill, could do nothing else; he was, in fact, himself little better than an old-type machine. To day even the traces of this stage are fast disappearing. Processes take the place of trades.

The tendency of modern improvements is no longer to abolish hand skill, because, in the old sense of the word, there is scarcely any hand skill left. It is, on the contrary, in methods to eliminate the training and cunning of the muscles, and substitute for them the training of the intelligence, that most inventions find their proposed utility. Compare the sweat and dust-covered toiler of a hundred years ago with the lordly engineering mechanic of to-day, calmly superintending his obedient mechanical slaves, and ask whether great good has come out of all these changes or no. To be consistent, the militant unionist should clamour, not for the closing of the floodgates of improvement, but for a return to the glorious days of handicraft, when every man could do one thing only, and little of that.

THE MEANING OF SCIENTIFIC MANAGE-MENT

By A. Hamilton Church

During the time while Mr. Gantt was introducing the task and bonus system at the Midvale Steel Works, and even earlier than that, while the historic work of Mr. F. W. Taylor was being carried on at Bethlehem, Mr. Church was associated with J. Slater Lewis in his pioneer undertakings to reduce the commercial organization of factories to the form of a practical science. For more than twenty years Mr. Church has been closely associated either with the making or recording of the science of management. His conception of it, therefore, rests upon the ground of intimate knowledge and has the broad perspective given by familiarity with many divisions of the field. It is interesting in its conception of scientific management as a means to an end—"Intensive Production"—which in turn is one of the ideals dictated by the philosophy of efficiency.—THE EDITORS.

A T this date, when "Scientific Management" has become a popular and favorite theme of the ready pens of the daily journalist and magazine writer, it cannot be too clearly pointed out that the modern theories of industrial administration represented by that newly coined term are no magic formulæ, but are the fruition of decades of slow and steady progress and of the laborious work of highly trained and experienced investigators. It is hardly too much to say that the evolution of a science of management was inevitable as soon as the scale of industrial operations became so great that no single manager, however naturally gifted, could continue to control personally all the activities of a plant. Looking at all the circumstances, it may even be asserted that scientific management is, if anything, rather overdue in point of time, for many of its elements were known and understood at the beginning of the factory age.

In a contribution to THE ENGINEERING MAGAZINE rather more than ten years ago,* I said:

With the growth of competition the necessity for co-ordination and of an accurate and swift presentation of results is more and more imperative. The margin for waste is less, the necessity for detail greater. *Everything should be the subject of forecast as to financial results, and of prearrangements as to the actual carrying out.* And when it is completed, *the records of what actually did take plaec should be capable of comparison with what was intended to take place.* Control then becomes a living reality. Co-ordination implies prevision, of necessity. *The place where it pays to spend time and money on work is before it has begun the serious and irrecoverable expenses of production.* It is the place, too, where it is most efficiently applied *to produce a maximum of smooth working.*

This paragraph is reproduced here because it is a forecast in very condensed terms of the course of much of that progress which has finally become developed and actualised under the term "Scientific Management." The only point of interest about it is that it was written ten years ago, which helps to show that the evolution of this body of principles was bound to take place because it was called for by the necessities of modern industry. The want of it was perceptible even then. That want has been brilliantly supplied by the efforts of a number of workers whose work is still too recent to be perfectly co-ordinated and viewed in its correct perspective. Foremost amongst these the names of Harrington Emerson, Frederick W. Taylor and H. L. Gantt are

17

*"The Meaning of Commercial Organizations," Dec., 1900.

familiar to the readers of THE ENGINEERING MAGAZINE.

It is not, however, with the historical aspect that we are concerned at present. My purpose is to attempt a definition of what scientific management actually is, to discuss a few of its direct and indirect benefits, and to glance as far as possible at the directions in which progress may be expected to develop. In this discussion I shall consider the term to include all the modern views of production that are making themselves accepted at the present time, without referring to the share of individual investigators in their development.

Scientific management contains two basic ideas. One is the planning of industrial activity from the consideration of its simplest units; the other is the pre-determination of standards of efficiency. To a certain extent the second of these is implied in or rather is a bye-product of the first, but the former of these principles may be put into practical use without the other.

To take a concrete illustration: every piece-work price that is not a matter of sheer rule-of-thumb implies that a certain amount of thought has been given to the elements of the operation for which it is fixed. But this by no means implies that the second basic idea, that of setting up standards of efficiency, is being kept in mind. In one of the largest engineering shops in this country an enormous mass of data has been accumulated, covering scores of thousands of operations, and representing areas of machined surface on which to base piece-work prices. Yet that same plant has not begun to get even a glimmering of the second basic idea—that of standards of possible performance. It compla-cently accepts the fact that its men do increase their production somewhat under the stimulus of piece-work prices, but what fraction of the possible maximum increase they obtain, or how much of the existing manufacturing capacity is actually running to waste, they do not think worth finding out.

It cannot be too clearly emphasized that scientific management is a body of principles and not a "system." These principles may be applied in a great variety of ways, so long as the basic ideas are not departed from. It is not a particular style or method of organisation, or a particular way of laying out a shop, or of keeping stores and raw materials—still less has it any relation to a particular set of forms, cards or books. It is a particular way of looking at the whole problem of industrial production, and nothing beyond. It is even quite thinkably possible that a man may be imbued with a fairly correct appreciation of these basic principles, and fail to extract satisfactory financial results because he does not distinguish between the end and the means—he over-develops his mechanism (that is, his system) beyond the commercial possibilities of the situation, and swallows up his profits in the effort to be up to date. A remarkable case of this kind came under my notice some time since, where a superintendent reorganized a very large shop upon a falling market without keeping close watch of the relation of his changes to the overhead burden, with results disastrous to his reputation and his career.

There are several bye-products of scientific management that are sometimes identified with scientific management itself, but which in my opinion are not inherent in it, although powerful and even necessary auxiliaries. It must not be forgotten that "scientific management" is only a phrase—perhaps not a particularly well chosen phrase: the end and object of it is "Intensive Production." Intensive production bears the same relation to the older type of manufacturing that the modern French "intensive culture," raising several crops a year from the same area of soil, does to the old-fashioned horticulture. The pace is increased all round. Now it is one of the main advantages of scientific management that the greater intensity of operation it sets up has necessitated the "tuning up" of a number of subordinate activities in manufacturing plants that were not regarded as factors of great importance until intensive production found out their weak points. It has also brought into prominence the ethical, or as it is sometimes termed, the "human" element in management, as one of the most necessary subjects of study in the whole problem. Some of its more enthusiastic advocates claim that it has settled, once for all, the warring claims of capital and labour by some magic principle of subdivision of the proceeds of industrial operations, necessarily satisfactory to both parties. This claim is in my opinion a particularly dangerous one, and has no basis in fact. I shall revert to this claim later.

Chief among the subordinate activities which have gone through the process of "tuning up" are those that can be grouped under the term "co-ordination." In other words, they secure regular and simultaneous effort on the part of a number of individuals, or depart-

ments, for the execution of a common aim, viz., the manufacture of a given piece. They are variously known as Tracing, Routing, or Despatching. Although under scientific management very much higher efficiency is required in this direction, the idea itself is not the outcome of recent progress. Very complete and accurate despatching methods are known to me as having been used for at least ten years or more, quite apart from any question of intensive production. Nor as far as I am aware has any great advance been recorded in this respect of late. Another question that has been forced into attention by intensive production is the handling of stores and finished components intended for re-issue to the shops. This, again, is a matter on which it cannot be said that any startlingly new light has been thrown. But again, the necessities of intensive production make it a perfectly vital matter that stores keeping shall be carried on in an exact way, and good stores keeping may therefore be regarded as a bye-product of scientific management.

The same remarks may be understood as applying to the organisation of tool departments, whose importance in intensive production can hardly be over-estimated.

Given the first basic principle above referred to—the planning of industrial activity from a consideration of its simplest units—it follows inevitably that considerable changes in the organisation of every engineering shop that adopts this method must ensue, if it bases its actual manufacturing work on the unit operation, instead of on the complete part. The first department to meet the change will be the drafting room, on which a

19

demand for unit drawings will be made to an extent unknown to the older practice.

From thence onwards the principles of scientific management begin to make themselves practically felt by concentrating attention on the unit process, exhaustively studying it, getting to know exactly what in men, materials, machines, tools, and auxiliary helps of various kinds it requires, setting in motion simultaneously all the activities necessary to get these requirements completely satisfied at exactly the proper moment, and then, by the light of the second basic principle, comparing these results with the forecast *possible maximum* of results and thus determining the ratio of efficiency.

The essential features of scientific managment, then, consist of principles and not systems or methods. When applied, they require a very high average of good organisation, but as I have endeavoured to show, this organisation is not in itself scientific management, and may—it is not too much to say that it always *should* but rarely *does*— exist apart from it. What there is of scientific in it, is in applying, on a practical scale, the accurate methods of the physicist to manufacturing operations. The moral effect of it, in addition to the tuning up of all departments, is the raising all round of the average perception of accuracy of observation and of performance—accuracy, and ever more accuracy.

In brief, it is the application of accurate thinking, accurate planning, and accurate doing, so as to increase output, reduce cost, and by consequence render available a larger margin of surplus for division between employer and employee,

It would be proper at this point to offer a few further remarks on the expectations that have been raised in some quarters as to scientific management being a panacea for the settlement of all disputes between capital and labour. It is only so insofar as it encourages a spirit of fair and honourable dealing between both parties. Its one virtue in this respect is that it does bring into play a stronger spirit of co-operation between all grades of a large staff, and helps even the most unthinking to realise how dependent each is on the fair and square performance of allotted duties of others. It is possible that this may have an influence on the more thoughtful type of workman, by leading him to realise how wide from the facts are the claims of Socialism that labour is the creator of all wealth. He cannot help but realise that labour is only one of several factors equally necessary to one another. But that there is anything in the principles of scientific management to render disputes impossible is I believe a fallacious claim, and if this is so, then it appears an unfortunate one to encourage. It does not appear to remove the question from the region of mutual agreement and mutual compromise where it has always resided, though it may smooth the way for better mutual understanding by reason of the accuracy of its methods.

In offering these remarks upon scientific management I have not been animated by any desire to criticise the remarkable achievements that have been effected, or to minimise their importance. I have merely endeavoured to separate out the essential from the auxiliary principles comprised in the term. Many persons hesitate to adopt, or even to consider, intensive production, because they are afraid of having to throw all their present methods to the winds, and embark upon a voyage through unknown seas. It is important that this impression should be removed. Even in the most backward plant every change should be evolutionary—starting from what exists and developing it towards a higher state of efficiency. Root-and-branch changes are rarely satisfactory. When it is realised that true scientific management does not mean pulling everything up by the roots, but is largely a matter of tuning up to concert pitch of the existing organisation, and then the gradual introduction of accurate planning —always with an eye to the expense account—then it may encourage some who are now trembling on the brink.

Space does not permit of more than a brief allusion to the future developments of intensive production. It may be suggested, however, that it will gradually force into prominence the principle that the unit of production for costing purposes, must be, not labour alone, but as Mr. Gershom Smith put it, very succinctly, some time ago in these pages—*the operative plus his machine*. As the extension of a non-productive staff, engaged in planning out and other auxiliary services, becomes developed, the old principles of costing by "flat cost" *plus* a percentage or man-hour, will be seen to be dangerously fallacious, and the "scientific machine rate" which the present writer has had the pleasure of presenting to the readers of THE ENGINEERING MAGAZINE on several occasions will be seen to be the necessary complement of scientific management, just because by it alone can the relation of overhead expense to the unit operation be exactly determined. And if for no other reason, its elimination of waste of resources, due to idle time, from true costs must become a powerful aid in setting up standards of efficiency.

Generally speaking, the formulation of principles of building up from unit operation, and of determining a possible maximum of work as "efficiency" and any failure to realise this standard as waste, will rank as one of the epoch-making events in the history of the mechanical arts. Like the doctrine of Evolution, they sum up in small compass the work of a generation of investigators who were blindly groping towards the light, and they will form the starting point for further progress which may have greater developments, both economic and social, than we are now able to foresee.

21

Intensive Production and the Foreman

By A. Hamilton Church

A practical question that has hitherto escaped adequate discussion; namely, the relation of the ordinary foreman to the new methods of securing increased output, or "intensive production," has been raised in a previous article and deserves attention.

In certain quarters there is a tendency to systematize the foreman out of existence altogether. This is most popular with the "root and branch" reformers who insist that efficiency can only be reached by yielding control of a plant for an indefinite period to experts trained in a particular school. Personally I must confess to a certain amount of skepticism as to the necessity for such autocratic introduction of reforms, and still greater skepticism as to the permanence of the efficiency obtained in that way. But as very few owners will be found who do not prefer to trust to evolutionary rather than revolutionary methods, I shall deal here only with the question of plants that are feeling their way toward efficiency by healthy and gradual progress.

It will, therefore, not be necessary to discuss whether "functional" foremanship may under special circumstances and in the distant future, wholly replace the foreman as we know him now, but simply the more practical question as to what place in the gradual introduction of scientific methods the existing type of foreman is to occupy.

Under the older régime the foreman was one of the pivotal functionaries, filling an analogous position to that of Kipling's' "noncommissioned man"—the backbone of the army." In him was vested great authority, he acted as a "buffer state" between the executive and the operative force, he was the recognized court of appeal on all "practical" matters; he was the repository of a vast body of technical wisdom; he devised ways and means of handling unfamiliar work; he was responsible for discipline, time-

> *Systematizers are apt to ignore the shop foreman in working out their plans. His position in the new order of things—intensive production—has never been accurately pointed out. Mr. Church shows that he should not be a specialist but a man with a wide view of all the conditions in his department and constantly watching the broad results.*

*Consulting expert on factory administration. C. H. Scovell & Co., Boston, Mass.

keeping, quantity and quality of the output of his men—in short, it is very difficult to say what was or was not within the sphere of a strong and competent foreman of 20 years ago.

At the present day a foreman's job may vary in importance from nearly all the above down to that of closely limited powers more like a "leading hand," save that he may be placed over a large shop with several leading hands under him.

It is evident, not only that the position of the foreman has been passing through many changes, but that it is time that some serious consideration should be given to the status of so important an official, under the modern method of planning out, forecasting results and determining efficiency by comparison of "results actual" with "results expected." In justice to many most harrassed members of the craft something ought to be

done to define his sphere, preserve his usefulness and protect him from the inroads of reformers who have only a vague idea of what he is there for. Also, if this question can be adjusted even approximately many forceful and aspiring men will set themselves to acquire whatever new qualifications may be wanted, instead of regarding the new principles of management with silent hostility and uneasiness.

The abolition of the foreman may be briefly considered—and dismissed. There is nothing fundamentally *impossible* in doing this. It is obviously a matter of subdividing his remaining duties among others, as many of his old-time duties have been assigned to others. In some "factory" types of undertaking each foreman's responsibility is exceedingly limited, but in proportion as the product is less uniform he tends to assume greater importance. The reason is that the purely factory type of organization is absolutely rigid; it does not require, and could not effect if it did any modification of its daily round. Now, in spite of the trend toward standardization and specialization, the ordinary machine shop will never arrive at that condition of rigidity. Consequently, it would seem that too centralized and rigid an organization may have dangers. The whole idea of having a foreman is a delegation of control for certain purposes. Chief among those purposes is the maintenance of a certain *elasticity*, which will take up lost motion and *compensate for the machine-like character of even the best organization by subdividing the general supervision into sections small enough for all the current events in each of them to be grasped by the foreman concerned.*

WHAT IS A FOREMAN?

This consideration helps us to a definition of what a foreman is. He represents the last outpost of general control as distinguished from special control. In other words, the function of the foreman which must survive all others is the administrative function. His special knowledge is to some extent superseded, but not wholly, as we shall have occasion to observe presently. But within his department he is or should be the man to see that all the various functions now performed by other members of the organization are effectively performed. Briefly, and in old-fashioned language, he represents "the master's eye" in the department over which he is set.

Considerable support to this view of the foreman's functions may be found in an extract from a paper read before the American Society of Mechanical Engineers by John Calder, manager of the Remington Typewriter plant at Ilion, N. Y. Though the type of work referred to in this paper is an unusually complete example of factory or mass production . .

. . . being wholly confined to the making and assembling of an immense variety of interchangeable parts Mr. Calder, while fully alive to the importance of routing, instruction cards and so forth, seems to think that the shop foreman's day is not yet done. "The writer," he says, "does not favor the restriction of the ordinary shop foreman to productive supervision, but prefers to encourage them to compete freely with the time study staff for the best results. If pains are taken to give publicity to all good suggestions adopted from foremen, a surprising amount of very profitable coöperation can be obtained from them, which enhances instead of diminishes their administrative ability."

The Foreman's Qualifications Will Tend to Rise

These remarks of an advanced and progressive manager go far to indorse my own view, namely, that so far from the introduction of scientific methods tending to improve the foreman out of existence, his qualifications, on the contrary, will tend to rise, notwithstanding that his active duties are less extensive and less varied. It may be that he will have to direct less and to observe more. If planning out, rate-fixing and similar specialized functions are taken from him and committed to special persons or departments he must still remain the active observer and intelligent critic of their operations. If exact records of each man's performance are a matter of routine quite apart from his personal observation, his personal relations with his men must always remain an important factor. *Surrounded by specialists and making use of the material they prepare, it must be the particular value of the foreman that he is not a specialist but is capable of looking at the whole life of his shop with a well balanced eye.*

Obviously, to perform this function successfully, the foreman must make himself acquainted with the routine of the specialized departments, to know how and when he may use individual discretion without throwing the machinery out of gear. In an emergency he must know just what to do, not only in regard to the work but also in regard to the specialized departments. Just how to accommodate the exercise of discretion by the foreman without disturbance of routine is a fine problem which requires very careful consideration at the hands of reformers. Hitherto the tendency has appeared to be a conjugation in the imperative mood—"thou shalt not interfere." Very convenient for the systematizer, but not quite, I venture to think, a final or satisfactory solution of the question.

The "Line and Staff" Plan

Among the valuable generalizations that have helped to develop the manufacturing problem, that of Harrington Emerson, borrowed from military organization, is one of the most illuminative; namely, "line and staff." It should be noted in this connection that the development of staff services in military affairs has not rendered less important the work of the company officer and the sergeant. In the same way, properly balanced, the development of specialized staff services in the machine shop should not diminish the value of the company officers and sergeants; that is, the departmental officials in charge of the practical affairs of the shop. The object of staff service is to serve. It cannot be at the same time a successful executive, or at least such a state of things would be contrary to all experience and, though it might work for a time, it would obviously be liable to break down very hopelessly if anything happened to derange the exact routine it follows. It appears to me that good foremanship is intended to obviate just this danger.

Is Planning and Operating a Function of Foremanship?

Some of the questions raised in connection with this phase of foremanship must, I think, be answered in the negative. Some writers call for the planning and operation departments being made a subdepartment of foremanship. There are several reasons why this cannot well be done. In the first place such departments, if properly organized, have a different viewpoint from that of any single foreman. They take, or should take, not the shop but the factory as the productive unit. They should be in close touch with the designing departments. They have to arrange for coöperation, or, as it is better called, coördination of the work of every executive officer in the plant for every single job. Such work could not be scattered here and there without loss of efficiency.

But there is a still more weighty reason why they must work independently of the foreman, though in collaboration with him. Under the definition of his work arrived at above the foreman represents the "master's eye." He has to see that his men do the work in the way approved by the specialized departments, but in addition to this he has to watch the broad results attained. He must not groan in spirit if some little thing is done in one way, when he thinks it should have been done in another. He must think in averages not in particulars. If he sees instances of inefficiency he must note them and place them alongside instances of efficiency. If he is sure that the balance when struck is unfavorable then he must speak up, not in a captious spirit and in a "I-could-have-done-it-much-better-myself" strain, but with a view to helping the executive to strengthen the weak element and bring it up to full working strength.

The Broad View To Be Taken

It is, no doubt, true that both the foreman and his employer have to shift round to a new viewpoint of his duties under modern methods of shop administration. A little friction in settling on this new viewpoint is perhaps unavoidable, but that is all the more reason why the subject should be thoroughly discussed. When things have settled down, it is probable that the foreman will have no reason to be dissatisfied with the change. Of course, I am speaking of foremen as a body, and especially of the many members of that body who are progressive men and only too willing to help along any methods that promise greater efficiency. For every advance in efficiency, every lowering of cost, widens the area of the engineer's operations, brings more work of a remunerative character to the machine shops of this country and provides greater future rewards for every kind of skill and experience in manufacturing.

23

Distribution of the Expense Burden *

By A. Hamilton Church†

What I have to say to you really involves a new way of looking at the facts of production, and consequently of the whole question of shop statistics and costs. This new point of view is the outcome of the results of a study of expense burden over a number of years, and I have to offer to you not so much a specific system of record, as a set of principles, the practical application of which can be and indeed must be varied and adapted to suit individual cases.

I advocaté a method of charging the hourly operation cost of machines by what I term machine rents, which differ from the old arbitrarily fixed machine rates. The machine rate as ordinarily employed was an attempt to give expression to the obvious physical differences between machines, and to bring an element into costs that would reflect this difference. But these old machine rates were, for the most part, arbitrarily fixed, and not based on anything like a complete survey of the facts of shop production. Usually, in fact, they expressed only the capital value of the machine. They failed to solve the problem, because they took account of some and not all, of the immensely varied items of the expense burden.

Cost of material is left entirely out of this discussion. In the early days of manufacturing industry, attention was not so much concentrated on doing things economically as with the much more difficult problem of doing them at all. The story of Nasmyth's invention of the steam hammer in response to a sudden demand for a machine that would forge the crank shafts of ocean steamships is a case in point. And a good deal of the history of industry during the last century consists of similar incidents, but each resulting in a new triumph over natural obstacles and becoming the starting point of a whole range of new progress in other industries.

Operation Costs Overlooking

I believe that this is the reason why the perfectly obvious idea of taking out the operation costs of machine tools was overlooked by the early manufacturers. To them, the operation cost of a new kind of machine was a small matter compared with the fact that it enabled them to do something that had never been done before. In other words, the progress of the last century was almost wholly in the direction of promoting technical development . . . . leaving to us, of the present day, the almost equally interest-

*Paper presented before convention of National Machine Tool Builders' Association, slightly condensed.
†Industrial engineer, Boston, Mass.

ing task of increasing economic efficiency.

There is another reason why the natural idea of taking out machine-operation costs was overlooked. It is only within a comparatively recent period that the question of costs began to force itself on the attention of engineering manufacturers . . . . the older school were in the happy position of being able to satisfy themselves by a glance at their bank books that they were all right. I am afraid that those halcyon days have passed. Increasing competition and the diminution of the margin of profit, to say nothing of the. necessity of minutely studying operations, have for some time past made it imperative for manufacturers to look into the cost of their product and I think it will generally be found that the most successful firms are those that have looked into it most closely.

By the time that the urgent demand for knowledge of costs began to be felt, manufacturing has already assumed a high degree of complexity of organization, and the fundamental mistake made by the early cost men was that in observing the complex activities of a busy machine shop they analyzed the wrong things. They analyzed figures instead of analyzing the facts that lay behind them. Had they, instead of dealing with book values, gone behind these and endeavored to undertake for what specific economic purpose each item of expense has been incurred, the machine-rent method which I present would have been born a generation ago.

Passing the Tool Point

I hope you will agree with me that the salient feature in machine-shop activity—the end toward which it is created and maintained, is the getting of work past the tool point. However numerous and complex the subsidiary activities, they all of them serve or should serve to this end and no other. It need hardly be pointed out that the functioning and maintenance of the tool is also implied in this definition, since if the tool were not at work we could not get the work past it in any useful sense.

From this definition as a starting point we may develop our first general proposition, viz., That every legitimate expense in a machine shop is incurred for the purpose of getting the work up to, under or away from the tool point, in one way or another.

One class of this expenditure is easily understood and mastered. The cost of the machine-operator's labor—and his labor is at the tool point—is in most cases a perfectly straightforward problem, and is handled successfully by existing cost methods. All the remainder, amounting to anything from 100 to 200 per cent. of direct operative labor is usu-

ally jumbled together into a common fund termed expense burden.

Now, while we persist in regarding this great mass of expense simply in the light of a lot of figures to be tabulated, analyzed, twisted or tortured in various ways, we may succeed in finding out a number of curious facts worthy of being put on exhibition in a museum, but we shall never get anywhere near knowing the very thing we ought to know—what is the operation cost per hour of each of our machines? We may figure our consumption of coal in terms of pounds weight of product, or ascertain the amount of lubricating oil used and its relation to each hundred dollars of wages paid, to a few decimal points—and I have known things done in an elaborately useless way almost as absurd as this—or we may do what is quite common practice and figure our expense burden as so much per cent. of our directly productive wages. I hope presently to have you agree with me that this latter proceeding is quite as meaningless as the other imaginery instances of the uses of "analysis" as applied to expense-burden figures.

Analyze Actual Activities

Suppose, however, that instead of applying our analysis to expense-burden figures we begin to analyze the actual activities which these figures represent—suppose, beginning with the principle that every item of expense has been incurred for the purpose of getting the work past the tool point, we go behind the figures and consider the things—asking ourselves, item by item, how this or that expenditure is related to the getting of work past the tool point.

The first, and in many ways the most important, discovery that results from such an analysis of manufacturing activities is that every manufacturer does a good many things beside manufacture. Some of these he does from necessity, others he does from choice, or because he sees a distinct economic advantage in doing them for himself. Stated in more abstract language—actual production is the last organization in a chain of related but separate organizations.

This is such an important point to grasp that I will restate it in another form. In order to manufacture economically, most manufacturers (and we may say all large manufacturers without exception), take on a number of nonmanufacturing functions, some of which are preliminary to production, such as that of landowner, landlord, or power supplier, and some of which are concurrent with, but subsidiary to, production, as, for example, storekeeping and costkeeping. The first three of these are entirely separable, and as a matter of practice are not always exercised by the manufacturer; the last two are, of necessity, always exer-

25

26

cised by him without recourse to outside aid.

THE COST OF CAPACITY TO PRODUCE

Now everyone who has given any consideration to the question of expense burden is aware that one of its most prominent characteristics is that it does not rise and fall proportionally with the volume of work in the shops. You pay for labor as and when you require it, but you have to foot the bills for expense burden whether you require it or not. If, therefore, you treat burden as an item of cost, you introduce a fluctuating element which very soon ceases to have any valuable significance when work is not steady in the shops. This is largely because the analysis of facts, the division of the functions of the organized factory into manufacturing and nonmanufacturing functions has been overlooked, and consequently the true meaning of expense burden has been missed. I will try to express what I believe to be its true meaning in a single phrase:

Expense burden represents, not the cost of production, but the cost of *capacity to produce.*

I will now carry the definition one stage further by saying that expense burden represents, in the main, the aggregate cost of the capacity to produce arising out of the nonmanufacturing functions exercised by the manufacturer, and that the true solution of the problem lies in our ceasing to think of expense burden as a whole, but in turning our attention to the various nonmanufacturing services and observing their relation to capacity to produce and then to actual production.

I would say that really, there is no such thing as expense burden—that there are only a number of separate expenses incurred to maintain various departments of the capacity to produce. The aggregation of expense-burden figures in a lump sum is, in fact, an inversion of the natural process. The cost of the different nonmanufacturing services rendered to production should never have been mingled at all.

TAKING A SIMPLE CASE

In order to make clear to you exactly what is meant by nonmanufacturing functions, I will repeat a favorite illustration, which elsewhere, I have termed the "parable of the little shops." In a large plant these functions and their ramifications are in fact not easy to identify without considerable study, but in the progress from the most primitive form of industry up to the modern scale of manufacturing efficiency it can easily be seen how, one after another, these functions are assumed and incorporated with the direct manufacturing function.

An elementary form of manufacturing industry is more common in some European countries than in this. A man may work by himself on some specialized

product which he sells either to some larger manufacturer or direct to a merchant. He will probably rent a room in a large factory building which is given up to such uses. His plant may consist of a single foot-power stamping press, and when this is the case we have manufacturing industry reduced to its simplest elements. The expense burden of such a worker consists of practically but two elements: rent of his shop and depreciation on his machine. Even here it is possible to imagine that expense is a serious matter to him. He pays a certain rent for his capacity to produce and for each kind of work there is a limit beyond which the work cannot afford to pay a higher rent. A stage further is the use of power. In these buildings power can be rented at so much per horsepower, and the question of the price of his power is a serious one to these "little masters" as they are termed. Even at this stage it is easy to recognize that two elements have entered into the cost of the worker's capacity to produce, quite irrespective of his actual production.

Let us assume now that he becomes ambitious. He thinks he could do better for himself by ceasing to buy his power, and he puts down a gas engine in a corner of his shop and makes his own power. By so doing he passes beyond the stage of a simple producer, and assumes nonmanufacturing function No. 1, viz., that of a supplier of power.

When he has installed his gas engine the problem takes on a more modern and familiar aspect. It has become relatively complex—if we like to make it so. What, we may inquire, is the proper method of arranging his cost accounts? The familiar way would be to analyze his indirect expenses—so much for rent, so much for gas, for lubricating oil, for ignition tubes, for repairs to the engine (which, we may imagine to be a second-hand one in poor condition, requiring frequent repair); to throw all the separate items into one "burden" or "establishment charge," and to allocate it as a percentage on wages cost by one or other of the well known and much debated methods. In other words, we confuse his function as producer with his function as supplier of power and, having mixed them up inextricably, we contentedly express the result of the jumble as a percentage on wages or time.

KEEPING FUNCTIONS DISTINCT

The alternative to this is obvious. It is to keep the two functions he has assumed perfectly distinct. Instead of consolidating his indirect expenses, he would do much better to preserve the more primitive form of his costs, and continue to recognize three factors as before, viz.: Time, rent and power. In order to do this satisfactorily he need take no more trouble. All he requires is to keep all his

expenditure on power (that is, all the cost entailed by his function as supplier of power) separate and distinct from his other expenditure, and to express it not as a percentage on time, but as a rate per horsepower consumed. He will then obtain his power factor exactly in the same form as he originally had it when he rented his power.

If three or four such "little masters" may be supposed to meet together to talk over their methods and compare notes as to their relative efficiencies, it is obvious that if each of them knows only two facts about his production—his labor cost and the percentage of his total expenses to his labor cost—they will not be able to compare results favorably. For even though one of them discovers that his percentage is higher than that of his friend, he will not know why. But if the three production factors so far introduced are kept entirely distinct, intelligent comparison becomes at once possible. The rent factor of one is perhaps higher than that of another. The power factor of a third may be greater than that of his fellows. The introduction of the gas engine, for example, when reduced to a power factor, may easily be seen to be a mistake, whereas if treated in the ordinary way and made part of an expense burden, that unpleasant truth would have had a strong tendency to conceal itself.

Again, our supposititious worker may rent a piece of ground and erect upon it an iron workshop for himself. This introduces a further complication and is another step toward the complexity of modern manufacturing concerns.

From this illustration of the gradual adoption of nonmanufacturing functions, in the evolution from primitive forms to the large scale of modern industry, a general idea of the method of dealing with expense burden that I am advocating will easily be understood. Its characteristic lies in *keeping separate* the cost of the various non-productive functions exercised by the manufacturer and in ascertaining the rents payable by the direct manufacturing department for the services thus rendered.

I wish to outline how, in practice, this principle is made effective. The essence of it consists in carefully disentangling all the different items of nonmanufacturing services, and in observing how each of them, taken separately, bears on capacity to produce, first by departments, and then by individual machines. About the simplest case is that of a rented building, the rent of which is obviously easily reducible to an annual rent per square foot of available shop space, and this is charged up to the machine according to the space the latter occupies. Now where the land and the buildings are owned by the manufacturer, all the expense and outgoings on the property

(Continued on page 999)

Distribution of the Expense Burden

(Continued from page 992)

are kept by themselves, and commuted into a rent exactly as if the property were rented from an outsider. They are not thrown into a general collection of similar charges and called expense burden. The exact bearing of that particular nonmanufacturing function called property-owning on capacity to produce is ascertained just as it would be ascertained if the property were rented from an outsider. All the group of expenses belonging to it are segregated and merged in an annual rent. Further, it has been found to be quite as easy to segregate all the other indirect or nonmanufacturing services and reduce them to rents chargeable for such services, instead of throwing them into a general expense-burden fund.

CHARGING INDIRECT SERVICES

When all such indirect services have been segregated and reduced to rents, these are charged first against departments, and then against individual machines on various bases of allocation. The total charge standing against each machine is then divided by the number of working hours in a month or year and so an hourly rent for the use of that machine is determined.

I should like you to understand that this determination, though it may be unfamiliar to you, is a purely logical process. That is to say that there is nothing arbitrary in it, but logical reason can be shown for the presence of each item of expense just where it is placed, so that there is no possible appeal from the final result. The final machine rents are actual or natural rents payable for the capacity to produce.

When all such rents for indirect services have been determined, and given an outlet on to jobs in the form of machine rents, a further and most important principle of my method comes into play. The capacity to produce may not always be utilized to the full. In the case of a given machine having a rent of 25 cents per hour, whatever work is done at it is charged at 25 cents an hour whether the shop be full or slack. That is to say that on this method, alone among expense-burden methods production cost is unaffected by conditions in the shop. You must not punish the job because part of your capacity to produce is being wasted. You have only used 25 cents worth of the capacity to produce which that particular machine possesses, and that is all the job should be charged with.

WHAT BECOMES OF IDLE TIME?

This idle time represents *wasted* capacity to produce, first of the machines individually, secondly of the machines collectively in departments, and thirdly of the plant as a whole. In practice the total of idle time by departments is the significant figure. The total of this idle time is ascertained and expressed as a supplementary rate or percentage on the monthly total of machine rents already charged to jobs. You may think that here we get back to a percentage after all. So we do. But consider what this percentage is. It is the ratio of wasted to utilized resources. Something quite new and very important to know.

This supplementary rate may or may not be charged to individual jobs, as preferred. Personally I do not think that there is any great use in doing so, as long as the ratio is determined and made known month by month. For it represents waste and nothing else, and has no real connection with particular jobs at all. If you do charge it up, then you have total costs made up of direct labor, cost of indirect or nonmanufacturing services as expressed in machine rents and a third figure which gives you a more or less arbitrary allotment of the waste. But I prefer to consider such waste as a separate job, and a very bad job, and keep it as a separate item in the shop accounts. For the sake of "rounding off" the costs it is sometimes distributed, but I regard this as a concession to the old idea of getting rid of figures by distributing them somewhere and somehow, regardless of whether the result has any true significance or not. In my idea waste is waste and when you have separated it out, face it squarely and admit that it is none the less waste if you arbitrarily spread it over jobs. I allow that this is sometimes an uncomfortable thing to have to do.

THE PRINCIPAL ELEMENTS

To sum up, I will briefly enumerate the principal elements of this method of ascertaining true costs of production, separated from wasted capacity to produce.

First, instead of throwing all indirect expenses together into a common fund of burden, and then elaborately analyzing them in the despairing effort to make something significant out of them, we segregate and keep separate the cost of all nonmanufacturing services.

Secondly, having segregated each group of expenses we determine the rent charge that must be made for it, precisely as the owner of a terrace of houses settles what rent he will charge individual tenants. But, of course, in the case of these service rents, there is no item of net profit included.

Thirdly, each department is charged up with its due share of each of these service rents.

Fourthly, the share of individual machines in each of these different service rents is ascertained.

Finally, at the end of this process, each machine will have been found to be charged with a number of annual rent charges, which represent the annual cost of that machine's capacity to produce. These separate charges are aggregated and commuted into an hourly machine rent, which is charged against all work done at that machine.

This completes the cycle of true costs. The residue which is left over because idle machines have not charged the whole of their "capacity to produce" onto jobs is collected together monthly, and represents waste pure and simple,

27

Has "Scientific Management" Science?

By A. Hamilton Church *

Eight years ago, at the spring meeting of the American Society of Mechanical Engineers, Mr. Taylor presented a paper on "Shop Management," the first words of which are: "The writer's chief object in writing this paper is to advocate the accurate study of 'how long it takes to do work,' or Scientific Time Study as the foundation of the best management." In the course of years this definite and modest claim has been expanded, until today Mr. Taylor and his associates have put themselves forward (or have allowed themselves to be acclaimed without protest) as the inventors or sponsors of a special system of industrial administration which they term "Scientific Management," thereby obviously implying that all other management is unscientific.

WHAT IS A SCIENCE?

A science is a perfectly definite thing. It consists of a long series of ascertained facts connected by tried theories that have stood the test of time and criticism. In an established science personal authority goes for very little, but logical proof counts for a great deal. Whoever undertakes to speak in the name of science must be prepared to prove his right to do so up to the hilt, however wide his experience or however great his reputation. In the present case the matter is one of more than ordinary importance, since Mr. Taylor appears to claim that he and his associates are the special repositories of this science, which cannot be successfully applied without their assistance.

This claim is such a remarkable and unusual one on the part of any body of men claiming to be exponents of technical progress, that we must first of all make sure that it has been clearly and unmistakably made. That it has been made the following extracts will show:

In paragraph 296 of "Shop Management"—"The first step after deciding on the type of organization should be the selection of a competent man to take charge of the introduction of the new system, and the manager should think himself fortunate if he can get such a man *at almost any price.*"

In the Art of Cutting Metals, page 26, we read:

"In fact, the correct use of slide rules involves the substitution of our whole task system of management for the old-style management, as described in our paper on 'Shop Management.' This involves such radical, one might almost say such revolutionary changes in the mental attitude and habits both of the workman and the management, and the danger from strikes is so great and the chances for failure are so many, that such a reorganization should only be undertaken under the direct control (not advice, but CONTROL) of men who have had years of experience and training in introducing this system."

A study of "The Principles of Scientific Management" leading to this conclusion: "After carefully dissecting Mr. Taylor's writings, one is forced to the inevitable conclusion that the term 'Scientific Management' has nothing tangible behind it, apart from certain very useful mechanisms which Mr. Taylor has done great service in bringing to general notice."

*Consulting Industrial Engineer, Boston, Mass.

(Note that the word CONTROL is placed in capital letters by Mr. Taylor himself.)

In Mr. Taylor's latest publication, "The Principles of Scientific Management," he says, on page 132.

"It is not enough that a man should have been a manager in an establishment which is run under the new principles. The man who undertakes to direct the steps to be taken in changing from the old to the new (particularly in any establishment doing elaborate work) must have had personal experience in overcoming the special difficulties which are always met with, and which are peculiar to this period of transition."

And just above, on the same page, he says:

"Inasmuch as the writer has personally retired from the business of introducing this system of management (that is from all work done in return for any money compensation) he does not hesitate again to emphasize the fact that those companies are indeed fortunate who can secure the services of experts who have had the necessary practical experience in introducing scientific management."

Naturally, the present writer would be the last to argue against the advantages of employing experts when projects of reorganization are on hand. The position and the value of the expert in such cases is well understood. It arises from the fact that to introduce changes in an organization demands somewhat different qualifications from those which make a successful manager, and further that changing an organization is such a delicate and intricate job that few executives have the time to devote themselves to what is naturally very absorbing work. It is also perfectly true that every reorganization presents a crop of special difficulties—difficulties which the expert with his special point of view and experience in just such matters can overcome much more efficiently than men whose regular business is routine management.

THE DEMAND FOR CONTROL

But Mr. Taylor obviously means more than this. He demands, in fact, what very few experts would demand, namely; not advice but CONTROL, and he demands this on account of the great dangers otherwise attending the introduction of "Scientific Management" into a plant. If he means anything at all it is that the principles of scientific management are so obscure and their practical application so difficult that an experienced and competent expert is unable to assimilate and apply them without years of experience and training in introducing that particular system.

From what does this obscurity and this difficulty arise? Is there really something so obscure in the ordinary elements of industry, in questions of pay, of giving instructions, of handling stores, of getting work up to and past the tool point, that after eight years of discussion about them, they still remain surrounded by a haze of obscurity through which only very competent and specially trained pilots can guide us? Or does the obscurity lie in the demonstration of what scientific management really is. Does the difficulty arise from conflicting claims and a general vagueness about what the principles are? Few men can be found to agree as to what scientific management really consists in. Some will regard it as time study, some as functional management, some as a particular method of "incentive" by extra pay and some will say that it is not any separate one of these things, but merely means a collection of the best methods and practice of the last two decades.

To clear the matter up we must obviously "appeal to Cæsar." We must obtain a decision from headquarters,—a definition that will set the matter at rest once for all. The means we select for doing so will naturally be a reference to Mr. Taylor's publications on the subject. The sources from which we obtain a knowledge of scientific management are three, namely: "Shop Management," 1903; the introduction to the "Art of Cutting Metals," 1906; and "Principles of Scientific Management," 1911. If on examining and comparing these authoritative statements we find, consistently, a definite and clear insistence on some central principle, the claim that scientific management is "one, whole, and indivisible" may be admitted, but if we find on the other hand that the stress and emphasis is constantly being shifted from one feature to another, then that claim will not be established.

Definitions of Scientific Management from Mr. Taylor's Writings

The first paragraph (of the Index) to "Shop Management" has already been quoted. It states specifically that the object of the paper is to advocate scientific time study as the foundation of the best management. (Here scientific management appears to be identified with time study.)

Paragraphs 92-94 declare that all ordinary systems of management ("including the Towne-Halsey system, the best of this class") are based on "ignorance and deceit." And the statement is made that by accurate time study "surprisingly larger results can be obtained *under any scheme of management* from day work up." (The italics are mine.)

In paragraph 135, "the writer most sincerely trusts that his leading object in writing this paper will not be overlooked and that SCIENTIFIC TIME STUDY will receive the attention it merits. (Capitals are Mr. Taylor's own.)

Up to this point we have a consistent idea, namely, the reduction of all operations to their elements and the time study of these elements by means of a stop watch. This idea is a very old one. It was well known to the early manufacturers in their researches into the proper "subdivision of labor." The use of the stop watch was described by Babbage in his book on "Economy of Manufactures," issued in several editions from 1832 to 1846. This does not, however, detract in the least from Mr. Taylor's rediscovery of the idea, nor from the credit due to him for his persistent advocacy of such an important instrument of industrial analysis. In itself it does not constitute a science. It is merely a very useful method for studying a limited class of facts. It is not management of any kind whatever.

Paragraph 21, however, asserts—and the whole paragraph is set in capital letters by Mr. Taylor, to mark its importance:

"This paper is written mainly with the object of advocating high wages and low labor cost as the foundation of the best management, of pointing out the general principles which render it possible to maintain these conditions even under the most trying circumstances and of indicating the steps which the writer thinks should be taken in changing from a poor system to the better type of management."

In this paragraph a new "chief object" of the paper is declared, and a new element as the "foundation of the best management" is put forward. It hardly need be pointed out that time study has no necessary relation to high wages and low labor cost, and that one is a practical instrument and the other a theoretical aim of management.

With paragraph 148 we enter a new phase of the subject. In this it is declared that management is an art, with four principles: (1) A large daily task.

(2) Standard conditions and appliances. (3) High pay for success. (4) Loss in case of failure. A subsidiary principle for future use is added, namely: That the task should be so fixed that only a first-class man can do it. Principle (1), however, appears to be superseded later (in paragraph 191) where the superior advantages of SHORT tasks is demonstrated. The main purpose of the paper appears to be modified once more, and these principles take equal rank with time study as the foundation of management. Time study is in fact relegated to a somewhat subordinate place among 14 or 15 changes necessary to realize the art of management.

In paragraph 232 another principle makes its appearance. It is declared that "a great part of the art of management lies in subdividing duties, and this is to be accomplished by ABANDONING THE MILITARY TYPE OF ORGANIZATION and introducing two broad and sweeping changes into the art of management." (Capitals are Mr. Taylor's own.) These changes are in the direction of what is known as functional foremanship.

The Planning Department Is Management

This idea is given definite shape in paragraph 257 on which the somewhat startling statement is made that

"The shop (indeed the whole works) should be managed, not by the manager, superintendent, or foreman, but by the planning department. The daily routine . . . . . should be so carried on . . . . . '. that in theory at least the works would run smoothly even if the manager, superintendent and their assistants outside the planning room were all to be away for a month at a time."

If there is any meaning in this statement at all, it certainly seems to infer that the planning department is not only the central feature of the art or science of management, but that it IS management in itself. This is a pretty large order and we seem to have gone a long way away from the original statements,

(1) That time study is the foundation of management;

(2) That high wages and low labor costs are the foundation of management;

(3) That large tasks, standard conditions and high pay are the fundamental principles of management, and have come down to the proposition, virtually, that

(4) The planning department IS management.

Space does not permit of dealing with the 17 elements of the planning department enumerated under the letters *A* to *Q* in paragraph 258. But we may note that *H* is "The mnemonic symbol system;" *K* is "Maintenance of system and plant and use of the tickler" (!!); *L* is a "works postal system" and *O* is a "mutual accident insurance association." These are gravely declared to be among the "leading functions" of the planning department.

This is a very surprising result: The planning department, held up as a creation so powerful and intelligent that it can run the plant without the assistance of the manager or superintendent, turns out to be merely a new group name for a number of administrative activities, some of which, as, for example, *G* the pay department, are as old as the relations of employer and employee.

Either Mr. Taylor has here failed, and very badly failed, to make himself clear, or this is a case of inability to distinguish between broad principles and mere practical devices. Functions *H, K, L* and *O* may be excellent things but that they are worthy of being ranked as fundamentals of management is more than doubtful. Their use is certainly not logically derived from the principles already laid down.

In paragraph 288 yet another principle makes its appearance. This is the "exception principle" which declares that each executive officer should deal with masses of reports and papers in a routine way, but have his attention called by an assistant only to those points which form exceptions to the past averages or standards. This is an excellent idea and is very frequently adopted, and it closes, as far as I have been able to discern, the series of principles selected for adoption in "Shop Management."

The introduction to the "Art of Cutting Metals" need not detain us. It contains little on the subject of management beyond the paragraph already quoted. We will, therefore, turn to Mr. Taylor's latest book, "The Principles of Scientific Management," published this year, and contrast its contents with those extracts from "Shop Management" given above.

Before doing so, however, let us endeavor to understand what the object of the paper on "Shop Management" really was. Although it began by declaring (1) that time study was the all-important thing in management and then went on to declare (2) that high wages and low labor cost was the leading feature, (3) that the art of management really consisted of four principles, (4) that the proper type of management was that known as functional, a specific instance being given of a planning department with 17 subdivisions—the chief idea which Mr. Taylor appears to have in mind was a development of the old principle of the "subdivision of labor." Had he made this the central feature of his paper and developed this idea by itself without tacking on to it so many subsidiary and insignificant details, so much cut-and-dried system, he would have performed a far greater service. But Mr. Taylor was not content to develop principles, he insisted on particular detailed arrangements, and the whole attitude of himself and his friends has been to cry "hands off" to any modification of these details, as if they were absolute and logical developments of some

29

30

well defined principle. That they are not is sufficiently obvious from what has already been presented above. That a comprehensive generalization is possible that shall include both time study and functional foremanship, and form a *real working principle* independent of arbitrary details is, I believe, not unlikely, but Mr. Taylor has nowhere given us such a broad and general statement, in the 464 paragraphs of "Shop Management."

THE PHILOSOPHY OF SCIENTIFIC MANAGEMENT AS SET FORTH IN MR. TAYLOR'S LATEST WRITINGS

Between the appearance of "Shop Management" and the publication of the "Principles of Scientific Management" neary eight years have elapsed—the latter may, therefore, be regarded as the matured presentation of Mr. Taylor's science.

The first chapter entitled "Fundamentals of Scientific Management," is mainly a dissertation on "soldiering." We are told, however (page 28), that the many papers written hitherto on scientific management have mistaken the mechanism for the essence, and a warning is given that scientific management consists of "a certain philosophy which can be applied in many ways; and a description of what any one man or men may believe to be the best mechanism for applying these general principles should in no way be confused with the principles themselves."

This seems hard on those of Mr. Taylor's assistants who after years of association with him have written books and papers on the "system" without, it would appear, being aware of the important philosophy that lies behind it. It is certainly discouraging for the rest of us that have not had this advantage of association, because it would seem to indicate that it is more than ordinarily elusive and mysterious. The only thing approaching the nature of a fundamental in this chapter is that,

"In almost all of the mechanic arts the science which underlies each act of each workman is so great and amounts to so much that the workman who is best suited to actually doing the work is incapable of fully understanding the science without the guidance and help of those who are working with him or over him, either through lack of education or through insufficient mental capacity."

As a deduction from this, he declares that "to work according to scientific laws . . . . almost every act of the men should be preceded by one or more preparatory acts of the management which enable him to do his work better and quicker than he otherwise would." Also that "close, intimate, personal coöperation between the management or the men is of the essence of modern scientific or task management."

Chapter II, however, does throw more definite light upon what scientific management is claimed to be. It contrasts the older plan of management—which Mr. Taylor calls the "initiative and incentive" plan (meaning that special incentives, piecework, premium, etc. are offered by the management to secure the workmen's interest and initiative)—with the new plan. The latter is declared to be a system by which,

"The management assumes the burden of gathering all the traditional knowledge which in the past has been possessed by the workman, and then of classifying, tabulating and reducing this knowledge to rules, laws and formulas."

In addition four "new and heavy burdens" are taken on by the management:

AN ANALYSIS OF THE CLAIMS

1. *"They develop a science for each element of a man's work which replaces the old rule of thumb method.".* What this high sounding claim means is not at all obvious. You cannot develop a science out of a single fact, and to say so is a misuse of words. Probably what Mr. Taylor means is that they develop what they believe to be the best practical method of performing each element of a man's work, basing this belief on the data as to performance they have already acquired by time study. That is a very different thing—a very human and fallible thing, extremely liable to errors of judgment, and not possessing any of the certainty and infallibility of "science" at all.

2. *They scientifically select and then train, teach and develop the workman, whereas in the past he chose his own work and trained himself as best he could.* This also is a very wide claim, unless we read into it limitations which Mr. Taylor has nowhere indicated. What is the meaning of the workman choosing his own work? Does it mean his trade, or the particular job? If the former, I think few workmen will change their trades at the bidding of any "scientific" manager. If the latter, then I do not know of any shop in which the workmen scramble for the jobs, or are able to pick and choose what they will or will not do. What Mr. Taylor really means—judging from his practice—is that each workman is made to do the job in a particular way, namely, that indicated by an official in the planning department. I have not been able to discover that this philanthropic-looking phrase means anything more than this.

3. *They heartily coöperate with the men so as to insure all of the work being done in accordance with the principles of the science which has been developed.* Here we have not philanthropy but idealism. The securing of "hearty coöperation" is an excellent idea—if it can be secured. But can it be secured by any system? Does Mr. Taylor claim that he can raise the average of human nature, because if so, and the claim be justified, many more urgent problems than shop management will have been solved. But if "hearty coöperation" is a necessary and inherent ingredient of this method, then practical men will do well to handle it with gloves. The millenium and a number of other things can be realized if hearty coöperation between man and man becomes the order of the day. This is another vague and rhetorical claim, the true meaning of which will be found in the eight separate "bosses" whose behests the man has to follow—and heartily coöperate with.

4. *There is an almost equal division of the work and the responsibility between the management and the workmen. The management take over all work for which they are better fitted, while in the past all of the work and the greater part of the responsibility were thrown upon the men.* Exactly how this fourth duty differs from the preceding duties is not at first reading very obvious. By the time that the workman has had a science developed for each element of his work, has been scientifically selected, trained, taught and developed and then heartily coöperated with into the bargain, there does not seem much more to be done for him by the management. Mr. Taylor seems to have perceived this dimly, as he says that this fourth duty requires further explanation. His explanation is that the development of a "science" requires numerous records and "a room in which to keep the books and a desk for the planner to work at." So that this fourth "new and heavy burden" means mainly an order system to transmit the "science" to the workman.

Finally Mr. Taylor sums up his four duties by remarking: *"It is this combination of the initiative of the workman, coupled with the new types of work done by the management that makes scientific management so much more efficient than the old plan."* It will be seen that this is yet another and totally different definition of scientific management from any before. It certainly makes us rub our eyes with wonder. Having gathered in all the workman's traditional knowledge, and indexed, tabulated and cross referenced it, so that as stated on page 58, "the records containing the data used under scientific management in an ordinary machine shop fill thousands of pages," having put the workman in such a position that his own personal knowledge is of not the slightest value beside that of the infallible mechanism, the planning department, having provided him with eight bosses (including a disciplinarian) to insure that he does not exercise his personal judgment in the slightest degree—Mr. Taylor calmly talks about scientific management "consisting in a combination of the initiative of the workmen with new types of work done by the management."

No sooner, however, have we become familiar with this definition than we are confronted two pages further on, by an entirely new view of the matter. "Perhape," says Mr. Taylor, "the most prominent single element in modern scientific management is the task idea." On examination, the task idea appears to be an old familiar friend, namely, payment by the piece (not necessarily piecework or premium as ordinarily used) with the proviso that,

"These tasks are carefully planned . . . . . that in no case is the workman called upon to work at a pace which would be injurious to his health. The task is always so regulated that the man who is well suited to his job will thrive while working at this rate during a long term of years and grow happier and more prosperous instead of being overworked."

And before we have had time to recover our judgment after the exhibition of this beautiful picture of the happy workingman—who is to receive after all an "incentive" of 30 to 100 per cent. extra wages if he comes up to expectations, Mr. Taylor presents us with yet another definition of scientific management. "Scientific Management," he says, "consists very largely in preparing for and carrying out these tasks." It might almost be said that, apart from the philanthropic motive, which is commendable, but not easy to realize, this is exactly what every advanced type of management consists in very largely also.

On pages 98-99 we have a definite statement of how scientific management was applied to a machine shop "in better physical condition than the average machine shop in this country." The demonstration of the superiority of the new system was made on one machine "by means of four elaborate slide rules . . . . also tools of the proper shape properly dressed, treated and ground," with the result that the gain in time ranged from 2½ to 9 times the original speed of operation. Here scientific management appears to imply simply an accurate knowledge of the "art of cutting metals."

A Confusing Situation

It is hardly too much to claim that all this is a little confusing. I have no wish to offer merely carping and destructive criticism, but probably few people will be found to assert that this is a clear, orderly and systematic development of "principles." Beginning with the essentially simple though very valuable idea of "time study" the claims of "scientific management" have been extended until they include practically every organic element of the mechanism of advanced management. Now this would be understandable if it could be demonstrated that these organic elements were threaded together on some exceedingly improved plan. But nowhere in Mr. Taylor's own writings do we obtain a definite idea of what this special plan is which differentiates his particular method of management from ordinary advanced methods to such an extent as to make it positively

dangerous to introduce into any plant without the CONTROL of a specially trained man.

To substantiate such a claim much more than mere rhetoric about "developing a science" or "hearty coöperation with the men" is necessary. Neither of these is either a principle or a method. They are simply a statement of two obvious and desirable aims, common in greater or less degree to every advanced management. To have high and desirable aims is good, but it is not a science of management in any sense whatever.

Some people may be inclined to think that this is not fair criticism—that I am selecting portions of Mr. Taylor's demonstrations and leaving out the explanatory and significant parts. To show that this is not so I will quote in full the matured and deliberate summing up presented near the end of his latest book. This will show that after having presented at various times, (1) time study; (2) high wages and low labor cost; (3) the four principles (large daily task, standard conditions, high pay for success, loss for non-success, and very difficult tasks) (4) functional management; (5) the planning department; (6) the four burdens; (7) the combination of men's initiative with new types of management work; and (8) the task idea, ... having presented these elements at various times, each in its turn as the most prominent and essential feature of his system, Mr. Taylor, on page 128, tells us that scientific management is NOT mechanism. he says:

"Precisely the same mechanism which will produce the finest results when made to serve the underlying principles of scientific management will lead to failure and disaster if accompanied BY THE WRONG SPIRIT in those who are using it. Hundreds of people have already mistaken the mechanism of this system for its spirit."

The quotation may be interrupted here to remark that scientific management here appears in an entirely new light, as a spirit. What does this exactly mean? We have been told of the necessity for a spirit of hearty coöperation, and by implication, of the desirability of cultivating the scientific spirit of inquiry, but by no ordinary use of words can a spirit—that is, an attitude of mind—be called a system of management. The cultivation of a particular spirit is the affair of moral and mental science, not a matter of practical management, except in the vaguest theoretical sense. This statement, however, does throw some light upon the necessity "not for advice but CONTROL" on the part of those introducing the system. Because it shows that, after all, scientific management is exactly like every other kind of management, namely: the outward expression of the peculiar and personal temperament—in other words, the spirit—of the manager.

TWELVE "MECHANISMS" OF SCIENTIFIC MANAGEMENT

Returning to our quotation, we find 12 elements of the "mechanism" of scientific management listed as follows:

(1) Time study, with the implements and methods for properly making it.

(2) Functional or divided foremanship, and its superiority to the old fashioned single foreman.

(3) The standardization of all tools and implements used in the trades, and also of the acts or movements for each class of work.

(4) The desirability of a planning room or department.

(5) The "exception principle" in management.

(6) The use of slide rules and similar time-saving implements.

(7) Instruction cards for the workman.

(8) The task idea, accompanied by a large bonus for the successful performance of the task.

(9) The differential rate.

(10) Mnemonic systems for classifying manufactured products as well as implements used in manufacturing.

(11) A routing system.

(12) Modern cost system, etc.

"These, however," adds Mr. Taylor, "are merely elements or details of the mechanism of management. Scientific management in its essence consists of a certain philosophy, which results, as before stated, in a combination of the four great underlying principles of management."

Even then, after this warning as to the essential importance of the "certain philosophy," Mr. Taylor does not enlarge at any great length on what this philosophy is. Instead, he presents us with a mere footnote of four lines, stating what the four underlying principles of scientific management are, viz: (1) The development of a true science. (2) The scientific selection of the workman. (3) His scientific education and development. (4) Intimate friendly coöperation between the management and the men.

Apart from the fact that these four underlying principles are nearly identical with the "new and heavy burdens" referred to in Chapter II, we are not much assisted in running down and identifying that very elusive "spirit" of scientific management by this footnote. Certainly the first principle that "scientific management is the development of a true science" does not throw much light on the subject. To say that the first underlying principle of a science is the development of that science seems to mean nothing. It is like saying that the first principle of the science of chemistry is to develop the science of chemistry. If we were engaged on a quest to discover what the science of chemistry really was, we should hardly be satisfied with a "principle" of that kind. It reminds one of the individual who asked for bread and was given a stone.

31

32

Finally on page 138, Mr. Taylor makes an altogether new definition of scientific management. He says:

"It will doubtless be claimed that in all that has been said no new fact has been brought to light that was not known to someone in the past. Very likely this is true. Scientific management does not necessarily involve any great invention, nor the discovery of new and startling facts. It does, however, involve a certain *combination* of elements which have not existed in the past, namely, old knowledge so collected, analyzed, grouped and classified into laws and rules that it constitutes a science, accompanied by a complete change in the mental attitude of the working men as well as those on the side of the management toward each other, and toward their respective duties and responsibilities. Also new division of the duties between the two sides and intimate friendly coöperation to an extent that is impossible under the philosophy of the old management. And even all of this in many cases could not exist without the help of mechanisms which have been gradually developed.

"It is no single element, but rather this whole combination, that constitutes 'Scientific Management' which may be summarized as:

"Science, not rule of thumb; harmony, not discord; coöperation, not individualism; maximum output in place of restricted output; the development of each man to his greatest efficiency and prosperity."

A GRAVE PROTEST

It is in no flippant mood, but in grave protest at this sort of thing being presented to practical men as a business solution of an every-day problem, that I would point out the vague and rhetorical character of these claims, which remind one of nothing so much as the writings of the "benevolent socialist" school of Robert Owen, and the "mechanical projectors" of the last century. What Mr. Taylor describes here, is neither a science nor an art, but simply a set of ethical propositions and moral aspirations. Having disclaimed the "mechanism" of time study, "functional foremanship," etc., as NOT constituting in themselves scientific management he leaves us no wiser than before about what are the steps that should be taken to bring about "changes" in the mental attitude of both sides, and to secure that "intimate friendly coöperation" which is to produce "harmony not discord" and "coöperation, not individualism."

AN INEVITABLE CONCLUSION

After carefully dissecting Mr. Taylor's writings, one is forced to the inevitable conclusion that the term "scientific management" has nothing tangible behind it apart from certain very useful mechanisms which Mr. Taylor has done great service in bringing to general notice. He has failed to show the path to the very desirable moral aspirations that he voices so eloquently, because he, like the rest of us, has no golden key to change human nature, or to bring about an industrial millennium. He admits on the one hand that there is little that is new in the *practical* elements of his system, and his claim for a new *combination* involves new and intangible elements which not only have

never existed in the past, as he admits, but are of such a nature that only the most concise and definite evidence will make us admit their existence in the present. It will take more than a simple claim, even on the part of so eminent a man as Mr. Taylor, to convince the rest of us that, in this imperfect world, he can banish discord, and substitute coöperation for individualism, except in the very limited sense that any well managed system of payment by results covers the same ground.

Even if we were inclined to admit this, Mr. Taylor has wholly failed to give us a glimmering of how it is to be done. He has specifically warned us against imagining that practical methods—that is, mechanism—will lead to anything but "failure and disaster" unless fructified by his "underlying philosophy" and when we come to examine that philosophy, in the very few phrases he devotes to it, we find nothing more definite than vague allusions to "changes in the mental attitude," and "intimate friendly coöperation." Neither of these is a means, they are only ends to be attained.

If a public man must be judged by his writings, then there is some justification for the assertion that Mr. Taylor has failed to make out his case for the possession of any specific method of management that really stands out so clear and distinct from all other advanced modern methods, as to warrant the distinctive title of "scientific management." Nor, except in the sense that he personally is a gifted man, with a natural talent for administration, is it at all clear what feature of his system it is that demands "not advice, but CONTROL." Indeed such a claim seems to imply that "scientific management" as expounded by Mr. Taylor, like every other kind is simply a projection of the personal temperament and ideas of the manager. If it were really a science it would not need to be "personally conducted" in quite such an imperious and arbitrary manner; its facts, laws, and principles could be grasped by any technically educated and qualified man.

No one will wish to deny that modern advanced management owes a great debt to Mr. Taylor. He has fought a hard fight through many years in improving methods and in contributing to the perfection of "mechanisms." Thus for example his "time study," his "functional management" and his "differential rate" are three wholly separate and independent conbributions of value that he has made to our store of useful "mechanisms." But in regard to this claim for the development of a "science" or a philosophy of management, it is hard to avoid the conclusion either that Mr. Taylor is struggling unsuccessfully to explain himself, or that he has mistaken a statement of aspirations for a statement of how to realize those aspirations.

Direct and Indirect Costs

By J. Edtterson*

The cost of a job is made up of three components: 1 Material; 2 direct labor; 3 indirect labor. It is desired to show, from the plant superintendent's standpoint, that the direct-labor cost is the most important of the three and the one of which he must have the most intimate knowledge and which at all times must be available. By the plant superintendent is meant that officer of an organization who has a plant under direction, from which he is required to produce work.

REFERRING TO MATERIAL CHARGES

It is at once apparent that the cost of material is not controlled by the plant superintendent, but rather by the designer, customer or maker of the specifications which the plant superintendent is required to meet. So far as the plant management is concerned, the material cost is a fixed one. In general, as regards material, you get just what you pay for.

Considering the indirect charges against a job, it is to be noted that of late great stress has been laid upon the necessity of determining the indirect charges most accurately, and if an accurate, absolute cost of the job is required for estimating or selling purposes,

---

> The plant engineer is more particularly concerned with the direct cost of production and less so with the material and indirect charges.

*Assistant Naval Constructor, U. S. N.

GENERAL EXPENSE

Maintenance of miscellaneous buildings	Drafting expense
Maintenance of elevators	Inspection department
Maintenance of furniture for offices	Testing and inspecting
Telegraph and telephone system	Testing and inspecting stores
Maintenance of roads, walks and gutters	Maintenance of testing laboratory equipment
Maintenance of tracks	Handling material not chargeable to shops
Maintenance of railroad rolling stock	Examination of apprentices
Weighing apparatus	
Maintenance of hoisting apparatus ashore	
Maintenance of live stock	
Maintenance of vehicles	
General office expense	
Insurance and depreciation	
Maintenance of sewer system	

SCHEDULE SHOWING DISTRIBUTION OF INDIRECT CHARGES

this is necessary. This is of vital importance to the establishment where the value of the indirect charges may be the determining factor in the award of a contract. Thus it happens that commercial firms are sometimes influenced to swing a portion of their indirect expense from that class of their production upon which they must meet competition to that class of their production upon which they have a monopoly. In other cases their inability to determine accurately the cost of articles of production has resulted in a loss of business.

Furthermore, the matter of indirect charges is a most attractive field for the accountant, as the accurate distribution of them offers a very interesting problem. Likewise, the business manager, the estimator and the salesman are interested in the matter of indirect charges. However, it must at once be apparent that the indirect charges are of very little concern to the plant superintendent. This is best demonstrated by the fact that the greater part of these indirect charges is

---

not under his control; this is evident from a consideration of the schedule.

ITEMS THAT FIX INDIRECT EXPENSE

There may be some difference of opinion as to whether these items have been placed under their proper headings, but the exactness of this is not important for a consideration of the point in question. It is sufficient to say that a large part of the indirect expenses is practically fixed by considerations other than those of plant management; as, for instance, the location of the plant, involving rent, insurance, interest, on capital invested, etc., and further the layout of the plant, the relative positions of the buildings as to convenience, accessibility, etc.; the age and type of machinery and equipment; the extent of such equipment and its layout; the location of the plant as regards the labor and material markets. These and other items are decided by business or military considerations, and are quite beyond the scope and control of the man who is charged with operating the plant.

In other words, we have our navy yards laid out to suit military needs. The location of the plant, the layout and distribution of buildings, the character of the grounds; all these are fixed by military considerations. The conditions are set; the plant superintendent must meet them and work with them, obtaining such average efficiency as he can develop under the circumstances.

SUPERVISORY AND OPERATING CHARGES

There is a portion of the indirect expenses of the plant which properly comes to the plant superintendent and is controlled by him. This portion may be considered as consisting of supervisory charges and operation charges. Both of these, in the matter of their control, are more clearly allied to the direct charges than to the indirect charges, and are only placed under indirect charges for the reason that it is difficult to assign them to any particular job, as they represent small amounts of labor expended on a great number of jobs. The efficiency of the supervisory force and of the operating force of the plant represents a problem in the handling of direct labor, and neither offers an exception to the statement that the plant superintendent is concerned primarily with the direct charges in his efforts toward efficiency. The supervisory and operating forces are handled exactly the same as the force working on job orders of production.

MAINTENANCE CHARGES

A reference to the schedule shows that certain of the indirect charges are listed

---

SHOP EXPENSE

Under Control of Plant Superintendent	Not Under Control of Plant Superintendent	Partially Under Control of Plant Superintendent
Supervision		Maintenance of shop equipment
		Maintenance, shop furniture and fixtures
		Maintenance, loose and hand tools
		Maintenance of machine tools
		Maintenance of Elevators
		Miscellaneous shop expense
		Power
		Fuel

POWER EXPENSE

Attendant to on light and power plants Supervision	Maintenance of power plant buildings	Power plant, boilers, flues and stacks
	Maintenance of substation buildings	Power-plant machinery
	Power-plant piping	Fuel
	Distributing system (heat)	
	Distributing system (electrical)	
	Distributing system (air and hydraulic	
	Water system	
	Substations; motors and accessories	
	Maintenance of tools, furniture and fixtures	
	Power-plant, supplies; oil, grease and waste	

33

as being "partially under the control of the plant superintendent." This will, in general, be true of the class known as "maintenance charges." The age and construction of buildings, machines and equipment generally must influence the maintenance charges. This portion is not under the control of the plant superintendent. The proper care of such buildings, machines and equipment may be said to be a part of the duties of such superintendent; but suppose that they do receive the proper care, there will be a certain fixed charge for their maintenance proportionate to their age and proper construction.

In other words, the plant superintendent does not have it in his power to greatly influence the indirect charges. Therefore, he is not particularly concerned with them, and they do not enter into a consideration of the efficiency of any given or established plant. With a plant established, improvement and efficiency must come through a reduction of the direct cost of production.

Having taken the material charges and the indirect charges out of the control of the plant superintendent or, rather having pointed out that they are not under his control, it leaves him only the direct charges with which to obtain his efficiency. The important thing to determine, therefore, is the proper method of recording these direct charges as to form, substance and availability.

STANDARD MACHINE OPERATIONS

Every job may be divided into certain standard machine operations. The job may never recur, probably will not; but the standard machine operations will continually recur. Therefore, the important thing to determine and record is the accurate cost of these operations. Further, they should be recorded in such form and in such place as to make them comparative, and available for the constant daily use of the plant superintendent. The first step, therefore, is to install a system that will give you these records and make them available. The next step is to study and compare these records. You will then arrive at a determination of your present efficiency.

Then must follow a careful and detailed time-study of each standard operation, breaking it up into such factors as will permit of its analysis. By a time-study of these factors it will be possible to determine wherein time is being wasted or energy lost. Each change in method gives us new records which we can compare with those previously obtained, and the curve of efficiency is readily sketched in and followed. It is to be noted that this can be accomplished only by a consideration of the standard operations and not by a consideration of the job as a whole. Therefore, the plant superintendent is not interested in the cost of the job as a whole. He is in-

terested in the cost of the operations. The job-order number merely connects his work with the work of the accountant.

RECORDING MACHINE OPERATIONS

There is a disposition to lay too much stress on the cost of the job orders, as the job orders usually issued in navy yards are of such general character as to give no data which are valuable for comparative purposes. It may be argued that these job orders should be issued in such detail as to make them comparative, but this is quite impracticable, as issuing a separate job order for each machine operation is necessary under it. Let the job order be quite general in reading if you so desire, and let the detail be in the form of "instruction cards" to machines or operators, and having preserved these "instruction cards," file them away according to classes.

You thus at once have the desired record of machine operations. For instance, it is only of general interest to the plant superintendent to know the cost of installing a bulkhead on the U. S. S. "Illinois," for the reason that when bulkheads are installed on any other ship the cost of the installation on the "Illinois," furnishes him no guide to efficiency, as there is no probable chance that any two bulkheads will be alike; but if he obtains a record of the cost of laying out a certain number of plates per bulkhead on the "Illinois," of drilling a certain number of holes, of driving a certain number of rivets, of calking a certain number of feet of seam, of painting a certain number of square feet of bulkhead, he can readily compare these operations with other operations of their class, whether they be performed on bulkheads, on decks, on bridges and side plating, or upon any other job.

If he desires to install bulkheads more efficiently, he attacks the problem by first taking his laying-out gang, studying their process, and guiding them toward greater efficiency. Then he takes his drilling gang; endeavors to increase the number of holes that can be drilled per day, per hour, or per minute. Then he attacks the problem of riveting and endeavors to increase the number of rivets that can be driven in a day. Then the problem of calking, of painting, etc., treating each operation separately, analyzing it, studying it, devising improved methods for performing it, eliminating delays, lost motion, and all that tends toward inefficiency. Greater efficiency on a job is thus obtained by improving the efficiency of the separate operations. Take care of the operations and the job will take care of itself.

Whatever system is installed, therefore, must be such as to enable the plant superintendent to attack the operations. Such a system must provide for the division of jobs for the standard opera-

tions; for issuing instructions to the men or mechanics covering these standard operations; for recording the time spent by the men or machines on these standard operations; for filing these instruction cards by classes, so as to permit ready reference and comparison; for detailed study of these operations. These are all merely a part of proper or scientific management.

LABOR RECORDS AND JOB ORDERS

What has preceded is intended to illuminate and lay particular stress upon the following two very important points incorporated:

The relative value of indirect and direct labor records, from the standpoint of the plant superintendent. There can be no question but what the plant superintendent has merely a general interest in the indirect charges and a vital and constant interest in the direct charges.

The very small importance of the job order, from the standpoint of the plant superintendent, and the extreme importance of the operation, from the standpoint of the plant superintendent. There can be no question either but what the plant superintendent has merely a general interest in the job order as a whole, and a vital and constant interest in the detailed operations. The problem therefore is, how to put the direct labor charges and the operation records in the vest pocket of the plant superintendent.

sition, and however convenient it may be under the special conditions obtaining in a government plant, it is certainly in direct opposition to modern methods of handling burden. I will first cite some opinions on the point.

A CLEAR STATEMENT OF BURDEN

One of the clearest statements of the case is made by Gershom Smith, late comptroller of the Pennsylvania Steel Co. Writing in the *Engineering Magazine* recently he said:

> Wage costs, heretofore so largely relied on as a basis for estimate and distribution of indirect charges, are steadily waning in relative value in the industrial formula, and are constantly becoming more inseparably bound up with machine costs. It is not the operative, but the operative plus his machine that we must regard as the producing unit. Hence, as far as manufacturing costs are concerned, our fundamental measuring rule becomes increasingly inaccurate if we continue to divide it by the scale of men's wages or men's time. We need a new scheme of graduation, which will be commensurable throughout with the scale on which our costs of production are actually being built up. This new unit of division is found in the machine-hour.

Another aspect of the question is given by D. Newman Collins. Writing on the subject of Design of Industrial Buildings, he says:

> A comparative glance at an old and a modern shop will show the latter to be characterised by the absence of men and the substitution of ponderous machines. . . . . It requires $25,000 invested at 4 per cent. to maintain one man in service at $1000 per annum.

MACHINE COST OF OPERATION WANTED

Space forbids other citations, but those given will serve to show that there is another side to the question, overlooked by Mr. Edtterson. What every plant wants is not the true wage cost of operation, but the true machine cost of operation, of which labor is only a part. When it is considered that burden may vary from 90 to 150 per cent. and more, of direct labor, the importance of an accurate connection of burden with individual jobs, at the tool point, can be estimated.

The object of a plant is to manufacture, and in pursuit of this aim, various subsidiary activities are undertaken, all of which, in so far as they have any justification, are in the nature of services to direct production. Each machine is a "production center" making use of the subsidiary activities in a proportion different from its neighbor.

It is obvious, therefore, that work done at one such "production center" costs more or less than work done at another center which makes a different demand on the "services" to production maintained by the plant. To ignore these differences and keep track only of wage cost is a backward step.

Under the old-fashioned methods of lumping all the indirect costs into one general fund called burden, and then expressing this as a percentage of labor, there is something to be said for Mr. Edtterson's plan, which has the advantage of simplicity though not of thoroughness or accuracy. But since the introduction of the "scientific" machine rate, in 1900, these percentage methods are falling into disuse, and most modern authorities on cost accounting favor the machine-hour plan.

If Mr. Edtterson will refer to the two books, "Proper Distribution of the Expense Burden" and "Production Factors in Works Management," he will probably be inclined to take a new view of the importance of connecting burden with job costs, instead of seeking to divorce them.

A. HAMILTON CHURCH.
New York, N. Y.

35

Direct and Indirect Costs

The paper on this subject by J. Edtterson in Vol. 36, page 387, provides a very easy way of dealing with the vexed question of burden, namely by taking no notice of it, as far as the shops are concerned. This is a somewhat novel proposition.

The Principles of Management

By A. Hamilton Church and L. P. Alford

An earnest attempt to discover and declare the basic regulative principles of management, with special reference to the shop and factory. The principles are:

The systematic use of experience.

The economic control of effort.

The promotion of personal effectiveness.

This article is intended as a contribution toward the fixing of a systematic basis for a definite art of management. It does not pretend to be either a dogmatic or a final statement of details. The stage which has been reached by the art of management is the outcome of a slow evolution during a period of at least 150 years.

The division of labor has been a well recognized principle since the days of Adam Smith, in the middle of the eighteenth century. The detailed study and analysis of processes began with the factory development of the textile trade, and had reached a high state of evolution by 1832, as recorded in the writings of Charles Babbage.

The considerable expansion of manufacturing operations during the last 20 years, owing to the enormous international commerce fostered by the steamship and the telegraph, and the uprise of an unprecedented civilized community of 100,000,000 people in America, has introduced much more complex problems than were known to the manufacturers of the nineteenth century, and has rendered the settlement of the art of management on well defined principles a matter of very great importance and urgency.

Many notable contributions to the question have been made of late years, yet it is not too much to say that their authors have been more occupied with urging special systems on the attention of the industrial world, than in developing the skeleton of a real scientific art of management.

In other words, many *solutions* of the problem of management have been offered, representing personal points of view, but these solutions are merely empirical combinations of methods, some good, others of distinctly doubtful value, and their importance is based rather on the authority possessed by their authors than on close logical reasoning.

Management is very far from having attained the dignity of a science at the present time. Yet it has progressed sufficiently in an orderly, though strictly tentative, statement of fundamental principles to be highly desirable. The logical development of these principles to the point where they touch practice may also be undertaken, and in the present paper this is all that is attempted.

The search for fundamental principles is, of course, of great practical importance. They would bring to light the gaps in our knowledge, and focus attention on the weakest links in our chain of practical applications. The mapping out of related fields of activity would become possible, so that every proposed improvement in method could be seen in its re-

lation to the whole—a condition absent at the present time.

In Vol. 36, page 612, Congressman W. C. Redfield ably outlines the present situation and need thus:

But there has not yet been established a science of management. And yet, if a science were ever needed, meaning definite rules or principles, based on exact knowledge of facts, it is in this very matter of management.

No apology is therefore necessary for an attempt to formulate some definite basis on which to build a truly scientific art of management. The regulative principles of the art of management are three:

The systematic use of experience.

The economic control of effort.

The promotion of personal effectiveness.

If these three principles are correctly stated, then the scientific basis of management is capable of being derived from their development and extension.

THE FIRST PRINCIPLE—THE SYSTEMATIC USE OF EXPERIENCE

Experience is the knowledge of past attainment. It includes a knowledge of *what* has been done, and also *how* it has been done. It is inseparably associated with standards of performance, that is with the ideas of quantity and quality in relation to any particular method of doing something.

The great instrument of experience, which makes progress possible, is "comparison." By systematic use of experience is meant the careful analysis of what is about to be attempted, and its reference to existing records and standards of performance. In many cases it may be found that gaps in existing experience occur. In such cases the experimental determination of data may be undertaken, so that we have a full covering of the ground, either by the experience of others or from our own experimental determinations.

In setting out to examine any work it is necessary to ask:

What experience, in the form of methods and standards of performance, already exist?

Is our performance equal to these standards?

Is it so far behind that it will pay to expend time, energy and money to approximate more nearly?

Are existing standards based upon the use of the most advanced practices and methods of the present day, or is there reason to suppose that experimental redetermination of such standards would show a new maximum of effectiveness?

In the experimental accumulation of experience the economic value of such experience must be kept in view. If the inquiry relates to operations which will be repeated many times, as in the processes of manufacturing staple articles, detailed experimental investigation may be worth while. In other cases it is well to consider the total economic value involved, the possible maximum that could be saved, and the probable cost of the investigation.

Experience tends to pass into traditional practice. That is its most useful form. Every kind of experience must pass into the mind of a man before it can be utilized practically; hence it follows that new experience should be crystallized into new traditions of practice as fast as possible.

In the shop, men are not always running to textbooks to see if they are right—at least the competent practical man is not. Even if it be conceded that practice in the present day is all wrong, and needs to undergo exhaustive study and reform, this only means that we are engaged in developing new standards of practice, which will take the place of the old traditional practice, and will in turn, form a new tradition. The proper place for these new traditions or standards of practice is precisely the same place as where the old ones were kept, namely, in the minds and memories of those who do and are responsible for doing the work. Further, it is impossible to record it all—something must remain with the man.

New experience can be transmitted in one of two ways, either in minute instructions of which individual workers do not perceive the drift, or as a connected body of new practice. The latter form is the better, though it demands educational efforts somewhat apart from ordinary shop routine. Not until the new experience has become fixed as a habit will its full value be realized.

THE SECOND PRINCIPLE—THE ECONOMIC CONTROL OF EFFORT

Effort is experience in action. Before we can do we must think, that is, dig into our stores of experience relative to

37

38

the proposed undertaking. Having taken thought, we proceed to action.

In order to produce organized action it is necessary to control effort in various ways. These are, "division," "coördination," "conservation," and—in industrial undertakings — "remuneration." Most of the discussions about management are, in fact, discussions about the various methods and degrees of controlling effort and fixing its reward.

It is possible to manipulate effort so as to produce an organization of the utmost flexibility or on the other hand, one of hard and fast rigidity. In certain special cases, rigid organization is permissible, but in general manufacturing, flexibility is really essential.

By flexibility is meant the power of self-adjustment to unforeseen events.

The divisions, "coördination," "conservation" and "remuneration of effort" will now be considered in the succeeding paragraphs.

Division of Effort

Division of effort is largely controlled by design. This is the principle of the unit part or component. Modern practice regards the complete machine or device as an aggregation of parts, and it is one test of efficiency when these parts come together in perfect shape, without requiring readjustment to correct faults of workmanship in their progress through the shops.

In modern manufacturing, design cannot be considered apart from operation. Not only must the exigencies of shape and dimensions with a view to economy in molding and machining be kept in view, but reduction of work by means of jigs, fixtures, etc., must be kept in mind. Usually also, standard dimensions, or fits, are a controlling feature in design.

All types of management are pretty much in agreement as to design. Concentration of attention on the unit part may be regarded as settled practice. There are, however, two important ways in which subsequent activities are built up. In one case the drawing sets things in motion; in the other case the model does it. Even a small characteristic like this tends to produce some variation in the type of organization, but consideration of these variations must be postponed.

It will be evident that design is a wholly independent function. It may be efficient or inefficient, quite apart from other functions. We may have very high efficiency of operation, for instance, and very poor design, or vice versa. As we proceed we shall see that all manufacturing operations consist of the combination of this with several other functions—all of which are independent, and contribute their quota of efficiency or inefficiency to the total result.

"Division of effort" is a universal principle throughout all the activities of man-

ufacturing. Starting with design, which controls the maximum limit of operative division, it is usually found desirable that operation should also be divided into processes. These usually correspond to machines. To some extent they are controlled by "settings."

It is important to have as few settings as possible, as nothing else is so wasteful of time. One setting in a jig is, therefore, made to subserve several processes in some cases. In other cases one setting in a machine holds the work for a series of consecutive processes, which may be of a different character, as turning, boring, threading, etc., at one setting.

From this it is apparent that there are limiting considerations to the division of effort. It is not merely a question of dividing to the bitter end. There are cases in which it is better to combine operations, and in fact execute them simultaneously.

This is worthy of attention, because it will be found that in all the principles of management that have yet been ascertained the limiting conditions are not yet formulated. Every such principle has limitations and it is neither necessary nor advisable to push it to its farthest possible development. For example, the provision of jigs for repetition work and where it is required to secure dimensional relations of exactness, as in drilling holes, though a very old idea, has not yet been definitely settled as regards its limiting conditions, and there are frequent cases in which doubt exists whether the expenditure for such jigs was after all, a wise one.

By many of the enthusiastic advocates of particular systems of management, the existence of limiting conditions is hardly suspected, consequently they ride their favorite hobby to exhaustion, till many useful ideas become discredited in the eyes of practical men. It is not enough to know that a principle can be applied—it is even more important to know when not to apply it.

Management cannot substantiate its claim to be a science until all these problems are cleared up. At present, it is not too much to say that very few of the problems of management have been recognized and defined, much less settled. Much of the present clamor is actually leading attention astray from the true essentials of the science of management.

The third great field of division of effort is in connection with administration or control. This is the great battleground of the systems at the present moment. Thus, to mention only two, we have Taylor's functional system, and Emerson's line-and-staff plan. Also we have the old method of simple, delegated authority in hierarchical form, from president to manager, manager to superintendent, superintendent to foremen and so on. Which is the best?

Obviously, the question cannot be answered until we have ascertained what principles have been applied in each case to produce these forms of organization, and what are the limiting conditions that control, or should control them. The subject is a tempting one, but it must be postponed until, at least, the remaining modes of manipulating effort have received attention.

Co-ordination of Effort

The coördination of effort is an inseparable counterpart of the division of effort. By coördination is meant the prearrangement of a number of separate efforts in such a manner as to produce a definite end. A still more perfect coördination is attempted when this end is to be attained in a definite time. Coördination in design means that unit parts are so designed that, ultimately, they fit together. Coördination in division of operations means that when all the operations are performed certain definite shape and dimension are given to the part. Both kinds of coördination are part of everyday practice, and are generally realized with a good percentage of success. Coördination of operations in regard to time, is however, a more advanced matter, and in many plants is still in a very unsatisfactory stage.

The coördination of administrative effort is the most complex and debatable problem of all. The moment we begin to divide effort, we must also begin to provide for its coördination. Administrative effort does not possess the same tangibility or definiteness as do design and operation, because it is wholly made up of spheres of influence of personal authority.

Therefore, in proportion as we divide administrative effort (executive functions) its coördination becomes more difficult. The more we subdivide authority the less flexible becomes our organization.

There is a point midway between simple delegation of all authority and the method of analyzing it into component functions and handing out each of these functions to a separate man, that is probably the most effective way of dividing administrative effort. The limiting conditions to excessive functionalism can, however, already be seen as shown above.

Conservation of Effort

Effort requires not only to be divided and coördinated, but also conserved. The conservation of effort means proceeding along the line of least effort to attain a given end.

In regard to design, the conservation of effort implies standardization of parts. In regard to operation it implies standardization of tools and equipment. In regard to administration it means using only so much complexity of system as is absolutely necessary. The conservation of effort, though of very great practical importance, is so simple an idea that it hardly requires either emphasis or illustration, at this stage.

REMUNERATION OF EFFORT

The remuneration of effort has very little relation to any of the other manipulations of effort, for these would still be necessary if no remuneration was offered at all. But as no plants are manned with staffs who work for the mere pleasure of working or "for their health," the question of remuneration, is very important.

THE FUNCTION OF COMPARISON

It has already been remarked that the great instrument of experience is comparison. In practical matters, this is also a department of effort, and requires as careful treatment. It includes the comparison of actual product with set standards commonly termed "inspection," comparison of results as expressed in figures of various kinds, including works statistics, and cost accounts, as well as the accumulation of data of the efficiency of individuals with a view to justice in promotions.

Design is at the beginning of the chain of production and decides what is to be done. Comparison is at the end of the chain and records what has been done, and also in some cases decides whether it has been done according to design. The effort, or activity, devoted to comparison is, of course, subject to the general law of effort, and requires division, coördination, conservation, etc., just like other branches of activity.

Although somewhat intimately connected in many cases with the mechanism of administration or control, it must be clearly perceived as a quite different kind of activity. Administration sets and keeps things going. Comparison merely records the results. The distinction is important, because it is quite possible to have an excellent system of comparison, and a wretched system of administration, and vice versa. Comparison is, therefore, one of the independent functions of manufacturing activity, and its efficiency is not inter-related with that of other functions.

THE THIRD PRINCIPLE—THE PROMOTION OF PERSONAL EFFECTIVENESS

The ideal plant is one which has good equipment, good methods, and good men. It is a comparatively modern discovery that the welfare of the plant and the welfare of its employees are closely connected. By welfare, we do not mean however, the semi-philanthropic ideals which result in model villages and other "social welfare" experiments, but only

the application of the principle of the "square deal" to working relations during working hours.

The Latin poet defined happiness as the possession of a healthy mind in a healthy body. The definition is perhaps a somewhat pagan one, but eminently practical at that. If the plant cannot secure these gifts for its people, it can at least see that all conditions shall be favorable, or at any rate, that they shall meet few conditions in their working hours inimical to either health of mind or body.

Remuneration stands, of course, at the head of these conditions, but it is not the only one, nor does it stand unconnected with others. In spite of Thomas Carlyle the "cash nexus" is far from being the only link between employer and employee, even today—that is, if he is wise. In every considerable organization *esprit de corps* is always latent, and if it remains latent or is turned into latent, or open, discontent it is a mark of the very worst management. Every human being desires to feel that his work is important. Even the criminal frequently has pride in his criminality. With certain kinds of creative work the mere doing of it is associated with a high degree of personal satisfaction, because the author or the artist is only following out the law of his being. The worst enemies of progress and contentment are those who are always crying from the house tops that mechanical work is dulling to the intellect, that men are becoming machines, and so on. It is a shock to any man to hear that his work is unimportant and destructive of the higher faculties. It may be so in certain cases, but it is not necessarily so. That largely depends on circumstances. The control of such circumstances is to some extent in the employer's hands.

Considered on the lowest platform the subject is one of importance, since all errors of policy have to be paid for, whether by an individual employer, or, in the case of a general practice, by the industry as a whole. It is one of the most hopeful signs of modern times that these matters are being actively discussed from many different points of view.

In proportion to the number of elements in a problem the difficulty of its solution augments. Personal effectiveness, and its favoring conditions, contain innumerable elements, many of which probably defy human analysis. Therefore, we must proceed modestly and cautiously on the path of discovery, and far from attempting to lay down the laws, it will be well if we succeed in observing the interplay of a few of the most obvious conditions of personal effectiveness.

To begin with, we must assume physical health. From this it is but a

step to recognizing that shop conditions must be such that health can be conserved. This point is beginning to be understood, and modern shops avoid the dirt, darkness and obscurity and extremes of cold and heat that a generation ago were accepted as good business. We have progressed so far as to be aware that, on the contrary, they are very bad business. Closely allied is the question of affording facilities for personal cleanliness, dining halls for the midday meal and other auxiliaries to physical needs of shop existence. The most widespread application of this third principle today is in the safeguarding of machines and operations.

The real center of the problem, is, however, not on the physical plane, or only incidentally so. The physchological elements are not so obvious, but they are much more important. As in most of the analyses we have made, it is observable that these two groups are nearly independent of one another; that is, their efficiency can vary independently. We may have very bad physical conditions and yet a fine *esprit de corps* or, on the other hand, a finely arranged modern shop and a sullen, discontented population within its walls.

The independence is not quite complete, since bad physical conditions must affect the psychological side to some extent, even though not observably. But on the other hand, the finest psychological adjustment will not make a dark shop light, or a cold shop warm.

Some of the conditions of personal effectiveness are these: The individual must feel leadership; have adequate encouragement and reward; be physically fit and under good physical conditions; and receive a definite allotment of responsibility.

These conditions apply not only to the operative force but to all grades of employees. In fact, some of them apply with greater urgency to the man "higher up" than to the actual worker. It is evident that they have, or should have, a considerable and controlling influence on the arrangements made for the division and coördination of administrative effort.

A good deal has been made by some of the modern schools of management doctrine of the claim that this or that system creates a fine spirit of coöperation between the plant and its men, but for the most part these claims are merely statements of a desirable end to be attained, and not indications of a method by which it can be attained.

The truth is, of course, that no single element of a system, or even a combination of half a dozen such elements, as methods of payment, functionalized authority, etc., more than touch the fringe of the question. Highly organized systems may coexist with fine *esprit de*

40

corps, but the latter is not dependent on any form of system or organization.

Of all the conditions controlling a fine working atmosphere, leadership probably plays the most important part. In warfare men prefer to serve under the general who wins battles, though that entails hardships without number and toil without end. In industralism, mechanism is a mighty unimportant thing compared with an "old man" who is a born leader of men.

The weakness of one prominent school of management doctrine is that it pretends that it has superseded leadership, by substituting therefor elaborate mechanism. Such a contention betrays a complete misapprehension of how men are constituted, and of what the true functions of elaborate mechanism really are. All such mechanism is but a collection of mechanical tentacles or feelers, to enable the controlling mind and spirit of the management to be in several places at once. If the personality behind these tentacles is a feeble one, the mechanism will not supplement its deficiencies in the slightest degree.

This is not to say that such mechanism is useless; on the contrary, it is essential in the large-scale operations of modern industry, and it is, therefore, highly important that it should be carefully arranged and well balanced, but it is in itself inert and lifeless—a purely passive channel through which the capacities of leadership may exert themselves.

A favorite illustration of the folly of "perpetual motion" is the reflection that a pound will not lift a pound anyway, and that the chances of making it do so are not increased by putting gears, levers, and other mechanism between the first pound and the second one, however artfully and plausibly these may be arranged.

The same truth applies to the mechanism of the organization. All work is born of effort, and all effort is controlled by the personal reaction of one man on another; therefore it is evident that no greater results can be attained by putting a vast array of blanks, forms, cards and books between the first man and the second, however plausibly and artfully they are arranged.

In other words, organization and system are something forced on us by the necessities of the case, and that something has no virtue either in itself, or in any possible combination of its components. It does not add one single cubit to the stature of leadership, though on the other hand, its absence, or its bad arrangement may detract considerably from the full realization of what would otherwise be possible to leadership

It is more than probable that types of organization depend for their success on their harmony with the particular type of leadership that is endeavoring to make use of them. This would explain why systems are successful in one case and fail down in what appears a similar case.

At the present stage of the analysis of management we can do no more than make a note of this. It must always be remembered, however, that organization is a tool, and that it is our duty to fit it to the leader, and not try to compress the leader to fit the system. Understanding of the limiting conditions of this part of the problem must be left to future progress to compass.

RECAPITULATION

This necessarily highly condensed and skeleton outline of the main regulative principles of management must end here. It will be observed that we have enumerated three regulative principles dealing respectively with "experience," "effort" and "personal relationships." Effort is further subject to certain modes of action; namely, "division," "coördination," "conservation" and "remuneration." This action is applied in certain definite divisions: "Design," "administration," "operation" and "comparison."

The truth or error of these expansions of the three principles must rest on the idea that each of these subdivisions is independent of the others. One can have good division with bad coördination; a high degree of conservation with a faulty basis of remuneration. Similarly the practical applications are also independent. Good design may coexist with every subsequent inefficient element. Operation may be, and commonly is, well in advance of methods of administration. All these may be good, and yet the remaining function of comparison may be only rudimentary.

These considerations point to the fact that *these are not arbitrary or accidental classifications, but are really fundamental*, and can be used in the practical analysis of the activities of any business. Improving one of them does not improve the other, and may even in some cases be wholly wasted effort. This latter consideration shows why reorganizations sometimes fail of effect, and general efficiency is not improved.

Finally we have dealt cursorily with the question of personal relationships. In their very nature these are more nebulous and difficult of precise definition, yet the conditions of personal effectiveness enumerated also pass the test of independent functioning, inasmuch as any one of them may be at a maximum while the others are lower in the scale, or practically nonexistent.

It may be interesting to subjoin here a brief comparison of the chief principles put forward by Taylor and Emerson, and show their place in relation to this tentative attempt to formulate the fundamental and constructive principles of management.

Mr. Taylor's Principles

As pointed out in Vol. 35, page 108, in an article entitled "Has Scientific Management Science?" Mr. Taylor's "scientific management" is a collection of axioms and an arbitrary combination of specific mechanisms rather than a body of principles. Among its leading features, time study, functional foremanship, standardization, planning in advance, and task-bonus may be selected as characteristic.

The place of time study is obviously under the first principle; namely, the systematic use of experience. It is a tool for supplementing and extending our experience, and its economic limitations have been discussed under that heading. Functional foremanship is related to the principle of the economic control of effort, and particularly to the division of administrative effort.

Standardization belongs to the same principle, and its particular niche is under the head of conservation of effort, is an avoidance of complexity where uniformity and simplicity can be maintained. In reforming old industries, standardization usually means cutting down, but in new industries it means the avoidance of unnecessary kinds, sizes and methods. It means building up along the lines of least effort—either result flowing readily from acceptance of the sub-principle of the conservation of effort.

Planning in advance is largely an application of the coördination of effort. A certain amount of planning is inherent in every established routine, because the very idea of division of effort necessarily implies some measure of coördination. The necessity for preserving flexibility acts as a limiting condition to planning too elaborated and intensive.

Task-bonus is, of course, a special variety of application of remuneration of effort. Its value as a practical device must rest upon the degree to which it actually promotes personal effectiveness. It is one of many methods of remuneration, but the conditions to which this and the other methods apply in the most effective degree have not yet been studied and compared in any serious way.

One more point of Taylor's system may be mentioned. It is his claim that the science which underlies each act of each workman is so great that no workman is able to fully understand it (and presumably give it effect) without specific and very detailed guidance from above. This point has been covered by what has already been said on the subject of forming new traditions and habits based on the new knowledge that recent progress has given rise to.

This is obviously a case of applied systematic experience. If Mr. Taylor had in mind the use of his slide-rules in making this claim then it is obvious that the use of such slide-rules, where they are useful, should become as much a part of the man's working habit, as is the use of shifting gears or other devices for controlling the working of the machine.

MR. EMERSON'S PRINCIPLES

Emerson's twelve principles will not detain us long. His first principle, "clearly defined ideals," is not especially an industrial principle. It is presupposed that a man knows what he wants, or he can do nothing successfully. It certainly comes, however, under the head of systematic use of experience, if we try to apply it practically. His second principle, "common sense," is hardly a principle at all. It is simply one of the basic conditions of all successful human endeavor, and might be ranked with "sound judgment," "perseverance" and other moral and mental attributes. It is not especially industrial.

His third principle, "competent counsel," must also be ranged under the systematic use of experience. It means from those best qualified to provide it. His fourth principle, "discipline," comes under the division of administrative effort.

One of the prime functions of administration is to secure discipline, that is, to prevent irregular activities which are not coördinated with the useful activities necessary to the work. Idleness, absence, disregard of instructions are examples of uncoördinated, and, therefore, harmful effort.

The fifth principle enunciated by Mr. Emerson is "the fair deal." This is a psychological matter belonging to the promotion of personal effectiveness. His sixth principle, "reliable and immediate records," is, of course, the function of comparison spoken of, though not the whole of it. The seventh principle, "dispatching," comes under, and in fact is, the practical mechanism of, the coördination of effort. The eighth, ninth and tenth principles, "standards and schedules," "standardized conditions" and "standardized operations," have been discussed under the Taylor system; so with the eleventh, "standard-practice instructions."

In these four cases standardization means conformity with the principle of conservation of effort, while standard practice instructions are a part of planning, and therefore of coördination of effort. Finally we have the twelfth principle given by Mr. Emerson; namely, "efficiency reward," which is simply another phrase for "remuneration of effort."

These illustrations have been made to demonstrate that as far as can be seen at present the three fundamental principles formulated in this paper, with their derivatives, do actually find a place for all divisions which modern analysis of industrial working has brought to light.

The important point is, of course, that by stating and fixing what are believed to be the three basic and fundamental principles of industrial activity, and deriving the subordinate details from these in logical order, a beginning has been made toward finding a truly scientific basis for the art of management, on which all its prime facts can be built up, later, into a coherent and understandable system of theory and practice.

41

The "Principles of Management"

I believe that nearly all who are interested in the problem of shop management will find themselves in hearty accord with the spirit of the article on the "Principles of Management," by Messrs. Church and Alford on page 857. If there is anything which the literature of this subject needs it is a clearing away of the underbrush that obscures the root of the matter and getting a clean-cut separation of the principles involved and their practical application.

The early literature of almost any movement is likely to consist, to a large extent, of a discussion of phenomena and results rather than of basic facts, and the literature of the principles of industrial management are markedly of this character. It is so filled with examples of systems, cards, forms and special methods that many have acquired the idea that it is possible to build out in the shop yard, a system that will answer all needs, lift it up with the yard crane and drop it down, a perfect fit, over shop, machinery, and personnel.

This lengthy discussion of *methods* has done much to obscure *principles*. The work of Mr. Taylor has done much to call attention to the fact that there *are* basic principles which can be formulated, and the article under discussion will go a long way in furthering this line of thought.

One of the most important points brought out in the paper is the distinction between the basic principles of management and human characteristics. No man can make a success of any business without such things as common sense and its correlated virtues. Yet the ardent advocates of system, in their anxiety to build up an imposing structure, have often included many of these human attributes as part of their structure with the result that the principles at the bottom are almost obscured from view.

As the article in question clearly points out, the fundamental principles on which the science of management (if indeed it be science) rests, are few and comparatively easy to understand. The difficulty lies in formulating methods of applying them, in recognizing their limitations, and in estimating correctly the desirability of some of the effects produced.

Granted that the principles are clearly in mind, it is not easy to apply them particularly when the matters of personnel and personality are to be considered, as in general they must be. It is disturbing factors like these which make it impossible to lay down methods which are universally applicable.

Personality and leadership are still, as these writers have pointed out, the great moving powers of all organizations. Many discussions by advocates of so called "systems" lead one to believe that these necessities can be obviated by card systems and blank forms, overlooking the fact that "organization" can *strengthen* a strong leader but never replace him.

I have always been inclined to believe that many of the systems which can lay claim to success have often succeeded, not so much because of inherent good qualities, but because of the leadership back of them.

The points which they have raised regarding the limitations of all *systematic* effort are well taken. It is not so difficult to plan manufacturing tools and methods where quantity of product can be secured, but it requires rare discrimination and expert knowledge to know where to stop the organized effort for simpler methods as quantity decreases.

It is as easy to overdo as to underdo in problems such as these, and many of them cannot be reached by mechanical systems, but require the keen judgment of the trained mind to properly evaluate new methods and standards in terms of its own experience.

And lastly the thread of thought that runs throughout the entire article bearing on the relations of these matters to human affairs should not be passed unnoticed. The time has already come when methods cannot be adjudged solely on the basis of whether they will produce dividends. Industry is being viewed more and more as a general means of supporting human existence and not as a means of individual profit; and as this sentiment grows, details of industrial methods are being judged desirable or not desirable, depending on how they affect human relations rather than on the ground of financial profit or loss.

I believe the statement of the basic principles of progressive industrial organization set forth in the article in question is not far from the truth, and we are in need of more literature of this kind. We need discussions which are neither destructive criticism of any earnest effort on the one hand, nor devoted to the exploitation of some one expert or system on the other, but which aim to find out if possible just what is at the bottom of this weighty matter. For if the basic principles can be made clear, methods of applications can usually be found.

DEXTER S. KIMBALL.
Professor of Machine Design, Cornell University.
Ithaca, N. Y.

The concentration of discussion, largely upon one particular scheme of industrial administration and control, has been the natural result of the exclusive claims of its promoters.

Many possible adherents of the efficiency movement have been lost by insisting that "scientific management" is the authoritative and final word upon the subject and that its principles and derived elements should be applied "with no modifications and no deviations" to every class of industry.

As a matter of fact no such program has been found practicable, yet the attitude remains and is a principal reason for the destructive rather than constructive criticism which this particular system has evolved.

The time is opportune for considering, analyzing, and formulating the general principles underlying successful industrial practice without tying these up to the preferred detail of any particular set of practitioners.

ATTITUDE OF THE PRACTICAL MAN

One thing is clear, namely, that the men who have "to produce the goods" daily, reject the idea that a pink pill has been discovered for all pale plants; they will not entertain it under any label. It offends their common sense. It also leads to injurious reaction against perfectly reasonable efficiency measures and hampers sympathetic and capable administrators in their promotion of betterment.

It would be a great pity if the very fertile generalization which we owe to the arduous labors of Mr. Taylor, should fail of acceptance because of intolerant or arbitrary insistence upon a system of detail which takes no account of the variety of industrial conditions and problems.

THE FUNDAMENTALS

For this reason the recent endeavor by Messrs. Church and Alford in your pages to outline the fundamentals of practice, without asserting any proprietary interest or introducing a mass of debatable details, is likely to interest the great mass of executive employees. The views set forth by these writers are lucid, well considered and concise.

They well deserve, and will receive the careful attention of progressive engineers and production managers. Their analysis covers the basic ideas and motives underlying all deliberate industrial coördination and also much, more or less unconscious, practice.

The fundamentals have been correctly reduced to three independent principles of action in management, namely: Systematized experience; economized effort; and developed personality; all raised to the highest power consistent with economy, and the business and human factors peculiar to any particular administrative problem. These principles and their natural derivatives are so fully and satisfactorily outlined that they call for neither criticism nor further expansion here.

The insistence, at great length, upon the details of particular shop manage-

43

ment systems has in the past merely darkened counsel or raised debatable issues. Your contributors have been well advised in their endeavor to find what is common to all such business problems, and their clear-cut analysis and philosophy is capable of very wide application.

LEADERSHIP

Your correspondents do well to emphasize the human elements in the success, or otherwise, of the best laid schemes of industrial economy. In the course of actual practice the existence of even a perfect scheme will not insure that the fundamentals and their derivatives will be all evenly developed. They rarely are and this may occur under the best system. To attain the ideal, the supervisory staff must be organized and competent to a degree which no mere system of actions can guarantee.

THE ULTIMATE GOOD

The ideal conception of work is that it should be the spontaneous expression of a man's best impulses. When it is, instead, a more or less grudging participation in what is felt to be daily drudgery there is something wrong with the man or the work, or possibly with both. There is nothing in the true principles of good management, or in their derivatives, from which the workman has anything to fear.

Less discussion of the details and more thorough practical application of them by wise and competent administrators will not herald the millenium but they will convince the largest and most reasonable section of our American workmen that they are getting at all times from such employers an absolutely square deal and that they ought to expect nothing less and nothing more.

Detroit, Mich.　　　JOHN CALDER.

46

A. HAMILTON CHURCH.[1] Of the two reports presented by the committee, the minority report raises the question as to whether the claims of certain groups of men to the possession of the key to all progress, have any measure of justification.

As it appears to me, the various schools of management have not presented to us any well-balanced theory of management capable of being developed in a hundred different ways according to special needs. On the contrary, it is as if they had presented to us a barrel of gunpowder, a telescope, and a magnetic compass and claimed these mechanisms to be the whole science of maritime warfare. Certain definite and concrete mechanisms such as planning departments, stop-watches, despatching boards, instruction cards of extraordinary complexity, and special methods of remunerating labor are interesting and useful, but do not make, either singly or combined, a science of management.

Moreover, the original claims, already generously broad, have been so expanded by some of the younger disciples that almost every modern method is claimed to be the direct outcome of the wisdom of one or another of the rival schools of scientific efficiency. It is because of this kind of thing that the minority report is important.

Turning to the majority report, we find that the prime underlying principle of management engineering is the transference

[1] Cons. Engr., 30 Broad St., New York.

of skill. This is an illuminative statement, and I venture to think, of great practical value. It is put very tersely in the sentence in Par. 8, "the skill in shoemaking is now in the mechanical equipment of the shop." That is a clear-cut picture of a change that is already complete, and it helps us to realize exactly what is meant by the transference of skill. It also helps us to understand why, in the engineering trades, there are such wide discrepancies in the amount of work turned out by individual operators. It is because, in these trades, the transference of skill is by no means so complete. For one thing, the capacity and range of the average machine tool is large, and to some extent indefinite. A considerable amount of skill is still vested in the worker. Still more, a remarkable amount of ignorance as to what the machine will or will not do is shared by the employer and the workman.

47

The report shows why this is bound to be so at the present stage. In the process of transfering hand skill to the mechanical fingers of the machine, the report emphasizes the fact that more attention has been devoted to designing it, than to the problem of using it afterwards.

The more I think over this problem, the more I am convinced that the true line of progress is the exhaustive study of machines, their capacities and limitations. I have held this opinion for many years, and the system of industrial accounting I have been advocating for the past decade was, I believe, the first step made towards bringing forward the machine to its true place as a factor of production. But I must confess that until this principle of the transference of skill was brought out so clearly by this report, I did not realize exactly why the machine tool was frequently so surprisingly ineffective under indifferent handling.

I will pass over the acceptance by the committee of the three regulative principles of management, viz: (a) the systematic use of experience, (b) the economical control of effort, and (c) the promotion of personal effectiveness, which were worked out by Mr. Alford and myself, except to say that the credit for the formulation of these principles belongs in a larger degree to Mr. Alford than to me, and I will conclude my remarks by calling attention to a phrase used in Par. 51 of the report, viz: "the habit stage."

All the mechanism of organization in the world is valueless

beside the steadiness of production that comes from the establishment of good habit throughout a plant. I will go further, and say that the whole object and end of organization should be to create the right kind and degree of habit in everyone of the persons engaged in production, from the president down to the shop sweeper.

It is not enough for the workman to be so instructed that he forms good habit. Every living link in the chain of production requires equally to be so trained that his acquired habit is harmonious with all the rest. The report has mentioned this aspect of the question where it insists that the executives and not the workman are the persons most important to be reached. Few people understand that the principal work of an expert organizer is not the designing of elaborate blanks and cards, but the fostering, with tireless patience, of correctly adjusted habit in each member of the staff.

As the new ideals of management engineering appear to me, and this view seems confirmed by the committee's report, they may be summed up in three sentences:

Take nothing for granted.

See that every effort is adapted to its purpose.

Cultivate habit.

These sentences are, of course, merely practical derivatives of the three regulative principles referred to in the report. Each of them in turn implies other things which will readily suggest themselves. Thus, the possibility of cultivating correctly adjusted habit depends obviously upon proper mental and physical conditions for the living forces. It implies "lead" and not "drive."

It is an interesting question where the new spirit that we find abroad in industrial management has come from. To some extent, I think, it is part of a larger movement, the realization of a sense of social solidarity, of social responsibility of each for all, that is so marked a feature of the times. But it also arises, in part, from another cause. Scientific men tell us that the great difference between a savage race and a highly civilized one is that the former remains in a condition of natural innocence, and the latter has arrived at self-consciousness. This, I think, is the real state of affairs in regard to management engineering. We are passing from a stage at which there was a simple and unconscious following of tradition, into a stage of self-consciousness in which we are moved to subject our habits and our motives to severe self-scrutiny, and examine afresh every item of our daily practice. It is a very painful stage to have arrived at. Most of us are so content with our comfortable natural innocence that we do not like to part with it, but it is a process that once commenced, must continue.

The examination into new methods of remunerating labor, the adoption, with caution, of searching instruments of analysis, such as time study, the use of precise methods of accounting— these are not causes, but *consequences*, of this newly awakened self-consciousness. It is beginning to be recognized that production is an aggregate of infinitesimal separate acts, in each of which there are three main components. First, experience must be drawn on; secondly, the resulting effort must be intelligently adapted to the end in view; thirdly, this intelligent effort must become habitual. And to secure the successful performance of these acts, the living forces concerned must be maintained in the pink of condition, both mental and physical.

49

CARL G. BARTH. I am gratified with the report as an endorse-
ment of the kind of work I am permanently engaged in; particularly as I find among the names of the members of the committee who have signed the majority report, that of a personal
friend who, only through this investigation has become a convert
to scientific management. I am unable to take as broad a view
of the matter as the committee have attempted, as I am tied
down too closely to the daily details and difficulties of the practical introduction of scientific management to devote much time
to its broad historical and economic aspects. Part of the report,
also, has a rather amusing side for those of us who now for
several years past have been working with some success in this
field, in that it is virtually a declaration to the effect that the
committee have assured themselves that there really is such a
thing as " scientific management," and that it does accomplish
some of the things, at least, which its exponents allege that it
does. It reminds me of the farmer who came to town in the early
days of the automobile to assure himself that there really was
such a thing as a horseless wagon not requiring tracks to run on,
and that it actually did carry people around in the streets without running wild and upsetting everything in its way, except
when in the hands of a driver possessing more ambition than
experience and sense of responsibility.

As regards the minority report, I see no good reason for its
coming into being, as it contains nothing that I cannot agree
to, and to my mind nothing that it recommends conflicts with
the majority report.

It merely asserts that there are places in which, and conditions under which, the introduction of scientific management
would not be a paying proposition; a matter that I do not
believe anybody will dispute. In fact, experience has long ago
taught me that there is hardly an establishment in which there
is not some department or corner of the works which is not
better left almost untouched by the new order of things, except
in the matter of having its relations to the rest of the works
properly dovetailed into this.

To take the automobile for a second illustration, I have never
heard of anybody recommending its use to the extent of declaring that walking is no longer a profitable and sensible method
of locomotion, to be eventually given up entirely; though we
also know that some automobile enthusiasts do use the automo-

51

bile at times and in places where walking would be more appropriate.

As regards the attempt of the committee, and others, to give a more appropriate name to what we all now pretty well understand by scientific management, I like to state that I have until recently preferred to refer to what I am trying to do, as the "Taylor system of management;" and that Mr. Taylor himself was the first one to discourage me in thus using his personal name in that connection, and to suggest substituting therefor the term scientific management. However, as I am not only not ashamed of, but on the other hand exceedingly proud of, being accused of being Mr. Taylor's most orthodox disciple, I have stuck to the former until recently; though since numerous imitators have invented a number of substitute names, so far as I can see to no practical purpose, I have become more favorably inclined to the use of the term scientific management. Accordingly, I now refer to myself as an exponent of the "Taylor system of scientific management," and feel that in doing so I have just about the whole thing.

In his discussion Mr. Gillette tries to point out that Mr. Taylor and his disciples have not covered the whole field and mentions as an example, cost and accounting as a matter to which they have paid no attention. However, the mere fact that Mr. Taylor has not written on every subject of his activities, must not be taken as a proof that he has neglected any important matter connected with the management of an industrial institution. The fact is that Mr. Taylor's disciples also owe him a great debt for the cost and accounting system he has handed over to them, one which for completeness and flexibility stands absolutely unequalled even today, in spite of the great attention this subject has recently received.

Mr. Church also mentions that the study of machines is a matter thus neglected. However, this is also a subject which Mr. Taylor gave serious attention over 25 years ago, or about the same time that he first took up the study of the art of cutting metals, and this has played one of the most important roles in the subsequent work done by myself in the perfection of some of Mr. Taylor's methods.

Again, one speaker suggested that there should be a special purchasing agent for buying labor, as if that too were a brand new idea, whereas Mr. Taylor has also pointed out the desirability of that, and as long ago as 1895 gave us an example of it in a man employed by some Western company at a salary of $5,000 a year, who had the buying of labor down to a fine art.

Mr. Gantt has told us about the disastrous results of changing to piecework from his bonus system of paying, in a plant systematized by himself, and I fear that what he said might have been misleading to some of the audience.

There is no question that piecework based on careful time study is the best and most just form of contract between employer and employe, and though I have not introduced Mr. Taylor's differential piece rates for some years past, I still believe that system is the best suggested to date. However, it is so difficult to get employers to wait until all such standards have been provided, and such time-study men have been trained, as are absolutely essential for the introduction of a piece-rate system. that we are usually forced by circumstances to beg the question and to resort to the expedient of a bonus or premium system.

These systems have the advantage of any piece-rate system, and particularly the differential, in that they may be established and give some satisfaction to both parties concerned, long before it would be possible to make a success of a piece-rate system.

However, there is no doubt in my mind, that the differential piece-rate system conceived and used by Mr. Taylor some 30 years ago, is the ideal of all the schemes suggested to date for paying workers in any other way than by straight day wages.

Regarding the use of a moving picture machine for motion- and time-studies, it looks to me to be practically the same thing as was offered to the Watertown Arsenal at the time we took up that part of the work there. I do not remember the inventor's name, only that he was connected with the Navy or with one of the navy yards in one capacity or another. While the scheme was interesting, it was declined after a conference between the commanding officer Mr. Merrick, and myself, particularly on the opinion expressed by Mr. Merrick, who is one of the most experienced time-study men in the country, and because of the anticipated great expense both of procuring and operating such a machine. Perhaps this was a mistake, for no doubt the machine can be successfully used for motion study, and hence for the elimination of useless motions, but I am still open to conviction regarding the use of any machinery of this kind in connection with time study. The two main difficulties in time

53

study are: first, to judge when a worker is working at a proper rate and to make proper allowances when he is not; second, to make proper allowances for necessary rests, etc.; and I do not see how any kind of machinery can help us in these difficulties.

54

The Journal of Accountancy

Official Organ of the American
Association of Public Accountants

| Vol. 15 | APRIL, 1913 | No. 4 |

55

The Treatment of Interest on Manufacturing Investment

In a manufacturing business shall interest on investment be considered as a factor of cost, or shall it be treated as a deferred charge against profits? The matter is one of considerable practical accounting importance and one on which the views of prominent accountants are diametrically opposed.

The reasons for this divergence of view and of practice have been presented in scattered articles, in single addresses, and in discussions following these addresses, but they do not seem to have received at any time a connected, reasonably complete and comparative consideration. For the purposes of such a consideration the JOURNAL presents in the following pages for the first time a series of comparative articles for and against the inclusion of interest on investment in manufacturing cost.

Although the writers of these articles are well-known and able advocates, it is not probable that they have given all the reasons that can be adduced in favor of the one course or the other, nor is it likely that their arguments are all unanswerable. For the sake of a full discussion and, as far as may be, a practical settlement of the question, it is to be hoped that the statements of the present articles will be supplemented or commented upon as may seem necessary. For this purpose the JOURNAL columns are open.

Interest on Investment in Equipment

By William Morse Cole

Assistant Professor of Accounting in Harvard University

Though it is common to speak of cost accounting as if it were different in nature from other kinds of accounting, virtually all accounting worthy of the name has for a prime purpose the determination of cost. Accounting should serve as a guide in three ways: in fixing prices so that they shall be adjusted properly to costs; in eliminating waste of material, of labor, and of burden charges; and in determining what had best be undertaken in the establishment itself and what had best be purchased or ordered outside. Since these three purposes are the recognized fundamental purposes of cost accounting, it is necessarily true that whether an enterprise is concerned with manufacturing, distribution, or service, its accounting should be, in a sense, cost accounting.

Let us examine these three aims in turn.

Prices must be fixed at such a point that they shall at least cover (1) materials, or goods; (2) labor, or service; and (3) expense burden, or what are commonly called "overhead charges." Obviously, if the last of these is not quite fully covered, the continuance of production or service is not economically advisable (unless, of course, the work serves other purposes than those which are immediately connected with the initial enterprise). If, again, the income provided by the price gives less than a proper amount as interest on the investment—investment in the form of capital locked up in machinery, facilities, material, or waiting product,—the return is not economically sufficient to make the enterprise self-supporting. If this interest is not included in the expense burden, therefore, it must be added later, somewhere, before one can know whether the return is adequate to make the enterprise self-supporting. Since one of the purposes of accounting is to show whether the return is adequate, the interest would seem necessarily to be involved somewhere in the accounting.

Efficient management always attempts to eliminate as much as possible of excess consumption of material, excess expenditure of labor—both mental and muscular,—and excess investment in machinery, in other facilities, and in supplies. The best guide for such elimination is an analysis of these various elements, so that comparison may be made between different methods and between different managements. To use a simple illustration, there may be a choice between two methods as follows: machinery at a cost of $35,000, materials at a cost of $5, and labor at a cost of $20; or machinery at a cost of $5,000, material at $5, and labor at $30. We may know, perhaps, that the maintenance, insurance, and taxes on the machinery, while the article is in machine process (that is, the share of maintenance, insurance, and taxes chargeable on this particular production), will be $10 in the first case, and $1.50 in the second case. These figures give us with the expensive machinery a production-cost of $35.00 (that is, $5 for material, $20 for labor, and $10 for maintenance, etc.), and of $36.50 ($5 for material, $30 for labor, and $1.50 for maintenance, etc.), with the less expensive machinery. Taking no account of the interest, therefore, the investment in the expensive machinery appears worth while—if, at least, our production is so large that a margin of $1.50 reduction in cost on each article of product is worth while when set against the possibly greater error in our estimate of depreciation, etc. Yet we have clearly left out of account one element of the problem, for, until we know the length of time for which these different equipments are involved in production we do not know whether interest on the greater capital in the first case will more than eat up the margin of saving over the second. If, for example, the machinery is employed a day in producing this article, even though we use as low a rate of interest as 3 per cent, there is in the expensive machinery an additional element of $3.50 in interest for the one day involved (on a 300-day basis), but there is an additional charge of only 50 cents in interest, on the same ground, for the inexpensive machinery. This difference in favor of the less expensive machinery turns the scale of advantage; for the costs are now $38.50 compared with $37. If, on the other hand, the machines were employed in this production only one hour, on the basis of a 9-hour day, the more expensive machinery with the lower labor cost would be a more economical means of production; for, since the interest element is now only 39 cents, its total is $35.39, but the total for the other machine, with interest of 6 cents, is $36.56. It is absolutely

57

233

essential, therefore, that interest be taken into consideration in determining which of two methods of production is more economical.

The same sort of consideration of interest is essential in attempting to determine what we shall make in our own establishment and what we shall order outside; for if work at home involves investment in machinery, or other facilities, so that we must get a return of $38.50 from our ultimate product or service, but we can purchase the same product or service outside for $37, it is obviously foolish to do the work at home—unless, indeed, our freedom from outside dependence is worth to us more than the difference in cost, or unless we can find no employment for our capital elsewhere at a rate as high as that which we have used in our calculation.

No comparison is possible between different establishments, between different periods in the same establishment, or between different methods in the same establishment, if capital investment in labor-saving or material-saving machinery is neglected; for the very purpose of such investment is to save cost in other directions, and to neglect the capital sacrifice, made in saving other costs, is to neglect in part the very aim of cost accounting.

Opponents of treating interest as a cost may admit the need of knowing the figure of interest but may deny the desirability of showing it on the books. The function of an accountant is to analyze a situation and learn the facts; and the function of a bookkeeper is to record the facts which, if not recorded, will be forgotten. It seems, therefore, as if it is the function of a cost accountant to learn regarding interest the facts which will serve as a guide in determining prices, in eliminating wastes, and in determining what may best be undertaken; for one cannot otherwise easily get a safe guidance in these particulars. It seems, too, as if it is the function of the bookkeeper to record the results of such study, for surely they will be forgotten if they are not recorded.

Possibly some persons admit that, for such purposes as those just discussed, interest must be considered, but deny that it is a cost. Discussions of terminology are quite as likely to be fruitless as fruitful. Any practical value that they may have must lie in a possible better common understanding of one another's meaning when men use the terms in question. Today the word "profit," which is the complement of "cost," is used in many senses. Under many partnership agreements, salaries and interest on investment are charged as expenses, and net profit is the gain arising from proprietorship pure and simple—from the *circumstance of responsible ownership,* aside from the salary of the manager as manager (not financially responsible) and from the income of the capitalist as capitalist (not personally responsible). The happy conjunction of ownership and personal responsibility often results in a gain not otherwise realizable, and that gain is profit. When there is no provision for interest and salaries, on the other hand, the term "profit" is commonly applied to the difference between the gross income and the charges incurred for purchases and outsiders' (non-partners') services; so that the profit shown is a compound of return for proprietors' services, for interest on partners' investments, and for the circumstance of responsible ownership. In corporation accounting, again, salaries are always included in expenses, and the net income is the return to the stockholders as owners of capital. In common parlance, therefore, the word "profits" means much or little. Knowing this, men always interpret it with a mental foot-note.

59

On the announcement of the figure of profits under an agreement which makes no provision for interest, the first mental act of anyone interested in the business is to see what relation those profits bear to the capital—so as to see what are the excess profits over a reasonable return on the investment. Instinctively interest is a first deduction—partly because it has a definite basis that can be figured, and partly because it is the one thing that everyone counts on. One does not think of terminology: one thinks only of the fact. Virtually everyone admits that in partnership or other settlements the most satisfactory agreement is one that provides for a definite interest charge. This is mere practical convenience. Though the accountant is not much concerned with theoretical economic distinctions, he is at least interested when he sees that economists use a term in a sense that happens to be, for his own practical purposes, most convenient for him. Professor F. W. Taussig, in his *Principles of Economics,* a recently published and standard authority used in many universities, says, "So much only of a business man's income is to be regarded as profits as is in excess of interest on the capital which he manages." *

We have seen that for analytical purposes, in studying operations, practical necessity requires us at least to consider interest in virtually all calculations when investment is involved; and we have seen that in financial statements practical convenience is served by the treatment of interest as a charge, or cost, rather than as a residue, or profit. It seems reasonable, therefore, for accountants to adopt a terminology that will serve their own ends, will agree with the terminology of economists, and will mislead no one. Business men are likely to be misled in the future, as they have been in the past, by statements of profit which assume that no cost is involved in the use of capital.

60

On the Inclusion of Interest in Manufacturing Costs

By A. Hamilton Church

Consulting Industrial Engineer, Patterson, Teele & Dennis

The question whether interest should be included in shop costs is frequently obscured by a certain indefiniteness as to what is meant by "interest" in this connection. As a matter of fact, interest as met with in accounting is of two kinds, viz.:

(1) Interest paid out by the concern for the use of borrowed capital, as on mortgages, debentures, loans and otherwise. The bearing of this kind of interest on the profits which will ultimately be distributable on the stock of the concern is of course very important. Bad financing may swallow up the profits, but this has nothing to do with the manufacturing efficiency of the shops. Whether or not the proprietors or directors elect to borrow, rather than to invest, capital, is entirely a question of how they are willing to distribute profits when earned. In other words, it is a question of finance, pure and simple, and affects revenue account alone.

(2) The second kind of interest is the only one now under discussion, namely, an assessment for the USE of capital values in the actual processes of manufacturing, represented by land,

* Vol. II, p. 179.

buildings, plant machinery, stores and work in progress, etc. I prefer to call this an "interest charge."

Not only are these entirely separate kinds of interest often confused, but it has happened that concerns have included in their costs percentages designed to distribute the interest incurred for mortgages and even for loans, while entirely ignoring any charge for the use of capital in the various forms employed in the shops. Such a practice has neither theoretical authority nor practical advantage.

The general principle that we must apply in discussing this question is that of utility. Older writers on the subject have frequently asserted that one or other of the aspects of the question was more "theoretically accurate," but have generally failed to state the terms of the theory involved. Probably, however, the older practice was on the whole against, rather than in favor of, including any interest charge for the use of capital in costs.

61

Until recent times, there was a good deal to be said for this attitude, for it must be clearly realized that such an interest charge does not affect the ultimate profits, however handled. If included, it increases costs, but this increase in costs is offset (when the whole course of the transactions is summed up in the profit and loss account) by the accumulation of a balance in the "Interest Earned" account. If not included, costs are lower by just the amount that would have been thus accumulated, and the net trading result is the same in both cases.

In such circumstances it is hardly surprising that many persons, looking at the ultimate result rather than at the intermediate steps, should have preferred the simpler method, and avoided the inclusion of interest in costs. It was of practically no service to the accountant, and from the nature of the methods by which the distribution over costs was made, it was scarcely of more value to the technical man or to the estimating or selling departments.

All indirect expense, including of course an interest charge where such was made, was formerly distributed over product in direct proportion to labor involved, or in proportion to time (hourly burden) taken to do the job. The informative value of such methods of distributing burden is very small, and as regards the item of interest-charge included may be said to be nil. The proportion of interest that became affixed to any given job bore no proportion whatever to the call on the use of capital made by that job. A purely hand-skill job might take just as much burden as a job calling for the use of the most powerful machines. All that was really attained was a rough idea of the bearing of indirect expense to direct labor *averaged over all the work*. When this figure was ascertained, the wholly unwarrantable assumption was made that each individual item of work might be safely regarded as taking neither more nor less than such average burden, whereas the truth commonly is that the real absorption of burden by different jobs is very unequal.

Practical intuition discerned this inherent vice of percentage systems long before any remedy was known, and burden figures have as a consequence been under a cloud, and have been treated with perhaps unconscious contempt by the technical men for whom alone they have any significance. If this was the case with all burden, it follows that the inclusion of interest charges in such burden had no practical value whatever.

Some attempts were made at various times, and even very early in the history of manufacturing, to remedy this defect. Machine rates were introduced to give some fairer incidence of the use of capital on individual jobs, but these were crude and arbitrary, and remained unsystematic until the present writer undertook an examination of the whole question of expense burden in 1899-1900. Since the publication of *The Proper Distribution of the Expense Burden* * there has been a steady growth of perception among accountants and manufacturers of the desirability of abandoning the practice of aggregating all kinds of indirect expense under the head of burden, in favor of a segregation of such expense into classes or "factors," and observing the relations of such factors to the actual operations of the shop.

Briefly speaking, the method of "production factors" is designed to give, among other things, due expression to the influence on costs of the USE of capital in manufacturing operations. This applies not merely to the capital involved in productive machines and tools, but also to that involved in auxiliary factors of production such as the land-building factor, the power, heating and lighting factors, the stores-transport factor, etc.

---

* First published in *Engineering Magazine*, 1901. In volume form, 1908. Reprinted, 1912. The subject has been expanded, from a more directly practical viewpoint, in *Production Factors*, published 1910.

Each of these factors represents a definite kind of expense, having a particular and definite bearing on the manufacturing processes. The cost of each factor is separately assessed against the productive machines making use of the services involved in, of course, exact proportion to the extent of the service.

Under this arrangement it is evident that each productive machine will be charged with a series of factor rents according to its individual call on the different services (including interest charge on its use of capital) rendered by the factors of production such as the land-building factor, the power factor, the transport factor, and the interest and depreciation charges on the capital value of the machine itself—the resulting total being expressed as an hourly "machine rent." Large and costly machines, occupying considerable space, using much power, and calling on the transport factor for heavy craneage service, will naturally have a very different machine rent from light, cheap machines, calling in a less degree on any factor. Consequently also the jobs done on these respective machines will have a very different amount of burden affixed to them.

The method of costing by "production factors" removes what was the main objection to the inclusion of an interest charge in costs under former methods, *viz.*, its inutility. On the contrary, to include it becomes logical and even necessary, as soon as we are able to connect its incidence with the variety of processes performed on individual jobs.

While it is obvious that the manner in which capital is *provided* (as by means of stock, mortgages, loans, etc.) cannot affect the cost of shop processes, on the other hand the manner in which capital is *used* must have a strong influence on the efficiency of production from the point of view of cost. Just as soon as two processes are used in the same plant, it becomes necessary to delimit as closely as possible all the elements of cost of such processes. Where more than two are used—and in a modern plant they may be counted by scores and even hundreds—this necessity increases in proportion to the complexity thus introduced. One of the first questions that would naturally arise if we approached the matter from a logical and natural standpoint would be to what extent the use of capital is involved in the different processes. This can be shown in the simplest and most convenient way by charging production for the use it makes of capital, in each of the different processes.

63

It is only by doing so, and consequently by segregating all expense into factors and including a reasonable interest charge for the capital used in the services represented by the factor, that we can obtain the complete story about the cost of any process. Wherever capital is made use of, whether in the power plant, in the erection of buildings, or in the purchase of costly special machinery, the use of such capital has to be paid for, somehow and somewhere. *It is only rational that it should be paid for by just those processes (and therefore those jobs) which involve its use. To exclude interest charge from cost of these jobs is to ignore one of the most important matters that we should know, namely—how far this use of capital is economically justified.*

The matter is rendered more important than formerly owing to the steady increase in the value of plant relatively to the cost of labor. A recent study of manufacturing statistics by Mr. A. C. Popcke (*Engineering Magazine*, September, 1912) shows that the horse power to drive machines has increased, on the average, 40 per cent per operator in the last ten years. Similarly capital investment in plant has increased 46 per cent per operator in the same period. These changes are significant of the growing size, weight and capacity of modern machinery, and point to the necessity of connecting a charge for the USE of capital with the various factors of production, and so, later, with each individual line or item of product.

In particular, no purchase of new equipment should be made until its call on all production factors has been worked out, and due attention paid to the influence of its use of capital, as represented by a reasonable interest charge.

Interest Not a Charge Against Costs

By W. B. RICHARDS

The writer does not believe in the principle of charging into either cost of production or administrative expense interest on the capital invested in the business. Many concerns do so charge interest, and many reputable accountants and efficient engineers allow it; but it is hard to see the logic of their arguments in its favor. In the writer's experience he has found that it is usually done for the purpose of increasing the cost for some reason, such as influencing the selling department in securing good prices for their goods, or for the purpose of concealing the real cost of the articles made; the manager of the sales department, knowing the real cost and making allowances where necessary at the time of sale.

Among the reasons for not approving of this interest charge are the following:

Every properly conducted concern includes in its cost of production a regular charge for depreciation of its plant, property and equipment. This charge, if correctly figured, keeps the value of its property accounts at the convertible figure. In these circumstances it would seem that charging interest as well on the amount invested would be making a double charge.   65

The financing of a business should be kept distinct from both the production department and that of administration.

Money borrowed by a business, whether on bond and mortgage or unsecured loans, should be considered as part of the capital, and, while interest paid on this is a fixed obligation, it should not be taken into the production costs—but should be considered a part of the commercial expense.

Interest Not a Part of the Cost of Production

By J. E. Sterrett

It is. interesting and perhaps significant that cost accounting is commonly thought of as appertaining to the affairs of manufacturers only. It is, however, apparent that the principles governing the correct determination of the costs of manufacturers and other producers who must meet open competition also operate in ascertaining the cost of. services rendered to the public by utility corporations, and the need for a knowledge of costs is substantially the same in both classes. To the first class a knowledge of cost is essential in the fixing of prices, the maximum of which is regulated by the inexorable law of competition. The second class must be prepared to show the cost of the service rendered and the value of the property employed in order that just rates may be established.

In both instances it is necessary to fix a selling price, or secure a rate that will not only return the actual cost of production (or of service, as the case may be), but will yield a reasonable return upon the property employed. While there is thus a constant association of these two elements in prices and in rates, they are distinct and each is entitled to its own identity and position. It may be interesting in passing to remark the wide variations in the relative proportions of these elements in different circumstances. The ratio of cost to price, or rate, may be as high as 80, or even 90, per cent in certain types of merchandising, and will drop to say 25 or 30 per cent in a gravity water system. In the first instance the interest (or return upon capital) factor is comparatively small, while in the latter it looms much larger than the cost factor.

66

Public service commissions and other rate regulating bodies have uniformly maintained a proper distinction between cost and return upon investment; but those who have felt called upon to discuss manufacturing costs have not always approached the question with the same clarity of vision. Moreover, those who assert that interest is an element of cost seldom attempt to give any logical reason in support of their contention, and they fail to carry their theory to its ultimate conclusion.

The end commonly sought by them is the attainment of costs that will reflect the employment wherever used of expensive types of machinery. It is obvious that the use of a costly machine must increase the hour rate of cost even though it may reduce the total cost of the article produced; but an adequate adjustment in respect of the use of the machine is, or should be, secured through the charge for depreciation, or speaking more accurately, the expired outlay upon productive plant. It would seem too that if interest is a part of cost the principle would in nowise be dependent upon the value of the equipment, and in theory, at least, it should be just as essential to include a charge for interest upon the capital invested in small tools as upon that locked up in the most elaborate and expensive machine. Moreover, why charge interest upon fixed capital and omit to do so in respect of floating capital? The oil that lubricates the machine, and the raw material that enters the product may be in the storeroom for months before being consumed and during this period they represent capital invested quite as surely as does a lathe or drill press. Or, viewed from another angle, why not compute interest upon wages paid from the date of payment until the completion of the article or job? The procedure might indeed even become so fascinating as to lead to a further charge for interest from the date of completion to that of sale.

The theory that interest is a part of cost is as unsound in economics as in accounting, but, as a discussion of that aspect of the question would be largely academic and outside the present field, it is desirable to pass on to a brief consideration of some of the results which would follow the adoption of a cost system providing for the inclusion of interest as a part of the cost of production. In doing so, however, it is necessary to have clearly in mind the more important purposes for which costs are ascertained. The primary aim is undoubtedly to aid in establishing a basis for fixing selling prices, or rates; while the secondary and scarcely less important, is to determine a fair value for inventories. Other purposes, such as reducing cost, increasing efficiency, eliminating waste, affording comparative statistics, etc., are important, but, as they present no problems not developed in connection with the first two purposes named above, they may be dismissed without further comment.

The determination of a proper selling price or rate depends for its successful accomplishment upon several things, of which cost of production is only one, although a highly important one. Other determining considerations are the cost of selling or distribution, terms of credit, risk of loss, and rate of profit required to yield a return upon the capital employed. At this point interest must enter into the calculation, but to inject it at an earlier stage serves only to confuse and render more inaccurate the cost accounts which under the most favorable conditions contain a margin of error far too wide for comfort.

In many lines of industry the value of the material and labor that can be specifically allocated to a particular article or job forms a minor, rather than a major, part of the total manufacturing cost. In all cases a relatively large amount of indirect cost is incurred and must be distributed by some means that in the most favorable circumstances do not admit of entire accuracy. Everyone acquainted with the conditions inherent in productive processes knows how necessary it is to devise methods by means of which the largest possible measure of the total costs of production can be identified with and charged to a given article or

67

job. Thus at a time when the best efforts of every intelligent cost accountant are being put forth to reduce to a minimum the proportion of indirect costs of production the wisdom of introducing an interest charge requires a clearer demonstration than any of its advocates have yet given. When it is considered that such an interest charge, instead of being a small, perhaps almost negligible, quantity, may and frequently would be a substantial proportion of the entire cost, the danger of serious error in the results is enormously increased. Furthermore, as there is, practically speaking, no fixed rate of interest (the legal rates varying in our own country from 5 to 10 or 12 per cent) the charge itself as adopted by one manufacturer might vary from that of his neighbor to an extent of 25, 50 or even 100 per cent. Production costs determined upon such an uncertain basis could only be accurately described as speculative costs.

The correct basis for inventory valuations is universally admitted to be that of the cost to produce the goods in the stage or condition in which they are when taken in the inventory. The only exception to this rule is that where current market prices are lower than cost, then, in order to be conservative, the market prices should be taken. An auditor cannot properly give an unqualified certificate to a balance sheet in which the inventory prices include a charge for interest upon capital, and bankers naturally object to any attempt at anticipation of profit upon the part of a borrower. In short, the inclusion of interest in an inventory valuation would, and properly enough should, tend to impair the credit of any concern indulging in such practice.

From an accounting viewpoint, interest or return upon capital invested is a part of the profit to be derived from trade. In its proper place it is no more to be overlooked than the cost of production or the selling and management expenses, but to merge it with cost of production or with the expense of distribution tends only to confusion and error. Furthermore, there is a broad distinction between profits anticipated and profits realized, and to begin to take profits weeks or months before the goods can be offered for sale is not only unsound in accounting but censurable in finance.

PREMIUM, PIECE WORK, AND THE EXPENSE BURDEN

By A. Hamilton Church

Mr. Church's comparison of the best-known wage-paying methods and their respective results in unit earnings and costs was prepared some years ago. The topic was temporarily supplanted in immediate interest by more comprehensive considerations of schools, systems, and doctrines of management. Admitting fully, however, that wage methods are but one co-ordinate (or even subordinate) factor in a complete industrial philosophy, they nevertheless remain a most active interest in the mind of many managers, and that interest does not wane, but rather increases, as time goes on. Mr. Church's discussion, with its interesting graphic charts, is therefore brought forward exactly as it was first written. A succeeding article will take up the bonus and "efficiency" systems of payment.—THE EDITORS.

THE fundamental difference between premium and piece work has never, to my knowledge, been adequately discussed. As a matter of practice, premium is supposed not only to be superior in results but also different in principle. We shall test thoroughly the soundness of that view.

The exact bearing of both premium and piece work on "total" or "works" cost reduction has hitherto received but little attention, while much has been written on their bearing on wages reduction. Yet of the two, reduction of "works" cost, that is, wages and burden (disregarding material as being outside the question) is the more important, both theoretically and practically.

The obscurity in which this question remains is largely due to the habit of regarding costs as merely the aggregate of wages and material, and of looking on "indirect expense," or "expense burden," as a rather theoretical thing that may be, and sometimes is, tacked on to costs, at the fancy of the accountant or some other system-loving person. When, however, we recognize that indirect expenses are passing minute by minute into the real cost of an article under process of manufacture, we not only widen our point of view in a very useful way, but are able to grasp more clearly the economic status of piece work and premium.

The object of any system of payment beyond simple day work is to stimulate production by making the workman directly interested in lowering "time taken." With piece work we appear to contract with him, with premium we appear to take him into partnership. Neither of these popularly accepted ideas is strictly true. Neither of them takes into account what practically is always the chief, and in some cases the *only*, benefit to the employer, viz., a reduced works cost due to savings on burden.

The present inquiry was undertaken with a view to analyze the differences and compare the results of premium and piecework in the light of total cost reduction. Most people have assumed that the tendency to cut rates which is so marked a feature of piece work, which is so greatly diminished on the Halsey plan and totally absent on the Rowan plan, is due to some very marked difference in principle between the

7

first two, and a mere difference of detail between the last two. The result would appear to point the other way. Considering piece work and ordinary premium only, for the moment, there is no difference in principle between them at all.

Piece work is exactly the same thing as premium work, only, instead of the premium being 33 1/3 per cent or 50 per cent, it is 100 per cent. In all other respects they are fundamentally the same.

If we commence by disregarding expense burden altogether, or assume it to equal zero, it will be seen that a very important practical difference results from offering what is called premium instead of what is termed piece work. In the former case, only a half or a third of the total saving goes to the worker. In the latter, 100 per cent, or in other words, *all* the saving goes to the worker. It follows from this, that except in the light of expense burden, the employer's benefit from piece work is limited to advantages of no great economic importance—(1), the time limit or "price" set for piece work is usualy slightly lower than previous day work records; (2), a fixed instead of a variable cost is obtained for the piece; (3), the resulting concentration of the worker's attention generally produces, after a time, a more uniform and accurately wrought product; (4), a quicker output results, which is sometimes of advantage, but not necessarily always of advantage. The worker's benefit, on the other hand, is that he makes considerably higher wages.

The practical instinct of employers has, however, always realized two controlling elements: first, that expense burden has a vital connection with the question, and that an actual reduction in time taken means a reduced total or works cost, though it

does not mean a reduction in wages cost; secondly, that after a certain point is reached, excessive earnings on the part of the man are out of proportion to the benefit from reduction in burden realized by the employer. How these two elements are really interconnected will be shown later, but that the desire to cut rates is not merely jealousy of the worker's high wages, may be gathered by supposing a case in which the work was given out to a homeworker or a small outside firm. In such a case, very few employers, having once made their contract, would trouble themselves at all as to whether the outworker was making "a good thing" out of the contract—even though they were fully aware of it. But when by use of the employer's own organization, machinery, and facilities the worker's wages become excessive, he, the employer, is inclined to call a halt. This will always be so, by whatever term the worker's reward is designated, as long as the premium is a very high one, as it is in piece work.

As will be shown presently, the trouble with piece work is that, with the expense burdens usually existing in machine shops, the man's share relative to the fall in works cost is always disproportionately high, and that under piece work, cost can never be halved unless the burden is well over 100 per cent (practically 160 per cent or higher). Yet the doubling of the workman's wages takes place long before this stage is approached.

In all systems of premium payment, whether the rate be 33 1/3 per cent or up to 100 per cent, a reduction of the time allowance brings benefit to the employer in inverse proportion to the amount of the premium. He gains by a share in the saving of wages cost (except in the single case where premium is 100 per cent, as in piece work) and he also gains by saving the indirect charges or burden on the unexpended time. Obviously, therefore, premium is not equally remunerative to the employer in all cases. The higher the burden, the sharper is the fall of the works-cost line relative to wages, as cost is reduced. At very low burdens,—where the percentage of burden to wages is lower than the percentage of premium paid to the man—the fall of works cost becomes proportionately less sharp as cost is reduced. In piece work, therefore, where the percentage of premium is as high as 100 per cent, it may frequently happen that great inefficiency results though the worker may be making double wages. These points will be made clear by the diagrams which follow

later. A few numerical examples will first be given; a 100 per cent burden is assumed in all three cases. Unit prices for unit time are also assumed (one dollar or one shilling for one hour)—the figures can therefore be read in terms of price or time as necessary.

A further analysis of the employer's saving in Table III shows the relative influence of premium and burden in the result.

An examination of these three sets of figures will show that the employer's saving is made up of two elements—a saving of burden, which is of course strictly proportional to the incidence of burden only *and has no relation to the rate of premium*, and a share of the saving of time as ex-

71

MAN'S EARNINGS AND EMPLOYER'S SAVINGS AT DIFFERENT PREMIUM RATES

(Burden 100 Per Cent).

	Premium 33 1/3 per cent.	Premium 50 per cent.	Premium 100 per cent. (Piece Work).
I. TIME NOT REDUCED—			
Wages for full time............	100	100	100
Burden for full time............	100	100	100
Works Cost	200	200	200
II. TIME REDUCED BY HALF—			
Wages for half time............	50	50	50
Premium Earned	17	25	50
Burden on half time............	50	50	50
Saving to Employer............	83	75	50
Original Allowance	200	200	200
III. ANALYSIS OF SAVING—			
Saving in Wages (2/3 of 50)	33 (1/2 of 50)=25		(None) —
Saving in Burden (100 Per Cent on 50).....................	50	50	50
	83	75	50
IV. RELATIVE SHARE—			
Man's Share of Saving:			
Wages	50	50	50
Premium	17	25	50
	67	75	100
Employer's Share of Saving......	83	75	50
V. REDUCTION IN WORKS COST—			
Percentage of Reduction.........	41 1/2	37 1/2	25

pressed in wages, which share is wholly determined by the rate of premium. Where premium is 100 per cent, as in piece work, this share equals 0, and that is all the difference there is between piece work and any other premium rate.

It will further be observed that, in the case taken, where burden is 100 per cent of wages, the relative positions of. man and employer, when time is reduced by half, are very significant. See Table IV.

The disproportionate share of advantage obtained by the man under piece work is seen at once—when time is halved the man is getting twice the benefit that the employer gets, and though the man is drawing double pay the total or works cost has only been reduced by 25 per cent (50 on 200). The other two percentages show a different distribution of the saving as between employer and man, and therefore a different degree of lowering of works cost as shown in Table V.

The important bearing of expense burden on cost reduction under premium plans having been outlined, and, incidentally, the identity of piece work with premium in principle having been shown, their further relations may be examined in detail by means of the diagrams on pages 12 and 13, which represent four varieties of premium payment in their relation to burdens varying from 25 per cent to 150 per cent.

EXPLANATION OF THE DIAGRAMS

For purposes of comparison an allowance of 100 hours is assumed for the two premium systems, while for the piece-work system an equivalent price of 100 price-units is fixed—such price-units being 1 per hour. In other words, the ordinary wage rate is assumed throughout to be one shilling or one penny, one dollar or one cent, per hour—the monetary value being a matter of no conse-

quence, as long as we remember that it is *one* per hour. The vertical column of figures represents rise in cost from 0 to 250 of such price-units (dollars, shillings, etc.). The horizontal figures represent "time taken" from 0 to 100 hours.

The thick line running diagonally from 100 down to 0 represents wages cost on the job. Thus 100 hours cost 100 shillings or dollars, 30 hours cost 30 shillings or dollars, and so forth.

The dotted line represents the *total receivable* by the man, made up of (1) wages, (2) premium. The distance *between* the dotted line and the thick line therefore represents *amount* of premium (or piece earnings) expressed in price units.

The fine lines represent *total works cost*. This is obtained by aggregating (1) time taken, (2) indirect expenses or burden on time taken, and (3) amount of premium earned. Several of these are shown, giving the different total works costs at different rates of burden, from 25 per cent to 150 per cent.

GENERAL FEATURES OF THE DIAGRAMS

The first thing that will strike the observer is the different degree of steepness shown by the lines representing total works cost. As this particular item is the real object of the employer's care, it is more important than the others. It will be seen at once, for instance, that each of the three methods presents peculiar characteristics. In the piece-work diagram the lines tend more to the horizontal and terminate very high up (on the right-hand side). In the Halsey system they are steeper than in piece work, and go lower. In the Rowan system they possess about the same degree of steepness as in the Halsey, but tend to curve inwards as the time taken approaches a minimum, and they finally reach zero.

This steepness represents, of course, the rate of fall of total works cost, as less and less time is taken by the workman to carry out the job. It is a measure of the effectiveness of each system to produce the results wished for by the manufacturer, viz.: to reduce actual costs per piece. In each of the four diagrams it will be seen that the higher the burden of indirect charges, the steeper is the fall of works cost. But as between the systems there is much variation in the degree of this fall, and consequently in relative efficiency.

The second noticeable feature of the diagrams is the relation of the dotted line to the thick line. The distance between these two lines is the amount of premium or piece earnings at various "times taken." It will be seen at once how enormously the workman's share in piece work tends to increase as time is lowered; how in the Halsey system it tends to rise to a very much larger amount than direct wages shortly after production is doubled; and finally, how in the Rowan system its ratio to wages rises steadily throughout, up to 99 per cent and not beyond.

A third feature of the diagrams is that whether the premium is 33 1/3, 50 or 100 per cent, there exists a "critical" point at which the works-cost line tends to diverge from, instead of approaching, the wages line. This always takes place when the rate of premium is greater than the percentage of burden. It affords an argument for low rates of premium, particularly in specialty departments, where the burden is low. It also affords a demonstration of the weakness of so high a premium as 100 per cent (piece work), because a smaller rate of burden than this is not infrequent, even in machine shops. Except with burdens considerably over 150 per cent it is practically impossible ever to halve works cost on this system.

THE ROWAN SYSTEM

Before proceeding with a comparison of the data afforded by the diagrams, it may be desirable to give some details of the Rowan variety of premium payment. Although a writer* in these pages formerly stigmatized this system as "both fallacious and inhuman", it is included here because in the present writer's opinion it possesses important practical features which override any such hasty condemnation.

In the original Halsey system, the premium is based on our view of the facts of lowered cost; in the Rowan system a different view is taken. Mr. Halsey's method is, as already shown, a lowered piece-work rate of 33 1/3 or 50 instead of 100 per cent. Mr. Rowan's method is based on a different principle, viz.:—an increase of the man's pay proportionate to the reduction of the time allowance. Instead of saying to the man that he shall receive 33 1/3 per cent or 50 per cent of what he saves, the Rowan system puts it another way. It says, in effect, that if he reduces time 25 per cent or 50 per cent, his pay shall be increased 25 per cent or 50 per cent or whatever other fractional reduction of time he effects. Comparison of the Rowan with the Halsey diagram shows that an important difference in principle is here involved. The premium area in the former is bounded by a closed curve. In the latter it is a constantly increasing segment. Inferentially, we see that in the Rowan system no possible error in fixing time allowance can lead to a man's earning double wages. It is this feature that Mr. Bender describes as "inhuman," but, as will be shown later, this strong expression arises from a confusion of thought between what can be done and what ought to be done on any

73

*Mr. Carl Bender, System of Wages; The Engineering Magazine, December, 1908.

74

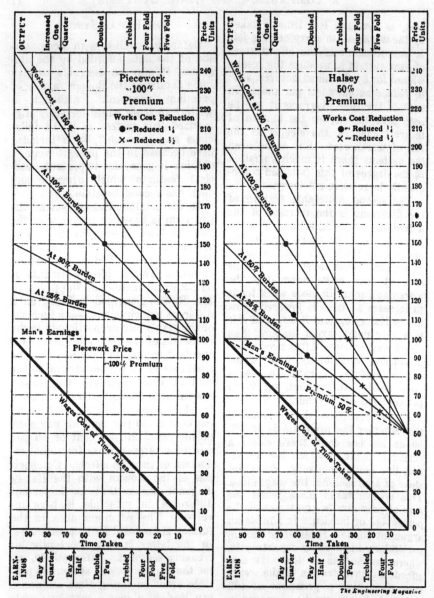

DIAGRAM NO. 1. PIECE WORK   DIAGRAM NO. 2. HALSEY 50 PER CENT

An allowance of 100 hours is assumed for the premium system, and an equivalent of 100 price units (wage hours) for the piece-work system. Diagonal thick line is wages cost of job. Dotted line shows total receivable by man—wages *plus* premium. Distance between thick line and dotted line on any vertical shows premium for the corresponding time. Fine lines show total works cost, made up of time taken, burden on time taken, and premium.

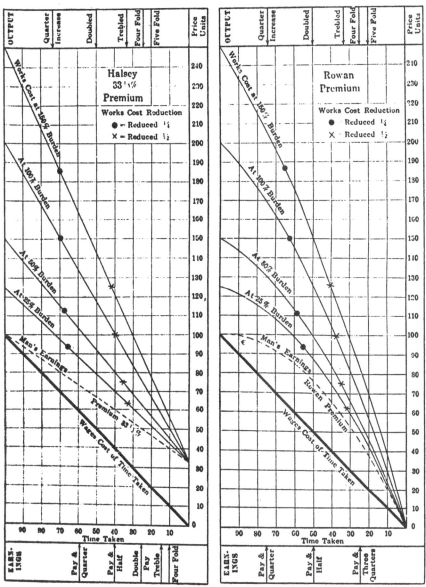

75

DIAGRAM NO. 3. HALSEY 33 1/3 PER CENT   DIAGRAM NO. 4. ROWAN

An allowance of 100 hours is assumed for the premium system, and an equivalent of 100 price units (wage hours) for the piece-work system. Diagonal thick line is wages cost of job. Dotted line shows total receivable by man—wages *plus* premium. Distance between thick line and dotted line on any vertical shows premium for the corresponding time. Fine lines show total works cost, made up of time taken, burden on time taken, and premium.

13

system of payment by results. The object is not to enable workmen to earn double pay, but to effect two things: (1) incentive to increase production at the right moment and under the right conditions; and (2) a just and equitable distribution of the saving so effected.

Fallacies with Regard to Premium Systems

In distinguishing between the practical results obtained from piece work, premium, differential, and bonus systems, credit is frequently given to a system for something that has nothing to do with the merits of that system. This is well brought out in Mr. Bender's very interesting and instructive comparison of wages systems already referred to. In discussing the Taylor system, for example, it is said that "Mr. Taylor scorns the suggestion that by any chance the worker could earn excessive wages." This, we find, is based not on any peculiarity of the system, but on the premises that "the method of standard-time determination is so rigorous that the worker cannot figure on curtailing his output." The Gantt bonus system depends for its successful working on a similar rigorous time determination. In the Emerson efficiency system also, Mr. Bender says, "the standard time required for every job should be scientifically ascertained."

Now we have here *preliminary* conditions that are the actual controlling features of the situation. With very accurately determined standard times, it is perfectly obvious that the right-hand halves of all our diagrams could never come into use. Yet it is towards the middle and right-hand half of the diagrams that the difference between the systems becomes most marked. For small increases in production the variation

in works cost between the different systems is comparatively small, and as everything in that case depends on incentive, it is quite an open question where burden is over 100 per cent whether the piece work system, with its 100 per cent premium, would not work out as well in practice as any other.

The success of a system which implies and necessitates a vigorous predetermination of standard times or a close and careful study of routine operations, cannot be compared with the success of other systems of which the chief merit is flexibility and ability to meet unforeseen conditions. In the writer's opinion the Rowan system fulfils this last definition more completely than the Halsey, for as will be seen from the diagrams, it offers its greatest degree of incentive for moderate cost reductions, and one of its chief virtues is that for such exaggerated results as five-fold production, which can be due only to the absence of a rigorous determination of standard times, it protects the employer while still adequately rewarding the man.

The Piece-work Diagram

Under piece work ($=$ a premium of 100 per cent) the ratio of premium earned rises from 11 per cent for a saving of 10 hours up to a 900 per cent premium for the saving of 90 hours. It will be noticed that halved works cost cannot in practice be realized by this system. It only appears once on the diagram, viz.: in the case of a 150 per cent burden, and more than five-fold production is necessary to realize it. In such a case the man would be obtaining a premium of 85 as against a wage cost of 15, or about 570 per cent. A reduction of one-quarter in works cost is only reached in practice at or about doubled wages, when burden is 100 per cent or over. It should also be observed that where burden is 100 per cent the works-cost line is parallel to the wages-cost line. Below 100 per cent they diverge, indicating that the rate of reduction in works cost is less than that of wages cost— also indicating a lessened efficiency just where the worker's reward tends to increase.

THE HALSEY DIAGRAMS

Separate diagrams are given for 33 1/3 per cent and 50 per cent premiums. They present advantages over piece work just in the degree that the percentage of premium is lower. It will easily be seen (and it is a conclusive argument as to the real identity of piece work and premium in principle) that intermediate diagrams of 90, 80, 76 and 60 per cent premium could be constructed and they would show a *gradual transformation* from the horizontal price line of the piece-work diagram to the inclined lines of the two Halsey diagrams. The circles and crosses, representing one-quarter and one-half reduction in works cost, would also gradually enter and pass from right to left in successive diagrams.

The principal point of interest in these two diagrams is in the fact that, by comparison with the piece-work diagram, they show the whole relation of higher or lower premium rates to the various elements of production, viz.: wages cost, man's total earnings, his share relative to wages, effect of increased production at different burdens, and the rate of fall of works cost relative to wages. It will perhaps be unnecessary to go over these points in detail because a comparative study of the diagrams themselves will reveal them, and their more important features will be summed up later. It may be remarked, however, that as in the case of piece work, where the burden rate is below the

premium rate, as in the 25 per cent burden on either diagram, works cost does not fall as quickly as wages cost, although—the premium rates being much lower—the divergence is proportionately less. Under special conditions, however, this divergence might have a practical significance.

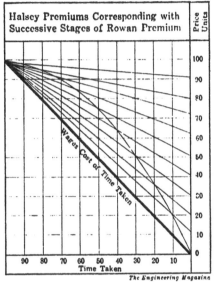

DIAGRAM 5. ROWAN SYSTEM

THE ROWAN DIAGRAM

The closed curve of the Rowan premium rate is *really equivalent to a gradually falling Halsey premium rate.* This point is so important that a special diagram may usefully be introduced to illustrate it.

It will be seen that so far from be:ng "inhuman", the Rowan system is actually more generous to the worker than a Halsey 50 per cent premium until wages cost *is halved,* and remains more generous than a Halsey 33 1/3 per cent premium until wages cost *is reduced two-thirds!* The radiating lines of the Halsey premiums corresponding to the various stages of the Rowan premiums do in fact exhibit, in practice, that

77

gradual transformation from very nearly 100 per cent premium down to 10 per cent premium that was spoken of above, when it was said to be quite possible to construct a successive series of diagrams showing such intermediate stages.

The practical value of this variety of premium is that it provides incentive just where incentive is wanted, viz.: at the left-hand of the diagrams representing progress from full time to halved time. It has the further advantage that a considerable error in time allowance which would bring the wages cost well over into the right-hand side of the diagram, say for example up to the point of four-fold or five-fold production, does not disproportionately increase the man's earnings and render it necessary to cut rates, however great the error.

The point of view of the Rowan system presents other practical advantages which I believe are not realized on any other method. Where premium has replaced piece work, an atmosphere of dissatisfaction is not infrequently found, as soon as the men see that the employer is obtaining the lion's share of the saving. Very frequently they fail to realize that rates will not be cut, and indeed an examination of the diagrams will show that after a certain point there is just as much temptation to cut a high Halsey premium allowance, as a high piece-work price. Moreover, it is very well known to have actually been done. Under the Rowan method, however, there is no question of an unequal *share* of saving introduced at all. The Rowan proposition takes the form of giving the man an addition to his hourly rate *proportional* to the time he saves. If he saves a quarter of the time, he receives time-and-a-quarter; if he saves half the time he receives time-and-a-half. It is a positive merit of the

system that it does *not* respond t the abnormal case propounded by M) Render, in which one man is suppose to take half an hour and another 5 $\frac{1}{2}$ hours to do the same job, becaus such a condition of things would b an absurdity, and would call for th prompt discharge of one of the mer and of the individual who fixed s wildly inaccurate a time allowanc(

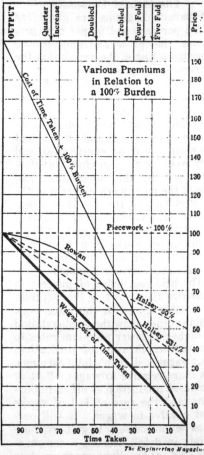

The Engineering Magazin

DIAGRAM 6. HALSEY AND ROWAN COMPARED

A careful examination of the diagrams will show that whatever merits the Halsey system has, the Rowan systems preserves all of them, and adds others peculiar to itself.

Conclusion

The great aim of any system of cost reduction must be to reduce "works" cost. This is effected in different degree by each of the four methods selected for examination. Diagram No. 6 shows all four premiums plotted together on the same wages-cost line, and a 100 per cent wages and burden line added, *based on the fall of costs only*, without taking into consideration the premiums earned.

This 100 per cent line shows what would be the actual works cost (at 100 per cent burden) if the fall of cost *were wholly due to improved methods of production and not to the extra exertions of the men*. Obviously this is the ideal condition desired by the employer, and from a certain point of view, the necessity of paying premiums to effect this reduction is a necessary evil. By plotting the premiums between this 100 per cent line and the wages-cost line, we see how they bulk in each case, compared with this ideal (but of course unrealizable) fall in works cost. It will be seen that the piece-work line soon passes outside the 100 per cent line, that the two Halsey premiums follow suit one after the other, but that the Rowan premium never does. The whole significance of this diagram lies in the fact that 100 per cent is generally supposed to be, and often is, an average burden, and it is suggested that the points at which the various premiums cross the 100 per cent line is where the practical instinct of the employer begins to make him uneasy, and desirous of cutting prices or allowances. I do not wish to lay too much stress on this diagram, but it is certainly suggestive.

The practical deductions from the foregoing study of the four methods are not many but they are important. They are:

(1) That premium methods gain in importance precisely in proportion to the burden (that is, in proportion to the size and value of machines used, cost of power, handling machinery, high value of land or buildings, expensive nature of supervision, etc.).

(2) That where *very accurate time allowance* can be thoroughly depended on, the system which gives the sharpest fall of works cost is, other things apart, the best. This condition is fulfilled by Halsey 33 1/3 per cent, in which the fall is sharper than Rowan until wages cost has been reduced between $\frac{1}{2}$ and 2/3—an event not likely to happen if time allowances are accurate. But this consideration is influenced by the question of incentive. For the same time allowance, the incentive to reduce cost is greater under both piece-work and Rowan system than under Halsey in the earlier stages. As it has been proved over and over again that added incentive (raising of time allowance) has proved the key to unlock the workman's ambition, the advantage of Halsey over Rowan is perhaps doubtful. If the man can be got to work equally energetically under each plan, then under the Halsey plan works cost falls more sharply, but as the Rowan plan, for the same time allowance, provides a larger incentive (and therefore a slightly higher works cost) its effect on the man is presumably greater. In the case of very accurate time allowances, therefore, there seems to be a certain balance of advantages between the two methods.

(3) Where time allowances are not scientifically and very accurately determined, then there can be no question which method has the balance of advantages. If the determination is very bad, then the Halsey premium, even when as low as 33 1/3 per cent, gives the man a wholly dispropor-

tionate share if he reduces the nominal time to its real working value. On the Rowan plan the falling premium rate automatically compensates for such errors, while still giving the worker a fair reward for extra effort. (The point at which the premium lines pass outside the 100 per cent. lines in Diagram 6 illustrates this aspect of the question.)

(4) For very low burdens, such as 25 per cent, only realized, of course, in very special work, a very small Halsey premium not exceeding the ratio of burden would perhaps lead to the most efficient results. The Rowan system does not seem to be adaptable to very small burdens, because the lines of its very high premium rates at the beginning diverge very greatly from works-cost fall. It is only with burdens of 75 per cent or 100 per cent and over that the best efficiency can apparently be obtained from the Rowan system.

Generally speaking, the results of this examination go to show that the merits of any system of premium payment are a balance between incentive and actual steepness of fall of works cost. Naturally, the nearer works cost approaches the ideal line in Diagram 6, the better. The best premium is that which raises this line as little as possible. Obviously, two considerations are involved: (1) Enough must be offered to effect the reduction in the first place; (2) it must not be so much as to make the resulting line as flat as is shown in the case of piece work. As a purely abstract statement, it may be said to be just as little as the worker can be

induced to accept, and yet keep his energies directed toward reducing cost further and further. This is the economic statement of the plain truth, but like most economic statements it has to be considered alongside human nature and with human sympathy before it becomes other than an engine of discord and strife. Of the four systems examined, the Rowan system seems to prevent, in practice, any arrival at a point where the interests of employer and employee come into actual conflict. It either produces or fails to produce sufficiently satisfactory economic results. In neither case does anybody lose; they only fail to gain. There is a psychological difference in that which has important practical bearings, and makes for industrial peace. And a remedy can generally be found, where interests do not drift into antagonism at any stage of their relations.

In the present article those systems of payment for labor are alone discussed which depend upon a simple time limit and sharing-out of the savings effected by the reduction of this nominal limit. A subsequent paper will deal with the relation of burden to "task" or "bonus" systems in which the worker's benefit either commences or is greatly increased at a predetermined point, and the success of the system in practice depends upon the proportion of workers who attain or pass this point. As this involves quite a different point of view from ordinary piece work or premium, it must be made the subject of a separate discussion.

BONUS SYSTEMS AND THE EXPENSE BURDEN

By A. Hamilton Church

In a preceding article, published last month, Mr. Church discussed the comparative results of premium and piece-work. He now takes up, in a similar way, the effects of bonus and efficiency wage scales. This contrast of the best-known wage-paying methods and their respective results in unit earnings and costs was prepared some years ago. The topic was temporarily supplanted in immediate interest by more comprehensive considerations of schools, systems, and doctrines of management. Admitting fully, however, that wage methods are but one co-ordinate (or even subordinate) factor in a complete industrial philosophy, they nevertheless remain a most active interest in the mind of many managers, and that interest does not wane, but rather increases, as time goes on. Mr. Church's discussion, with its interesting graphic charts, is therefore brought forward exactly as it was first written.—THE EDITORS.

IN the preceding article, those systems of payment were discussed which depend upon a simple time limit and an equally simple law of apportionment of the reduction made. In the present paper, the newer and more complex "task" or "bonus" methods will be reviewed in the light of their bearing on works cost, i. e., prime cost *plus* expense burden.

The two principal methods are the Gantt Bonus Method and the Emerson Efficiency Method. It is necessary to treat these two systems of remuneration from a different standpoint from that adopted for the examination of the others, inasmuch as they are the outcome of what might almost be looked on as a new philosophy of manufacture—a revolution which is, however, really a return to first principles, *viz.*, a close watch on the duration and circumstances of every successive operation in a process of manufacture, with a view to determining a theoretical maximum of productive output. It is curious to observe that the scrutiny of successive operations with this end in view was more familiar in early days than in later

times. In Babbage's "Economy of Manufactures", published in 1832, hints are given as to the precautions necessary in timing the details of operations.

It must be perfectly evident to every sober-minded observer that the ultimate success of piece-work, using that term in its broadest sense to indicate all kinds of remuneration by results, must depend upon the possibility of finding ultimate or "real" bases for calculation. The objections to piece work on the part of trade unions is founded on the perception that, as at present fixed, all prices are to a great extent arbitrary. When they are offered, there is no possibility of judging their fairness except by trial and error, or by the exercise of that very delusive quality, the practical man's judgment. This, by itself, is no great matter, but it becomes overpoweringly important in relation to the perennial bugbear of the relations between capital and labor—the cutting of rates, or, what is even more dreaded, the gradual whittling-down of rates.

In engineering manufactures, the enormous variety of pieces in shape,

81

size, weight, and material, and the great number of different processes which can be and are applied to any one piece before it is finished, render "standard" price lists of pieces impossible. Consequently as matters at present stand there is some degree of reason in the attitude of trade unionists towards piece work. Even though as regards any one shop there may be a fair and square understanding that prices, once fixed, shall never be reduced, that (in itself difficult to attain in practice) is no safeguard against other firms in the same line fixing slightly smaller prices—a process which has a tendency to continue in spite of the efforts of the better class of employers, and the theory that the best workmen will always gather round them.

Up to the present time all systems of piece remuneration must be considered as temporary and practical solutions of a problem of great importance—involving a c e r t a i n amount of dissatisfaction at times, but kept working by the common-sense and fair dealing of the parties to the bargain. The special interest of the task-and-bonus methods is that they are a considerable step forward towards a state of affairs when most piece-work prices will be referred to an ultimate or real basis and thus be beyond dispute, either at different times in the same shop, or at the same period in different shops; not because of the peculiar methods by which payment is reckoned, but on account of their minute survey of the maximum possible production, and their enumeration of every factor occurring in such production.

It is perfectly obvious that these new methods are leading up to an ultimate basing of prices on these known factors. For though these factors are numerous, they are not infinite in number. and it is only a

matter of time before they will become tabulated so that the price of any new piece of work will be a simple aggregate of the prices of its factors. When this desirable stage has been reached, the settlement of standard prices for these factors between employers as a class and workers as a class will become quite feasible, and a much higher degree of industrial peace will have become possible. The progress made of late years shows that this is no fanciful picture, but a sober possibility. It seems certain, therefore, that the best interests of trade unions would be furthered not by blind opposition to every kind of piece work, but by an intelligent and friendly co-operation with all attempts to continue and extend the work of finding and standardizing the unit factors of operative production.

The Gantt method of piece remuneration consists, in essence, of what may be termed a truncated premium price. It sets back the time limit in such a way that the early stages of increased speed on the part of a worker do not yield him small results, but no results at all. On the other hand, when this increased speed has, so to speak, acquired sufficient momentum, and has attained a certain predetermined efficiency, the worker finds himself in possession, all at once, of a substantial reward, the proportion of which, relative to his day wages, continues to be an increasing quantity as long as he continues to reduce the allotted time. In the Gantt method a time limit, or allowance, is set as in all other methods of payment by results; and precisely as in ordinary piece work, any reduction of this limit goes entirely into the pocket of the worker. But in addition to this, a bonus of 20 to 40 per cent on the time actually spent on the job is paid to him if, and only if, he succeeds in attaining or reducing the time limit. In all other systems hitherto examined, the passage from day pay to extra earnings is smooth and gradual. Whatever premium or reward is paid to the worker is given for reduction of a time limit, and is in strict proportion to the amount of that reduction. The only difference between those systems is in the relation of the reward of extra effort to the total works cost of the job. And this difference is mainly one of degree. As regards the worker their influence is also very similar. When he attains the limit set, his profits begin, and it is open to him to be content with any degree of profit, large or small, according to his ambition. The time limit set can hardly be described in such cases as a standard attainment, but rather as a milestone, because immediately on either side of it his earnings are much the same, and it is only gradually that they increase when he has passed it.

In the method we are now discussing, the milestone is set at the top of a hill, and a considerable reward is given for getting up to it. It is true that an increased reward follows for further progress, just as in the other systems, but that is not the principal object in view, which is to set a standard of attainment and not a starting point. Examination of the diagram (Figure 1) shows the peculiar feature of this system very plainly. The dotted line representing actual earnings corresponds with time taken until the task or limit is attained, when it rises suddenly, and continues to diverge from the time-taken line, representing an increasing rate of profit or earnings, as time is reduced.

Various interesting deductions can be made from a study of the diagram. In the first place, the meaning of the phrase "a truncated premium price," used above, will be made clear. It is obvious that if the dotted line representing earnings were continued right across the diagram so as to meet the line of time taken, this diagram would be precisely equivalent to a Halsey diagram with a time limit of 167 (166.6) price units, at a premium share of 60 per cent. Regarded from this point of view, the Gantt system is a method of holding back the early portion of profits due to increased activity, which on an ordinary premium plan would be divided from the beginning between employer and worker. This is confirmed by the works-cost curves, which fall sharply until the task set is attained, then rise suddenly, and fall again at a slower rate than before, owing, of course, to the inclusion of extra earnings in them. They are precisely equivalent to Halsey cost curves, except that the latter fall regularly without either the preliminary swift descent, or subsequent restoration to the normal by the sudden rise.

It will be evident from the general form of this diagram that any specific Gantt task can be converted into a Halsey premium job by a shifting upward of the time limit, and some comparisons based on this fact will be given later. First, however, the bearings of the Gantt method on works cost and production generally will be discussed. As regards expense burden, the principles worked out in the previous article when dealing with Halsey premium systems apply to the Gantt method also. The maximum effect on works cost (labor cost *plus* burden) occurs with high burdens. Where Gantt bonus is at the rate of 40 per cent the fall in works cost is parallel with that of time taken when the burden is 60 per cent on wages. With burdens over 60 per cent the fall is more rapid, and with burdens under 60 per cent less rapid, than that of actual time taken.

83

84

In looking at the results of the Gantt system as shown by the diagram, it must be borne in mind that this method sets a standard of attainment and its *raison d'être* is largely fulfilled when it has been attained. Consequently the curves on the right hand of the diagram have very little importance—much less importance than those in corresponding positions on the diagrams of the other systems. The time limit or task is set so low that most of the impulse given by the method takes place before and not after the limit is attained. Hence on this system the determination of the task is all-important.

In Mr. Gantt's recently published book on "Work, Wages and Profits", which must be regarded as one of the most important contributions yet made to the subject, the philosophy underlying his method is brought out in detail. If there is one thing more evident than another it is that the mere mechanism of reward—that is, the part of the method capable of being expressed in a formula or a diagram, is the least essential portion of it. This is very important to understand and to remember, because the temptation to identify the method with the mechanism of reward is necessarily great. But to instal the bonus or task-limit system without the rest of the method would be to court disaster on a big scale. Of all the systems of remuneration yet examined, the Gantt is the most dangerous in the hands of the amateur organizer, who is unable to view manufacturing operations as an organic whole.

The ultimate object of all these systems is to secure a reduction in works cost by providing some method of stimulating labor. In all the systems previously examined, this object is attained in a more or less empiri-

cal manner. No definite standard is in view at any time. The principle frequently recommended to those installing the premium system, *viz.*, to be generous with the time limit and parsimonious with the share or percentage of division, is a wise one in the majority of cases and represents a cautious advance into unknown fields. Where this principle is adopted, the consequences of an error in the time limit are not very serious, and are, indeed, reduced to a minimum on the Rowan system with its closed curve of share percentage. On the Gantt system, however, an entirely new principle comes into play, and the mechanism of the system though peculiarly adapted to its necessities, is quite secondary in importance.

The special and admirable feature of the Gantt method is that it commences by an enquiry into the possible maximum of production, and uses the information thus gained to set up a standard of attainment, difficult perhaps, and in fact impossible to the unaided worker, but just for that reason more than ordinarily valuable because it enforces the necessity and develops the faculty of intelligent and successful co-operation. All the previously examined systems confine their attention to the operative and work on the supposition that by the promise of extra reward his movements will not only be quickened, but his intelligence aroused. That is unquestionably the case, but how much they will be quickened or aroused is left entirely to chance, for the very good reason that no one has known (except the all-wise rule-of-thumb and judgment man) what possibilities were in sight.

It is, however, very much easier to determine a theoretical maximum of production than to guess at what is "a fair day's work". Given certain

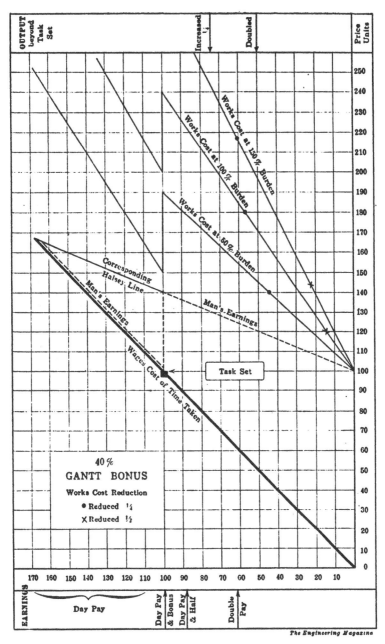

85

FIG. 1. EFFECT OF GANTT BONUS SYSTEM ON EARNINGS AND WORKS COST

An allowance of 100 hours is assumed for both systems. Diagonal thick line is wages cost of job. Dotted line shows total receivable by man—wages *plus* premium. Distance between thick line and dotted line on any vertical shows premium for the corresponding time. Fine lines show total works cost, made up of time taken, burden on time taken, and premium.

conditions, there is always a limit (and it is a mere matter of observation and calculation) beyond which production cannot possibly pass. But in determining this theoretical maximum, it is quickly seen that its attainment depends on a number of auxiliary conditions whose importance—whose vital importance—is otherwise apt to be neglected. This is precisely the point where the "magic touch" comes in, where the subtle difference of principle begins to have important practical results.

The older systems stimulated production, and were well content when they had done so appreciably. As there was a good deal of "trial and error" in their methods, they were very apt to rest on their oars when some progress had been made. In fact, too much progress became rather alarming as individual items of the payroll approached the point of "double pay". When a certain percentage of increase had taken place, everyone, whether master or man, was inclined to say "good enough" for want of knowing any better.

But the moment that a theoretical standard of maximum production is set up, everything is changed. It is an ineradicable factor of human nature to struggle toward a definite ideal—the real trouble of life being that few of us get hold of the right ideal. This applies quite as much in the prosaic atmosphere of the machine shop as anywhere else. The inevitable result of discovering a tangible goal, a maximum standard of attainment, is that only the lazy and incompetent will be willing to rest on their oars after a short spurt of advance. Instead of everyone exclaiming "good enough," the tendency will necessarily be for everyone to exclaim "might be better". The stimulation which the older methods apply to the workman alone is shared by

everyone concerned, and, what is most important, a much more intelligent appreciation of the whole of the conditions—main and auxiliary—pertaining to successful production will be aroused. Incompetence necessarily has a rough time when it is visibly holding back progress towards a definite and ascertained goal. It will be seen, therefore, that the psychology of the Gantt method is much more important than its mechanism.

It is true that so far all the progress that has been made is towards standardization of actual machine work—towards ascertaining the theoretical maximum output of the machinery and labor in conjunction. Yet, as the present writer has often shown in these pages, the relation of establishment charges or burden to production is one of the most serious problems in the attainment of a minimum works cost. It is, perhaps, inevitable that the importance of setting up definite standards of operative work must be recognized before the importance of standardizing indirect expense can be driven home. But no one who is familiar with the question can fail to perceive that the new view of production given by Mr. Gantt lies in the same straight line with the "production-factor" method of dealing with expense burden advocated by the present writer. In wholly independent fields they both tend towards the same end, and that is the predetermination of theoretical efficiency. The tendency in both is to consider each machine as a "production centre" and thoroughly to discuss, enumerate and record all the conditions of its maximum successful operation. They both seek to set up definite standards of work, by which the efficiency of all similar machines wherever placed can be judged.

Obviously this is no mere chance coincidence. It represents the existence of a very definite trend in principles of administration, inevitable as manufacturing operations grow in scale and complexity. It marks the introduction of a higher order of intelligence into manufacturing operations, *viz.*, the co-ordinating as apart from the merely directive, the staff officer as distinct from the regimental commander. There is no getting away from this. The principle of prevoyance, of accurate predetermination of the powers of production in all their aspects, has come to stay.

In this field the work of Mr. Harrington Emerson is also well known. Here again we find a system of payment of a peculiar character which borrows its importance from its association with a standard of theoretical efficiency. The main difference between the Emerson and Gantt systems lies in the nature of the curve traced by the "earnings" line. Whilst the latter partakes of the character of a "truncated" premium limit, the former (see Figure 2) is a 66 per cent Halsey limit, pure and simple, at the beginning and end of its operation, but between these, forms a parabolic curve (of which the likeness to an *inverted* Rowan curve will be noticed) corresponding to a whole range of Halsey limits as the actual time taken is reduced. The practical effect of the parabola is most noticeable in the earlier stages of time reduction, allowing only an almost negligible bonus to be earned until the nominal limit called 100 per cent efficiency is being approached.

In the Emerson system, also, the curves on the right-hand side of the diagram possess comparatively small importance. The whole field of operation is supposed, as an axiomatic condition of the adoption of the method, to be so exactly mapped out that no great reduction of the task set is likely. The psychological difference

between the two methods lies in the absence, in the Emerson system, of a sudden rise in earnings. On the contrary, earnings begin to grow when two-thirds of the task efficiency has been attained, although very slowly in the earlier stages. The question naturally arises—which of these two methods of approaching standard efficiency is best?

No definite answer is possible, or rather any attempted answer must contain several unknown or indeterminate factors. Personally, the clearness and definiteness of the Gantt standard seems to me to offer a greater leverage on average human nature than the gradual rise of earnings on the Emerson method. But in actual practice everything depends on the personality of those who are in authority—much more perhaps than on the workers themselves. Probably the Gantt method requires greater self-confidence and a clearer survey of the ultimate goal to be reached than the other, but just because of its definiteness one may be inclined to suggest that in the right hands its success would be more thorough and uniform.

Considered in relation to high burdens, it will be seen from the curves that the Emerson works cost does not differ to a very great degree, at any point, from an ordinary 66 per cent Halsey premium works cost. The higher the burden, the closer this approximation becomes. The practical deduction from this observed fact is that the principal value of these new methods of remuneration lies in their introduction of the "Standard of Efficiency" idea—that is, their placing of the task milestone at the top of a hill, and thus setting free the tendency inherent in all humanity to attain, if possible, a goal that is in sight.

In the foregoing examination of

these two methods nothing has been said about the remuneration which is given to other than direct-workers for attainment of task or standard efficiency on the part of these latter. Yet it will be obvious that bonuses to officials whose intelligent and active co-operation in their respective spheres is necessary to enable the worker to have an uninterrupted chance of success, is a most important feature of these advanced methods. Such bonuses are not new in themselves, but under the older methods of working have rarely been found satisfactory, leading, not infrequently, to aggravated forms of "driving" and general unrest. It is only when introduced as part and parcel of the standard efficiency or task idea that they promise success, because, and only because, the introduction of this idea leads to production being regarded from a co-operative point of view, in which manual skill, machinery and directive (or rather educative) effort, have each their appointed place. In other words, the bonuses are given not for "making" other men increase their production, but for "helping" them to do so—a very different ideal, signifying entirely different personal relations and a much more progressive atmosphere.

It has been shown above that, in relation to burden or establishment charges, these new methods of remuneration do not present any strikingly novel features; that is to say, they do not introduce any new relationship between the time actually spent on the job and the overhead charges the job has to bear. Nevertheless the introduction of the standard task or efficiency idea may have, as already briefly pointed out, an influence on the point of view from which burden is regarded. For if we assume a standard task and agree

to regard any failure to perform it as so much avoidable inefficiency, it is evident that we imply a standard quantity of burden, whether the latter is regarded as a percentage of time, or wages, or is treated on the "production-centre" system of machine rents. There is, then, a double degree of inefficiency in failure to come up to standard on any job. Not only is there a loss of time, but what is sometimes even more important, there is an undue absorption of burden. The modern principle of predetermination of standard time-cost requires to be supplemented by similar standardization of overhead burden, in order to bring all the elements of cost to a focus.

The inefficiency of a shop may take three principal directions, *viz.*:

(1) Wasted burden owing to idle machinery.

(2) Wasted time due to standard tasks not being attained.

(3) Unduly absorbed burden on this unnecessary time.

Items (2) and (3) are of course inseparable, and vary together. The question is complicated by the fact that while (2) is an obviously unnecessary expense, (3) on the other hand is a false *credit; i. e.*, it represents an amount by which burden, chargeable either against the shop or against the machine, has been improperly relieved.

Space does not admit of a fuller discussion of the general relations of burden to costs under a system, such as the Gantt or Emerson, of standardized task efficiency. Enough, however, has been said to show that the subject requires development if only because the *mechanism* of both systems shows no changed relationship of time to burden, although the *spirit* of each system really changes such relationship entirely. In other words, predetermination of standard

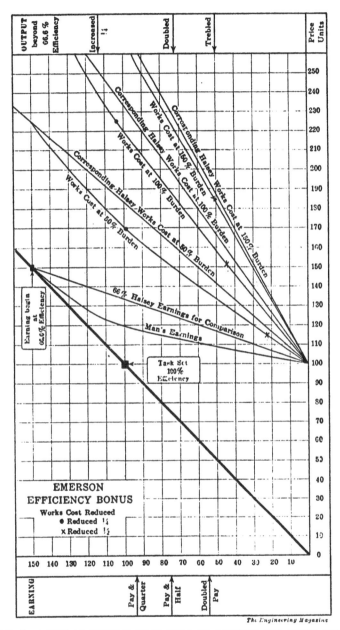

FIG. 2. EFFECT OF EMERSON WAGE SCALE ON EARNINGS AND WORKS COST

An allowance of 100 hours is assumed. Diagonal thick line is wages cost of job. Earnings line shows total receivable by man—wages *plus* premium. Distance between thick line and earnings line on any vertical shows premium for the corresponding time. Fine lines show total works cost, made up of time taken, burden on time taken, and premium.

costs, depending as it does on the close application of scientific methods of analysis of the elements of jobs, and the consequent accurate mapping out of all the field of production, throws, to a considerable extent, the relations of burden to cost into the melting pot. For it is obviously an incomplete programme to have one-half of productive expense accurately surveyed, and to leave the other, and possibly the larger half, on the old haphazard basis.

At the outset of this enquiry the question of equivalent time-limits on the different piece-work, premium and bonus systems occupied my attention. It is actually possible, and seemed useful, to determine these equivalent limits, which promised to afford a method of switching over from one system to another. Further examination has shown that though this is to a great extent possible, *e. g.*, every Gantt limit at a given rate of bonus has an equivalent Halsey limit at a given rate of bonus—nevertheless to lay any stress on this point would be mischievous and misleading. For as already remarked, the mechanism of the new methods is their least important feature, and to offer any details which might lead the unwary to think of adopting the mechanism without the far more essential spirit, would be a poor service.

The moral to be drawn from an inspection and comparison of the diagrams in this and the preceding article will now be recognizable. It is that between all these systems of remuneration there is a strong family likeness, and that there is not between them as great a difference in principle as is commonly supposed. Fundamentally and in all essential points, they attain closely related results by very similar paths. The differences between them resolve into the shifting backwards and forwards of time-limits and tasks, and the greater or less share which is retained or given as a reward for extra exertion. After a dispassionate examination, the closed curve of the Rowan system with its self-protection against the results of bad errors in limits seems to me to offer many advantages—considered merely as a *mechanism* of reward. On the other hand, the newer method of standard task or efficiency examined in the present article must in time supersede all others as to *principle*. The question arises, however, whether some combination of the Rowan closed curve for mechanism, with the standardizing idea as principle, is not possible, and if possible whether it would not form a happy and practical combination. Investigation along this line seems worth while.

The Scientific Basis of Manufacturing Management

By A. HAMILTON CHURCH

R-T Index; ARf

This paper is a brief résumé of the method which has been followed by Mr. A. Hamilton Church in his attempt to formulate the beginnings of a systematic science of Manufacturing Management. The practical working out of the basic facts and laws here outlined will be presented by the author in a new book, shortly to be published by the Engineering Magazine Co., New York, under the title of "The Science and Practice of Management." It is expected to be ready within a few weeks.

92

I

In undertaking to arrange the fundamental facts and working principles of manufacturing management so as to exhibit their definite relationship and interaction I have not had in view the elaboration of any new 'system' for commercial exploitation. The stage through which the study of Management has been passing in recent years bears about the same relation to sober science that Alchemy did to Chemistry. The eagerness to discover and exploit something new and wonderful has diverted attention from the desirability of getting a correct perspective of the whole facts of production, and has led to attention being focussed on one or two practical applications as if these were in themselves sufficient to form a science.

The time to pass beyond this immature stage has probably arrived. Some clearly defined facts are observable; some definite principles, amounting in their universality to Laws, are also observable; it is therefore necessary to combine these so that their interaction can be traced and understood. If they are correctly observed and stated we shall find ourselves in possession of the beginnings of a real science of Management. "There has not yet been established," said Secretary Redfield* in his recent book, "a science of management. And yet, if a science were ever needed, meaning definite principles, based on exact knowledge of facts, it is in this very matter of management."

---

* THE NEW INDUSTRIAL DAY, Wm. C. Redfield.

8

It must be understood that the science of management, like every other science, is abstract. It is not a series of "shop hints." It is not a collection of "short cuts." Just as there is no royal road to the mastery of mathematics, so there is no royal road to the mastery of management. A treatise on the science of management will no more give definite instructions how to manage a shop, than a treatise on strength of materials will give specific directions how to build a new Brooklyn Bridge. A science is an enquiry into first principles, it is not a book of recipes or even of plans.

What then, it may be asked, is the use of reducing management to an abstract statement of definite facts and laws? The answer must be, of course, that whatever is true is important. A knowledge, for example, of the very dry and abstract science of mechanics and the still more refined abstraction of the conservation of energy will prevent us from frittering away our time in trying to accomplish impossible things, such as the invention of perpetual motion. It will also enable us to apply our efforts intelligently to whatever practical problem we have. But it will not set aside the necessity for careful study and working out of each practical problem on its own merits.

93

Knowledge of the abstract but fundamental basis of management will also prevent us from trying to do, if not impossible things, at least inadvisable things. By uncovering relations not always visible on the surface, it will enable us to understand how our efforts should be applied and where they should be applied. It will enable us to analyze our practical problems, and correspondingly to direct intelligently our treatment of those problems. It enables us to do these things because it is abstract, and in proportion as it is abstract. In other words, it substitutes theory, which is the accumulated and systematized experience of many, for empiricism, which is the more or less shrewd guesswork of the experienced individual.

No apology can be made therefore for the setting up of theory, that bugbear of the "practical" man, in the arena of management. In any branch c knowledge, theory has to make its appearance, sooner or later, and when it appears progress is usually rapid because assured. Theory can never precede practice, because as just said it is merely systematised practice. but once established, it guides and controls the path of new practice. It does this in two ways. **First,** by showing in which directions practice is most imperfect, and secondly, by preventing the necessity for experiment along lines which have been already thoroughly explored.

II.

It is possible that some day a complete science of management will be formulated. By complete science is meant one so universal that it will apply to every kind of organized human activity. At present, however, this is far from our grasp. Our aim at the present day must be much more humble than this. We must be content to explore comparatively narrow sections of such activity, leaving the coordination of such sections to the future. I have found, for example, that no good results were attainable by attempting to include all kinds of management in one system. Nor has it even been possible to include all kinds of *Industrial* management in one system. At present the basic facts of *Manufacturing* activity are all that it is contemplated to cover. It has been found that the first necessity is to discover and formulate what I have termed the Organic Functions of management. Now these Organic Functions are wholly different in a manufacturing plant and in, say, a railroad or a merchanting business. My inquiry has therefore been wholly confined to determining the facts and laws of manufacturing management.

In the spring of 1912, in conjunction with Mr. L. P. Alford, editor of the *American Machinist,* I undertook an attempt to reduce the regulative principles of management to their broadest and simplest forms. The object of this was to provide a basic classification on which a detailed structure could subsequently be built up. In other words it was an attempt to provide the lowest course of the foundations for a true science of management. In the course of our inquiry we found that all the different working principles common in manufacturing (including those enunciated by all previous writers on the subject) could be reduced to one of three main groups, viz. :—

(1) The Systematic Accumulation and Use of Experience.

(2) The Economic Control (or Regulation) of Effort.

(3) The Promotion of Personal Effectiveness.

These three main regulative principles met with considerable favor. Such authorities as Prof. Dexter Kimball and Mr. John Calder wrote to the *Machinist* in approval of the effort to clear the ground, and substitute a discussion of principles for the already too long drawn out discussion of particular methods. Later also, the majority report of the special committee appointed by the American Society of Mechanical Engineers to investigate the new ideas in management endorsed and adopted these principles, with the addition of one of their own, namely, "The Transfer of Skill," which, however, I am unable to accept as an established regulative principle of *management,* though it is, no doubt, a salient feature of *industry.*

Following up the line of inquiry thus started, I developed the application of the principles in a series of articles contributed to the *Engineering Magazine* (Jan.-June, 1913). These articles were titled "Practical Principles of Rational Management," because at that time the peculiar feature of the modern systems seemed to be the introduction of *reasoning* into management, as opposed to the old rule-of-thumb school. To exhibit the regulative principles in work I found it necessary to delimit what I there termed "spheres of activity," in each of which the principles were applied, and had a different aim. But on reviewing the whole matter at leisure, I came to see that the specific and peculiar nature of any kind of industrial undertaking lay precisely in these "spheres of activity," which thus assumed new importance and merited close study and analysis. The "spheres of activity" were seen to be the fundamental *facts* which are necessary to a science because they form the matter on which the principles or laws act.

Once this important relationship was perceived, progress was possible. The whole point of view of what management really was became changed. Its existence was seen to be based on the existence of *specific organic functions each devoted to a special purpose,* and therefore that before any general science of management covering all forms of organized activity was possible the special forms in which it is found in practice must be studied, because in each of these the organic functions are necessarily different. In *manufacturing* these functions were found to be "Design, Equipment, Control, Comparison and Operation." In *other* kinds of management such as commerce or railroading, some of these would be missing and their places would be taken by wholly new ones.

This brief historical sketch of the way in which the inquiry grew up has been given because it will probably assist the reader to follow more readily the condensed description of the laws of effect and the organic functions they control, which follows.

<h2 style="text-align:center">III</h2>

In manufacturing there are five organic functions—Design, Equipment, Control, Comparison and Operation—which embrace all the different kinds or varieties of activity necessary to successful manufacture. It must be emphasized that these are purely *productive* functions. They have nothing to do with selling or with finance or with the higher administrative activities which determine the broad lines of policy of a plant. They are concerned only with that chain of activities beginning and ending with the transformation of material into new and more valuable forms, but within this sphere of production they embrace everything.

Compactly described, Design *originates;* Equipment provides *conditions;* Control specifies *duties* and gives *orders;* Comparison measures, records and *compares;* Operation *makes.* No kind of productive activity is found in a plant that does not fall exactly and completely into one of these organic functions.

The practical importance of these five organic functions lies in the fact that they are wholly independent. They form water-tight compartments. If a business is in ill health, diagnosis must be directed to finding out in which function the trouble exists. *It is of no use to tinker with one of these functions if the disease lies within another.* Moreover, if a condition of general disease exists, the order in which remedies are applied is exceedingly important, since if the wrong function is stimulated to begin with, the condition of the plant may be rendered worse instead of better. Many of the failures of modern methods may be attributed to the fact that the organic nature of manufacturing activity has been hitherto not clearly appreciated.

The way in which these respective functions originated is not without interest. Actually they are found to be a series of devolutions from a primitive condition of industry. Originally they were all exercised by the craftsman in his own person, and in the course of progress and expansion he has shed them one by one for very obvious reasons, and by very obvious stages that cannot be described here. The practical point is, however, that they are *natural* subdivisions of production, hence they are natural *facts,* not capable of being varied by any process of organization, or by any one's will or fancy. They form the prime, basic facts that are necessary to build up a true science of productive management.

Space forbids any demonstration of the actuality of these functions or even any definition of their exact scope. Having asserted their existence we must now pass to consideration of the regulative principles which control the phenomena of production as and when they are applied to the five Functions in daily routine.

The regulative principles worked out by Mr. Alford and myself, and quoted above, have been found to stand. For convenience, however, it has been found desirable to express them in mandatory form, and to expand them by certain main subdivisions in some cases. Further, it seems likely that they are much more universal in their application than the organic functions. While the latter are, as said above, strictly limited to particular kinds of management activity, such as manufacturing, the regulative principles seem likely to become true general Laws of Effort, and I have therefore ventured to give them this title. These Laws of Effort probably apply to any kind of activity where associated groups of men are organized for any definite work in common. It is at any rate certain, and this is sufficient for our purpose, that they apply to all forms of manufacturing industry without exception. They are now stated as follows:

97

(1) Experience must be systematically accumulated and applied.

(2) Effort must be economically regulated (in four ways).

    2a. Effort must be Divided.
    2b. Effort must be Coordinated.
    2c. Effort must be Conserved.
    2d. Effort must be Remunerated.

(3) Personal Effectiveness must be promoted.

This last Law of Effort is also subdivided so as to indicate the *directions* in which we must seek to promote personal effectiveness, but, as I have not yet completed the analysis, the subdivisions are omitted here.

We have thus furnished ourselves with a series of natural facts— the Organic Functions—and a series of Laws of Effort. We have in fact all the materials for constructing at least the beginnings of a

true science. It may be objected that these facts and these laws are
very general and that their mutual relations are by no means self-
evident. This is so, and under certain conditions this is their merit.
If they are correct, and particularly *if they are exhaustive,* their
generality is no bar, but is on the other hand an assurance that we
shall be able to develop them into as exact detail as we require for
practical purposes.

It is, of course, impossible to show, within the limits of a short
paper, how this development takes place. Only a suggestion as to
the method is possible. Each of the Laws of Effort with all its subdivisions is applied in turn to each of the Organic Functions. The
result is to uncover the relations of every kind of activity, every
kind of duty, and every kind of Effort that is found in a manufacturing plant. Wherever a duty has a justification for existing at all it
must be for the purpose of serving one of the five Functions and is
subject to the Laws of Effort.

We can apply this knowledge either constructively or analytically.
That is to say we can either develop an ideal organization to fit predetermined conditions, or we can consider the case of an existing
organization and observe how far its structure and routine is in
accordance with the natural Organic Functions and how far the Laws
of Effort are being applied or neglected. And we can do this almost
with the precision of a mathematical analysis.

It will be fairly obvious that the application of the first Law—
that Experience must be accumulated and applied—will have very
different outcome when applied to the work of the Function of
Design than when applied to, let us say, Equipment. In the same
way the Division, or the Coordination of Effort in regard to the
Function of Comparison, is obviously dealing with a different set of
facts from those involved when Control is in question. Moreover,
when we consider the second Law of Effort we see that its four subdivisions are mutually related. As soon as we begin to divide Effort,
it is necessary to take measures to Coordinate it. In practical language, if we give three parts of a product to three people to make,
we must take measures to ensure that they will meet together when
made. But this is not enough. It is also necessary to ensure that
no Effort is wasted, or in other words Effort must be Conserved.
Further in each Function, there will be some variety of Effort that

is peculiarly significant in its bearing on the efficiency of that Function. The subprinciple that Effort must be Remunerated makes it desirable to discover and isolate this significant variety of Effort for special reward.

Now, each of these subprinciples of the second Law of Effort deals with Effort in the abstract. It does not matter what th' Effort is, or what aim it has. Consequently, although the aim of Effort in each Function is wholly different, and represents an entirely different kind of work, and frequently a different class of labor, still the Law holds good in all. Wherever Effort, mental or physical, is divided, it must also be coordinated, conserved and special features of it marked out for special remuneration. If this Law is neglected, then specific ills arise, but these ills have different aspects in each Function—that is, they have different consequences, although their cause is similar.

99

These brief illustrations will perhaps serve to indicate both the theoretical reach and the practical value of a true theoretical science of management, built up on natural facts and subject to the regular action of general but definite laws of Effort.

"PREPARATION FOR TASK-SETTING. Among the steps to be taken before setting a task are: To get all machines and appliances in proper order; to establish a proper tool-room where suitable tools can be obtained for work; to arrange to supply the workmen with material in the order wanted; to plan work so that it is very seldom that one job shall be stopped to make way for another. In other words, before we begin the problem of task-setting for the individual, we should arrange conditions so that he can work to the best advantage, with proper ventilation and a comfortable temperature."—*H. L. Gantt.*

"I find in many factories that the amount of work in process, moving in a desultory way through the factory, is two or three times as great as there is any necessity for, if its course were properly planned. It not only takes up factory space, but it ties up a large amount of capital where work is not properly planned. The ordinary stock-keeper or foreman always wants to give himself about two or three times as much time as is needed to get the work done."
—*H. L. Gantt.*

100

The Evolution of Design

Professor Kimball's articles on design present a view of the matter that is, I think, as original as it is interesting. I remember, many years ago, contemplating that frightful monster called, I believe, "Puffing Billy," that stood in the museum of the British Patent Office. This was the prototype of the locomotive, and must have been, when working, as diabolical a sight as could be desired. It would certainly "go," and as certainly was devoid of any pretensions to shape or beauty.

By degrees the locomotive changed its outward appearance and passed through a few generations of what may be termed a "long-limbed" type, corresponding to certain stages in the growth of a child. It became all wheels and funnel—a queer straggling object. This was also, I believe, the period of gorgeous coloring, shining brass domes, polished handrails, and multi-colored enamels.

Then for a time there was a pause in technical improvement, and with each succeeding generation of locomotives, a nobler and grander form appeared. Colors were sobered down, and polished surfaces were restricted. What may be termed "stream lines," such as are visible in modern automobiles and well-designed steam yachts—lines that seem appropriate to a great mass rushing at high speed—were strongly marked.

Then came another burst of technical invention, compounding and so forth, and the locomotive fell back at once to the level of a hideous barbaric monster, from which it has not yet climbed up. The American locomotive in particular, which looks as if it had been dipped bodily in tar, is almost as awful as the original "Puffing Billy." But Professor Kimball's theory gives us some hope that it will evolve again into a thing of splendor and delight to the eye.

The question of decoration is a very subtle one. Can Professor Kimball tell us why ancient Flemish and German buildings, which are covered with ornament, delight the eye, just as much as French buildings, which depend chiefly on exquisite proportion for their effect? Why should curved legs to a sewing machine be hideous, and yet hammered-iron gates or grills full of curves and twists be beautiful? There is, I apprehend, no real reason connected with *use* that makes twisted iron appropriate to gates. Is it because sewing-machine legs are cast that makes them out of place—one process being used to simulate the effect of another process?

I wonder if it would be considered as trenching on politics to suggest that, as regards domestic articles, woman's influence has something to do with the matter. The household stove, the German tiled stove and the sewing machine possibly remain as they are because of this influence. Women love to embroider things; they rejoice in ornament for its own sake. I know of one case where the women of the family just worship a table with monstrous claw feet, like those spoken of by Professor Kimball, while the men of the family would cheerfully amputate them at sight. I once saw a typewriter that had been prepared for a European queen; it had been made gorgeous with gilding and colored enamels.

Modern steel buildings confirm Professor Kimball's views. They are mostly in the second stage at present, that of inappropriate decoration. Some of the recent examples, with polished marble façades up to the third story and the plainest of brick above, are as bad as anything in the history of machines. The London Tower Bridge—a steel structure masquerading as a stone Gothic castle—is equally horrible.

It does not seem clear whether the appreciation of an article unadorned, and merely admirable from its perfect adaptation to its end, is not a quite modern idea. It is noteworthy that in the case of body-armor worn by knights, development was from the simple and beautiful outline through willfully fantastic shapes to a final stage of elaborately damascened, inlaid and engraved ornament. Yet if there was ever an article of which the development was controlled by use it should have been armor. I am inclined to think, therefore, that the law of design and ornament pointed out by Professor Kimball is really evidence of the dawning of a new and more perfect sense of fitness, due perhaps to the great triumphs of modern science and invention that have given a new perspective to the world. For my part, I believe that the sight of a collection of chemical apparatus may give as much intellectual pleasure as contemplation of the Sistine Madonna; but it is doubtful if a medieval European or an ancient Greek would have been able to get that point of view.

A. HAMILTON CHURCH.

New York, N. Y.

the executive is just the person to do this efficiently. But let us consider the matter for a moment in the light of what actually happens with regard to the design of machines. We shall probably find that there is no true parallel between the two cases.

The difference lies in the kind of experience that is be-hind the knitting together of details into a completed whole. Machine design is expert design. A firm that is building a line of machines will acquire and keep always at hand the best technical skill available for its design. It can afford to do this because it is going to keep on with just this kind of designing as a regular part of its work. It will not one day close up its drafting room and consider that no progress is possible. It will not claim, if it is wise, that it has a machine that can-not possibly be improved on. On the contrary, it will always be keen to incorporate fresh features in its design and to bring it more and more uptodate. Machine de-sign has no finality.

Now it is possible to pick up a hint here and an idea there and weave them successfully into an improved design of machine, because the firm has experts at hand capable of knowing in advance just what the influence of any new proposal will be. Its men are not only famil-iar with machine design as a whole, but they are familiar with the specific kinds of machine they are always work-ing on. Moreover, they will be familiar with all the various ways of attaining the object for which the ma-chine exists; they will know what rival machines are like, and why they are different in some ways and similar in others; they will know that new suggestions are variable in value and that what might be an improvement in A's machine would not be so in the case of B's.

Why do they know all this? Because they are experts in their particular line, and an expert is merely a person whose experience is so wide that he knows much more about a particular matter than anyone who only gives it attention as a side line. There are, of course, degrees in expertship, and therefore there are degrees in regard to the facility with which one will perceive at once the rela-tion of any new suggestion or new device to previous practice. But successful machine design implies an expert designer.

There is another aspect of machine design that is im-portant to observe. If we have a good machine today, and some new suggestion comes up, we do not have to dis-card the good machine until we have tried out a new ex-perimental model. We do not rush to get out patterns and jigs for an imagined improvement until the su-periority of the new idea has been practically proven. That is, we do not do so if we possess business acumen. No doubt there have been many who have thus succumbed to temptation, but not among the firms that habitually make money.

How far do these conditions obtain in regard to the de-sign of "system"? It will be seen at once that the prime conditions are exactly reversed. Only very large firms have sufficient "system" designing to render it possible to employ experts in that line permanently. It is even questionable whether they gain much from so doing, be-cause a good deal of the organizing expert's value comes from his detached viewpoint. But as regards the majority of firms, large and small, they have no use for the ser-vices of a high-grade organizing expert as a permanent item. A good system should last from 5 to 10 years

Machine Design and the Design of Systems

By A. Hamilton Church

Is the design of "systems," that is, of organization methods, accounting plans and control arrangements, a matter at all similar to the design of machines? This question is often asked, and it must be confessed that the answer is one of practical interest.

For some reason or other not very clear to me many persons seem to think that the designing of systems comes by nature and is a necessary accompaniment of ad-ministrative ability. Because the manager has need of a properly designed system, he must necessarily have the capacity, skill and experience to design one for his needs. There is a missing link in the logic of this position, but from the nature of the case, the errors perpetrated are not very readily discerned. A badly designed machine will either not work at all or, by comparison with some other machine, can be seen to be inferior; but a badly de-signed system always works after a fashion, and the op-portunities for comparing it with *what it might have been* hardly exist at all.

At first sight, it seems quite reasonable to suppose that there are elements of system, just as there are ele-ments of machine design, which can be picked up here or there and incorporated with existing practice, and that

101

without serious modification, except in special circumstances. It may, in favorable cases, last for much longer.

THE FIRST DIFFERENCE

This, then, is the difference: The designing of a good system is a single and not a continuous operation, and consequently needs temporary and not continuous expert help. Next, we must consider the question of additions and supposed improvements to be incorporated in the system from time to time. Here again we have a totally different situation from that of machine designing. Improvements to a system should arise from new felt wants, but improvements to a machine have a distinct competitive and market value for their own sake. If a system has been intelligently designed in the first place and does not merely consist of a collection of devices and methods that have happened to be adopted, it should not be tinkered with for the sake of tinkering. New methods should not be forced into it because they happen to work well at So and So's. The less it is meddled with the better, except under the advice of the experts that designed it, or others of equal standing.

Novelties in machines have generally a commercial value; they become talking points. But system is a domestic and product is a public matter. What is good for the one is not necessarily good for the other.

ANOTHER DIFFERENCE

Even more important is the consideration that to inject new elements into a system is a much more serious matter than to try out new elements in a machine. To alter a system is like reconstructing a railroad terminal or a busy bridge. You must keep the traffic going and be sure also that you have foreseen exactly the range of your alterations. In tearing down, you must not tear down too much or too rapidly, for when the alteration is complete, if it is not what you expected, it will be very difficult to return to the old conditions.

The fact that every reorganization is of this nature indicates why the expert, quite apart from the question of designing the system, has great advantages over the non-expert. He is familiar with tearing down as well as with building up.

The extent to which non-expert alterations of system will go and the waste they incur are known to most professional organizers, but are not realized by executives as they should be. On one occasion I had conveyed to the boiler furnaces *three large cartloads* of beautiful printed stationary, loose-leaf books, etc., found as obsolete stores of a firm that had believed in home treatment for its complaints—and this was merely the waste incurred in five years of experimentation. Add to this the time of executives and the worries, blunders, delays, losses and exasperations, the effects of which could not be so easily observed, and the money value of the whole would be an uncomfortable total. Yet this same firm had an excellent product, fine modern buildings and good machinery. But to get these, it had employed experts.

This, it may be claimed, is a professional view of the matter, and so, of course, it is. But is it not also a reasonable view of the matter? When it is considered how very important a part the system fills in the smooth working of any business, does it not seem that the very best talent available should be secured when its welfare is in question. It must not be forgotten, also, that it is

no mere question of a design on paper—the professional organizer installs as well as designs, and this is the most delicate part of his work for the reason already given, namely, that all organization is reconstruction, during which the traffic must be kept moving.

How, then, does the professional organizer regard the efforts of the AMERICAN MACHINIST and other journals to report specific instances of how things are done at this plant or that? Has the publication of such details as regards system the same value as when details of mechanical design are in question? For my part, I regard this as excellent service, because anything that ventilates the subject is good for everyone. The firm that sees and adopts some new departure of system for the first time is already on the path which will lead it, sooner or later, to appreciate the value of expert services. The more that people come to discover that there are other methods of doing things than their own time-honored ones, the better for eventual perfection. Certainly this is important work, even though there is no very close parallel between elements of machine design and elements of the design of systems. Or rather, in the majority of cases, the divergence in validity is due to the very different degrees of expert knowledge behind the attempted application of each.

✱

The Relation Between Production and Costs*

By H. L. GANTT†

SYNOPSIS—It has been common practice to make the product of a factory running at a portion of its capacity bear the whole expense of the factory. This has been long recognized by many to be illogical, but so far there has not been presented a rational theory as to what proportion of the expense such a product should bear. Mr. Gantt offers the theory that the amount of expense to be borne by the product should bear the same ratio to the total normal operating expense as the product in question bears to the normal product, and that the expense of maintaining the idle portion of the plant ready to run is a business expense not chargeable to the product made. This latter expense is really a deduction from profits, and shows that we may have a serious loss on account of having too much plant, as well as on account of not operating our plant economically.

Manufacturers in general recognize the vital importance of a knowledge of the cost of their product, yet but few of them have a cost system on which they are willing to rely under all conditions.

While it is possible to get quite accurately the amount of material and labor used directly in the production of an article, and several systems have been devised which accomplish this result, there does not yet seem to have been devised any system of distributing that portion of the expense known variously as indirect expense, burden or overhead, in such a manner as to make us have any real confidence that it has been done properly.

There are in common use several methods of distributing this expense. One is to distribute the total indirect expense, including interest, taxes, insurance, etc., according to the direct labor. Another is to distribute a portion of this expense according to direct labor and a portion according to machine hours. Other methods distribute a certain amount of this expense on the material used, etc. Most of these methods contemplate the distribution of all of the indirect expense of the manufacturing plant, however much it may be, on the output produced, no matter how small it is.

If the factory is running at its full or normal capacity, this item of indirect expense per unit of product is usually small. If the factory is running at only a fraction of its capacity, say one-half, and turning out only one-half of its normal product, there is but little change in the total amount of this indirect expense, all of which must now be distributed over half as much product as previously, each unit of product thereby being obliged to bear approximately twice as much expense as previously.

When times are good and there is plenty of business, this method of accounting indicates that our costs are low; but when times become bad and business is slack, it

*To be presented at the spring meeting, June, 1915, of the American Society of Mechanical Engineers.
†Consulting engineer, New York, N. Y.

indicates high costs due to the increased proportion of burden each unit has to bear. During good times, when there is a demand for all the product we can make, it is usually sold at a high price and the element of cost is not such an important factor. When business is dull, however, we cannot get such a high price for our product, and the question of how low a price we can afford to sell the product at is of vital importance. Our cost systems, as generally operated at present, show under such conditions that our costs are high and, if business is very bad, they usually show us a cost far greater than the amount we can get for the goods. In other words, our present systems of cost accounting go to pieces when they are most needed. This being the case, many of us have felt for a long time that there was something radically wrong with the present theories on the subject.

AN ILLUMINATING ILLUSTRATION

As an illustration, I may cite a case which recently came to my attention. A man found that his cost on a certain article was 30c. When he learned that he could buy it for 26c., he gave orders to stop manufacturing and to buy it, saying he did not understand how his competitor could sell at that price. He seemed to realize that there was a flaw somewhere, but he could not locate it. I then asked him what his expense consisted of. His reply was, labor 10c., material 8c., and overhead 12c. My next question was: "Are you running your factory at full capacity?" and the reply was that he was running it at less than half its capacity, possibly at one-third. The next question was: "What would be the overhead on this article if your factory were running full?" The reply was that it would be about 5c.; hence the cost would be only 23c. The possibility that his competitor was running his factory full suggested itself at once as an explanation.

The next question that suggested itself was how the 12c. overhead that was charged to this article would be paid if the article was bought. The obvious answer was that it would have to be distributed over the product still being made and would thereby increase its cost. In such a case it would probably be found that some other article was costing more than it could be bought for; and, if the same policy were pursued, the second article should be bought, which would cause the remaining product to bear a still higher expense rate.

If this policy were carried to its logical conclusion, the manufacturer would be buying everything before long, and be obliged to give up manufacturing entirely.

The illustration that I have cited is not an isolated case, but is representative of the problems before a large class of manufacturers, who believe that all of the expense, however large, must be carried by the output produced, however small.

This theory of expense distribution is quite widespread and clearly indicates a policy that in dull times would, if followed logically, put many manufacturers out of busi-

103

ness. In 1897 the plant of which I was superintendent was put out of business by just this kind of logic. It never started up again.

Fortunately for the country, American people as a whole will finally discard theories which conflict with common sense, and when their cost figures indicate an absurd conclusion, most of them will repudiate the figures. A cost system, however, that fails us when we need it most, is of but little value, and it is imperative for us to devise a theory of costs that will not fail us.

Most of the cost systems in use and the theories on which they are based have been devised by accountants for the benefit of financiers, whose aim has been to criticize the factory and to make it responsible for all the shortcomings of the business. In this they have succeeded admirably, largely because the methods used are not so devised as to enable the superintendent to present his side of the case.

Our theory of cost keeping is that one of its prime functions is to enable the superintendent to know whether or not he is doing the work he is responsible for as economically as possible, which function is ignored in the majority of the cost systems now in general use. Many accountants who make an attempt to show it are so long in getting their figures in shape that they are practically worthless for the purpose intended, the possibility of using them having passed.

In order to get a correct view of the subject we must look at the matter from a different and broader standpoint. The following illustration seems to put the subject in its true light:

Let us suppose that a manufacturer owns three identical plants of an economical operating size, manufacturing the same article—one in Albany, one in Buffalo and one in Chicago—and that they are all running at their normal capacity and managed equally well. The amount of indirect expense per unit of product would be substantially the same in each of these factories, as would be the total cost. Now, suppose that business suddenly falls off to one-third of its previous amount and that the manufacturer shuts down the plants in Albany and Buffalo and continues to run the one in Chicago exactly as it has been run before. The product from the Chicago plant would have the same cost that it previously had, but the expense of carrying two idle factories might be so great as to take all the profits out of the business; in other words, the profit made from the Chicago plant might be offset entirely by the loss made by the Albany and Buffalo plants.

If these plants, instead of being in different cities, were in the same city, a similar condition might also exist in which the expense of the two idle plants would be such a drain on the business that they would offset the profit made in the going plant.

Instead of considering these three factories to be in different parts of one city, they might be considered as being within the same yard, which would not change the conditions. Finally, we might consider that the walls between these factories were taken down and that the three factories were turned into one plant, the output of which had been reduced to one-third of its normal volume. Arguing as before, it would be proper to charge to this product only one-third of the indirect expense charged when the factory was running full.

A GENERAL PRINCIPLE

If the above argument is correct, we may state the following general principle: *The indirect expense chargeable to the output of a factory bears the same ratio to the indirect expense necessary to run the factory at normal capacity, as the output in question bears to the normal output of the factory.*

This theory of expense distribution, which was forced upon us by the abrupt change in conditions brought on by the war, explains many things which were inexplicable under the older theory and gives the manufacturer uniform costs as long as the methods of manufacture do not change.

Under this method of distributing expense there will be a certain amount of undistributed expense remaining whenever the factory runs below its normal capacity. A careful consideration of this item will show that it is not chargeable to the product made, but is a business expense incurred on account of our maintaining a certain portion of the factory idle, and chargeable to profit and loss. Many manufacturers have made money in a small plant, then built a large one and lost money for years afterward, without quite understanding how it happened. This method of figuring gives a clear explanation of that fact and warns us to do everything possible to increase the efficiency of the plant we have, rather than to increase its size.

This theory seems to give a satisfactory answer to all the questions of cost that I have been able to apply it to, and during the past few months I have laid it before a great many capable business men and accountants. Some admitted that this viewpoint would produce a very radical change in their business policy and are already preparing to carry out the new policy.

It explains clearly why some of our large combinations of manufacturing plants have not been as successful as was anticipated, and why the small but newer plant is able to compete successfully and make money, while the combinations are only just holding their own.

The idea so prevalent a few years ago, that in the industrial world money is the most powerful factor and that if we only had enough money nothing else would matter very much, is beginning to lose its force, for it is becoming clear that the size of a business is not so important as the policy by which it is directed. If we base our policy on the idea that the cost of an article can legitimately include only the expense necessarily incurred either directly or indirectly in producing it, we shall find that our costs are much lower than we thought and that we can do many things that under the old method of figuring appeared suicidal.

The view of costs so largely held, namely, that the product of a factory, however small, must bear the total expense, however large, is responsible for much of the confusion about costs and hence leads to unsound business policies.

If we accept the view that the article produced shall bear only that portion of the indirect expense needed to produce it, our costs will not only become lower, but relatively far more constant, for the most variable factor in the cost of an article under the usual system of accounting has been the overhead, which has varied almost inversely as the amount of the product. This item becomes

(Continued on page 1061)

The Relation between Production and Costs

(Continued from page 1056)

substantially constant if the overhead is figured on the normal capacity of the plant.

Of course, a method of accounting does not diminish the expense, but it may show us where the expense properly belongs and give us a more correct understanding of our business.

In our illustration of the three factories, the cost in the Chicago factory remained constant, but the expense of supporting the Buffalo and Albany factories in idleness was a charge against the business and properly chargeable to profit and loss.

If we had loaded this expense on the product of the Chicago factory, the cost of the product would probably have been so great as to have prevented our selling it, and the total loss would have been greater still.

When the factories are distinctly separate, few people make such a mistake, but where a single factory is three times as large as is needed for the output, the error is frequently made, with results that are just as misleading.

DEFECT OF MAKING PRODUCT BEAR IMPROPER OVERHEAD EXPENSE

As a matter of fact it seems that the attempt to make a product bear the expense of plant not needed for its production is one of the most serious defects in our industrial system today, and farther reaching than the differences between employers and employees.

The problem that faces us is, then, first to find just what plant or part of a plant is needed to produce a given output, and to determine the overhead expense on operating that plant or portion of a plant. This is primarily the work of the manufacturer or engineer and only secondarily that of the accountant, who must, as far as costs are concerned, be the servant of the superintendent.

In the past, in almost all cost systems the amount of overhead to be charged to the product, when it did not include all the overhead, was more or less a matter of judgment. According to the theory now presented, it is not a matter of judgment, but can be determined with an accuracy depending upon the knowledge the manufacturer has of the business.

Following this line of thought, it should be possible for a manufacturer to calculate just what plant and equipment he ought to have and what the staff of officers and workmen should be to turn out a given profit.

If this can be correctly done the exact cost of a product can be predicted. Such a problem cannot be solved

105

by a cost accountant of the usual type, but is primarily a problem for an engineer, whose knowledge of materials and processes is essential for its solution.

Having made an attempt to solve a problem of this type, one of the most important functions we need a cost system to perform is to keep the superintendent continually advised as to how nearly he is realizing the ideal set and to point out where the shortcomings are.

Many of us are accustomed to this viewpoint when we are treating individual operations singly, but few have as yet made an attempt to consider that this idea might be applied to a plant as a whole, except when the processes of manufacture are simple and the products few in number. When, however, the processes become numerous or complicated, the necessity for such a check becomes more urgent, and the cost keeper that performs this function becomes an integral part of the manufacturing system and acts for the superintendent, as an inspector, who keeps him advised at all times of the quality of his own work.

This conception of the duties of a cost keeper does not at all interfere with his supplying the financier with the information he needs, but insures that information shall be correct, for the cost keeper is continually making a comparison for the benefit of the superintendent, of what has been done with what should have been done. Costs are valuable only as comparisons, and comparisons are of little value unless we have a standard, which it is the function of the engineer to set.

Lack of reliable cost methods has, in the past, been responsible for much of the uncertainty so prevalent in our industrial policies; but with a definite and reliable cost method that enables us to differentiate between what is lost in manufacturing and what is lost in business, it will usually become easy to define clearly the proper business policy.

106

Discussion of Previous Question

Mr. Gantt's Theory of the Expense Burden

I notice that Mr. Gantt has entered on the thorny path of the reformer with regard to burden charges (see page 1055, Vol. 42). I wish him success, more particularly because for 15 years I have made a special study of that field and have written two books on it that remain, I believe, the only works dealing exhaustively with the principles of burden distribution.

The general principle put forward by Mr. Gantt appears to be this: As actual burden is to normal burden, so is actual output to normal output. This is, however, only another way of saying that the rate of burden percentage chargeable when the shops are full is the rate that ought to be charged when the shops are slack. This is only partly true, and it only covers a small portion of the field occupied by the question, "What is the proper share of burden for this job?"

The idea of separating the "undistributed expense remaining whenever the factory runs below its normal capacity" from the full burden is the special feature that I originated in 1901, as the basis of my method of distributing expense burden. Such undistributed expense was handled by means of a "supplementary rate." On page 98 of "The Proper Distribution of the Expense Burden," I said:

Finally, there is the supplementary rate—the third factor of cost. This will be of chief significance as showing what proportion of the total cost was due to the accidental features of the commercial situation at any period. This factor has never been separated before from the general body of costs—the manufacturing efficiency due to method was intermixed with the commercial efficiency due to state of trade.

When Mr. Gantt points out that in slack times burden should be divided into two groups—burden actually and

108

properly incurred by the job, and burden chargeable to wasted production capacity—he is following the essential feature of my method. But if he wishes to apply this "general principle" to ordinary percentage methods of distributing burden, I fear he is on rather dangerous ground. In fact, he seems to be somewhat aware of this when he alludes to the necessity of finding "just what plant or part of a plant is needed to produce a given output, and to determine the overhead expense on operating that plant or portion of a plant." He does not indicate how this is to be done, further than by saying that it is primarily the work of the manufacturer or engineer.

The fact is, all these difficulties have been studied and solved long enough ago. Burden is a very complex subject, and half-measures are not desirable with regard to it. The ordinary percentage methods are known to be inaccurate, and as Mr. Gantt says, when the figures resulting from such methods indicate an absurd conclusion common sense repudiates the figures. But on the other hand, if a system is put forward that is assumed to be correct, it is most important that it should be really correct. I am not sure that Mr. Gantt's "general principle" is in itself so much nearer correctness than others that it can be relied on in all cases.

The reason for this doubt is that Mr. Gantt's principle leaves unaffected the great source of error that is in all percentage systems of distributing burden. What he says with regard to his three plants, namely, that the true view is obtained if one considers them all assembled on one lot and the dividing walls taken down, is even more true with regard to individual machines, or "production centers." That is the point Mr. Gantt has missed, or rather only alludes to in a vague way as being "primarily the work of the manufacturer or the engineer." No percentage method of distributing burden can give effect to the varying call of individual machines on the expense represented by burden, and it will easily be understood that if some machines absorb more expense than others, as they do, then the question of just which machines were idle and which were working on jobs is the very core of the expense-distribution question. The only way in which this problem has been solved hitherto is by the "production-factor" method, which gives rise to accurately determined individual machine rates and collects all undistributed burden into a "supplementary rate."

Under this system the cost of jobs done in the same time and in the same way is at all times the same. There remains in slack times an undistributed balance, which is not merely a vague average, but represents the aggregate failure to absorb burden due to the idleness of the machines that were actually idle. But there still remains the problem of how this undistributed balance is to be disposed of.

It is of course mere waste. It represents unused productive capacity. To charge this at once to profit and loss is an easy thing to do, but generally speaking, I find a great disinclination on the part of practical manufacturers to do it. My original solution, and I believe that it is still the best solution except under special circumstances, was to distribute this unabsorbed balance over jobs as a supplementary rate. If, for example, 25 per cent. of the burden was unabsorbed a separate charge is made to each order, being 25 per cent. of the amount actually charged by machine rates to that order. The production

cost of jobs thus remains steady whether the shops are slack or busy, but the total cost rises or falls in the way familiar to those who use percentage methods.

For estimating purposes the actual production cost is taken, but for accounting purposes the total cost is taken. This seems a safer plan than the drastic step of charging undistributed burden direct to profit and loss. Careless bookkeeping under such circumstances might lead to serious results. At any rate, there would arise a general desire in the shops to get as many charges as possible into that convenient hiding place, and I do not know a single advantage that would be gained by the practice. On the other hand, the presence of the "supplementary rate" in every costing order brings the fact of idle machinery prominently to the attention of everyone that handles the figures.

The amount of burden chargeable to supplementary rate (or to profit and loss) can be determined when, and only when, some mechanism exists to attach to each order the proportion of the burden that properly belongs to it. This can be done only through scientifically determined machine rates based on "production factors." When the shop is full of work all the burden is being charged to jobs through machine rates. When it is slack that portion of the machine rates not taken up by work is charged to waste or the supplementary rate, but this amount is not necessarily a simple ratio, as laid down by Mr. Gantt's general principle. It entirely depends on which machines were idle, and therefore on the class of work being done. To omit this factor seems to me likely to give rise to deceptive results.

A. HAMILTON CHURCH.

New York, N. Y.

Discussion of Previous Question

Relation Between Production and Cost

109

Mr. Church's comments on my paper on "The Relation Between Production and Cost" (see p. 209) are very interesting. Mr. Church is well known as one of the leading accountants in this country and as such his opinion should represent the best thought of leading accountants. He makes four points: (1) That the principle I have laid down is only partly correct; (2) that it is very difficult to find the proper burden for a job; (3) that there is a great disinclination on the part of practical manufacturers to charge unabsorbed "burden" to profit and loss; (4) that a feeling of resentment is aroused at my statement that an engineer and not an accountant is needed to say what the output of a plant should be.

With regard to the first item—that it is only partly correct to make a product bear only that part of the burden needed to produce it—I cannot see that he proves his case, or even tries to do so.

With regard to the second item, he bases his statement of difficulty in carrying out this principle on the theory that we use the ordinary "percentage" method of distributing "burden." He admits that it can be done if the "machine-expense" factor method is used, but seems to feel that because he has been advocating the use of "machine-expense" factors for 15 years and has written two books on the subject that he has a sort of monopoly of it. As a matter of fact, the late Frederick W. Taylor found, nearly 25 years ago, that his attempts at improving methods of manufacture were so hampered by the cost accountant that he was forced himself to become an expert accountant in order to foil their efforts. This he did in his usual thorough manner, and passed on to his followers what he had learned. It was from his teachings in 1897 that I got the idea of "machine-expense" factors, which I have since used whenever I had occasion to do so. He saw the hampering effect on the business of making a reduced product bear all the "burden" of a large plant, and devised the "limit-cost" method of finding the lowest figure at which it was proper to sell during dull times, rather than close the plant. The difficulties which Mr. Church sees are not so great, after all; in fact, in actual practice they appear to vanish quite rapidly.

The third item is that there is a great disinclination on the part of practical manufacturers to charge unabsorbed "burden" to loss. This statement on the part of Mr. Church seems to indicate that he has tried to dispose of the excess "burden" in this manner and has not been able to overcome the "disinclination" of the manufacturers to do it. His statement that it is "mere waste" seems not only to confirm this idea but to emphasize the correctness of my contention. A disinclination to do a thing that in itself is right should not be used as an argument for not doing it. As a matter of fact, a man who does the thing which is economically right, whether it is disagreeable or not will soon distance his competitors who do only those things that are both economically right and agreeable.

If this excess burden is mere waste, it certainly is an expense not of the part of the works being operated but of the part not being operated, and which is not turning out any product. Hence it is not a charge against the output we got, but should go against the policy which kept a portion of the plant idle. It should therefore be charged against the business as a *loss*, and the management should be induced thereby to study its policy. He states that it would be dangerous to charge this part of the "burden" to loss if the bookkeeping were careless. I agree with him absolutely on this subject, but feel that careless bookkeeping might produce equally detrimental effects under any system of expense distribution.

The fourth item I got out of his article was a feeling of resentment at my statement that an engineer and not an accountant was needed to say what the output of a plant should be. This seems the real cause of his writing the article, for I cannot imagine he really believes me to be as ignorant of the best present methods of cost-keeping as he assumes I am. I did not intend to make any criticisms of those cost accountants who confine themselves to their proper work of recording and reporting what has been done but only of those who assume that what has been done in the past is a measure of what can be done in the future. It is at this point that the cost accountant stops and the engineer takes up the work. The cost accountant necessarily looks backward: it is the duty of the engineer to look forward.

The industrial organization whose policy is guided by what has been done will soon be left far behind by the competitor whose policy is based on what can be done. It is the engineer who can look farthest into the future that is most useful today. A cost accountant who assumes to do this work must not only be an engineer also, but must be in the first rank of engineers. In conclusion I may say that my object in writing the paper in question was not so much to show how the ideals I had in mind could be carried out, which would be impossible in such a paper, as to set forth before engineers in general ideals which will be of value to them as they have been to me.

H. L. GANTT.

New York, N. Y.

Discussion of Previous Question

Relation Between Production and Cost

The subject of the connection of burden with cost is so important that I must try to make my position clear in regard to Mr. Gantt's proposals, as far as they have been disclosed by his original paper, supplemented by his letter on p. 385. So far as I can see, the whole claim made by Mr. Gantt is that embodied in italic type in his paper as a "general principle": *"The indirect expense chargeable to the output of a factory bears the same ratio to the indirect expense necessary to run the factory at normal capacity, as the output in question bears to the normal output of the factory."* Now it is to be presumed that Mr. Gantt supposed this discovery to be one either original with himself or at any rate (if really originated by the late F. W. Taylor, as implied in his letter) as yet unpublished, and unknown to the world at large. In my criticism of this paper on p. 209 I tried to suggest as mildly as possible that in so far as this "general principle" was true, it had been announced by me 15 years ago, but that as stated it seemed to me to be too broad a claim, and open to doubt, unless some more exact method than the ordinary percentage for burden distribution was employed. Mr. Gantt now says that some such system (devised by Taylor) was implied, but he certainly did not say so in his original paper.

The criticism I made was, therefore, that in so far as Mr. Gantt's principle is true, it is not new, but that, on the other hand, it is only partially true, or only true under certain conditions.

Mr. Gantt says quite correctly that if excess burden is mere waste, it is not a charge against the output actually realized in any period. Quite so! But we must be quite sure that we ascertain correctly what the amount of that excess burden is. A mere slide-rule calculation based on proportion of output today to output yesterday will not give it save under special circumstances. Judging from his original paper, that is precisely what Mr. Gantt failed to perceive.

Quite apart from the correct determination of what burden is actually wasted and what is actually used, another aspect of the case is commonly met with. In many kinds of business there is always a more or less floating loss of burden, due to idle equipment, which is inseparable from the running of the business, and must therefore be paid for out of profits—that is, it must be recovered through the cost of what was actually made. It is this aspect of the case that makes manufacturers chary of charging all unabsorbed burden to profit and loss, even though it be accurately determined. And there is much to be said for this attitude.

As for Mr. Gantt's imputation that my criticism was due to a feeling of resentment in the old quarrel—engineer versus accountant—this is rather amusing, seeing that I am generally accused of taking precisely the opposite side. From this I am emboldened to fancy that my standpoint is probably pretty nearly an impartial one. I was an engineer before I was an accountant, and as an engineer I obtained a knowledge of what the problem was; but it must be remembered that scientific accounting is a kind of engineering too, being in fact the science of the measurement of values. In cost accounting both these sciences meet, and the principles of both, arising out of special kinds of experience in each case, must be taken into consideration to effect a cure.

I fear that Mr. Gantt yielded to the temptation to establish a cut-and-dried formula for the solving of difficulties that are frequently far too complex to yield to any formula. A generalization is an excellent thing if we do not take it too seriously and attempt to apply it without the qualifications which experience suggests. Unfortunately the question of burden has been befogged already quite enough by the fatal facility by which the simple percentage method can be applied to all and sundry cases. Even the percentage method sometimes gives correct results, and when it does then Mr. Gantt's formula will be correct. But in a large number of cases it gives results very wide of the mark, and in such cases Mr. Gantt's formula will give results equally wide of the mark—unless indeed he applies it in some way that he has not disclosed.

A. Hamilton Church.

New York, N. Y.

111

Relation Between Production and Cost

I have followed the discussion between Mr. Gantt and Mr. Church with much interest, because the subjects of production and cost constitute my own business and I have looked upon Mr. Church as a master. Taking the four points in Mr. Gantt's letter, on page 385, in their order:

1. As to the principle being only partly true, it seems to me that the principle as laid down by Mr. Gantt is absolutely true, but I think Mr. Church did well to point out the danger of assuming that the segregation of expense should be upon a percentage basis, which Mr. Gantt's statement of the principle might seem (to some) to imply. Mr. Church points out very clearly that, if the means of separating the portion of expense belonging to the production from that chargeable to lost opportunity to produce be not a reliable means, the results may be dangerously misleading.

2. As to the difficulty of finding the proper burden, Mr. Church again calls attention to some features which, like thorns, guard against a too hasty grasp of an attractive principle. A case in recent practice illustrates this: In a sheet-metal industry several men (riveters) were replaced by a small electric welder. Shortly after the latter was installed, a director of the company made the criticism that the new tool was often idle. A hasty calculation showed him that, while the welder was earning 200 per cent., compared with hand riveting, the capacity of the rest of the shop would have to be more than doubled to put this small tool in balance. Under such circumstances, it seems hard to convince the "business man" that more than 50 per cent. of the overhead charge on this tool should be kept out of costs and charged directly as (part of) loss due to idle capacity; yet this is not only what the theory calls for, but in actual accounting procedure it is the more practical thing to do, as the "business man" soon realizes if he will but take the trouble to study the matter in actual practice rather than in theory. And I agree with Mr. Gantt that "in actual practice the difficulties appear to vanish quite rapidly"—that is, after the problems of installation have been squarely met and overcome.

3. As to the disinclination of manufacturers to keep the "unused burden" out of costs, I can agree with my master because, as a manufacturer, I took this view when making my first installation of the production-factor method. But after this practical experience with it and further study and practice in a variety of industries, my mind has settled to a strong conviction that it is wrong in principle and absurd in practice to add to the true cost of doing a thing the wholly misleading cost of not doing that thing or any other thing.

4. As to the proverbial friction between engineer and accountant, perhaps the less said the better.

Engineers commonly realize that the weight of moving parts may be such that, when working in one direction most of the necessary power is absorbed by the mechanism, while in the opposite direction no power at all is required.

A somewhat similar condition obtains in cost-accounting methods whereby seemingly impracticable but highly desirable statistical results may be carried by the current of necessary routine of payroll and other office work; while, if advantage be not taken of this, the simplest scheme may be working against gravity and the resultant duplication, confusion and friction damns many a well-laid plan. I think that many engineers who undertake cost-accounting installation fail to realize how much there is to be known on this side of the problem.

On the other hand we come across cost systems installed by accounting firms of the highest reputation as accountants, which fall down utterly either in actual practice or when subjected to an analysis carried out on modern shop-operating lines.

This subject is rapidly assuming the dignity of a science, and past pretensions are melting away. The manufacturer is demanding more ability to forecast and less and less of the historian in his cost man, and I cannot entirely agree with Mr. Gantt that the engineer should have a monopoly of the forecasting; rather, I feel that the cost man must recognize his position and see that he has some technical foundation to build upon.

WILLIAM E. M. McHENRY.

Philadelphia, Penn.

Discussion of Previous Question

Relation Between Production and Cost

Replying to Mr. Church's letter on page 431, it seems to me that he is industriously setting up a man of straw and then just as industriously trying to knock him down. Most of his argument is based on the theory that our method of distributing "overhead expense" is the usual percentage method.

I hardly thought it necessary to inform Mr. Church that we not only did not use that method, but never had used it. Moreover, we were using, under the direction of F. W. Taylor, the machine-factor method of distributing expense several years before Mr. Church claims to have devised it.

A careful reading of my original paper will show that I made no claim whatever to originality in my various statements, but simply announced the fact that the principles that I tried to elucidate were not in general use.

Mr. Church denies the truth of the general principle that the indirect expense chargeable to the output of a factory bears the same ratio to the indirect expense necessary to run the factory at normal capacity (or full capacity) as the output in question bears to the normal output of the factory; but I think he will agree that "the cost of an article can only legitimately include the expense incurred directly or indirectly in producing it," which is another way of stating substantially the same thing.

He will perhaps disagree with me in the method of finding that indirect expense. I can understand that he may have a method of determining indirect expense according to which the foregoing statement might not be correct, but in that case I think he should look into his method of determining overhead.

This is not the place to go into a long discussion of the details of cost-keeping methods, and the object of my paper, if I may judge from the discussions that it has provoked, has been accomplished, inasmuch as it has established in the minds of those who have given the subject careful thought the fact that the cost of an article can legitimately include only the expense incurred directly or indirectly in producing it. If there are other expenses incurred in the manufacturing plant, these must be incurred for some purpose other than the production of the article in question, and are therefore business expenses and chargeable to profit and loss.

I do not think Mr. Church and I are very far apart; but inasmuch as the accountant is, as a rule, "the servant of the financier," he has found it necessary to soften down the results that this method exposes in order to have them accepted by the financier. Mr. Church is really defending his method of putting the unabsorbed expense in a reserve fund to be distributed later, which he practically admits was a concession to the financier. I absolutely fail to see why this reserve fund, which is really an "idleness charge," should be spread over the product with which it had nothing to do.

H. L. GANTT.

New York, N. Y.

What Is a Cost System?

BY A. HAMILTON CHURCH

SYNOPSIS—A cost system may be approached from two view points—that of the accountant and that of the shop official. This article points out briefly what information the shop foreman, superintendent, executive, and proprietor should be able to obtain from machine-shop cost records.

Notwithstanding all that has been written on the subject for the last fifteen years, there is still a considerable number of persons who do not possess the same concrete picture of what a cost system should be as they have of most other problems of their daily business. It might almost be said that few people really know what they have the right to expect from a cost system, which is much the same as having an expensive machine in the shop of which the use is not fully understood.

This is partly because cost systems have several uses, each of which is as important as the others, but as usually designed one or more of these uses are emphasized to the neglect of the others. A cost system may give results that are excellent to the proprietor and valueless to the shop foreman, or vice versa.

Another cause of trouble is that the design of a cost system may be approached from two opposite viewpoints—that of the commercial accountant, who thinks in ledger accounts, and that of the shop staff, who think in terms of hours, men and materials. The accountant thinks of detail as a troublesome necessity; the shop staff know that detail is the life-blood of a cost system provided it is available at the right time and in the right place.

The object of this article is to mention very briefly what a cost system should provide for the principal officials in a fair-sized plant, and when it should provide it. The when is as important as the what.

As all productive expense begins in the shops, we shall consider the shop foreman first. What we have to say here will apply, of course, to as many departments or separate shops as there happen to be in the plant. To avoid repetition only one shop and one foreman will be mentioned.

WHAT THE FOREMAN WANTS TO KNOW

The foreman is concerned, first and foremost, with the cost of jobs. The "job" may be defined as a process or operation applied to one part or a number of identical parts. It is his business to see that jobs are done at a cost not greater than formerly, or where costs are already standardized, at a cost not greater than standard. As in a large shop there may be dozens of jobs, it is evident that a selection must be made. What, therefore, the system must bring to his attention is the exceptional job, one which has cost more or less, or is costing more or less, than expected.

This is easy to do, but it is not enough. When his attention is called, certain conditions must exist to make that attention worth while. The first of these is that his attention must be called as soon as the job or the first installment of the job is completed. In practice this means next day; not a week or a month after, because that is next to useless and only burdens the foreman with worry. The next condition is that he must be able to see

and handle the prime records—the original time notes, slips or cards, with all the information they bear. A mere accountant's abstract is very unconvincing to the average foreman, and often with good reason.

These original records should indicate the man, the machine, the nature of the process (if more than one process can be effected by the machine), the job number, and a complete record of the starts and stops, the interruptions, the overtime belonging to the job. Any time record worth its salt should provide all these details in readable form.

With this information placed before him immediately after the completion of the job, the foreman will usually be able to lay his finger on the reason for the unexpectedly high cost. He will indorse his opinion of the reason on the record, and in many instances his attention will end there. In other instances he will desire to take the matter up with the delinquent, armed with all the documents, while the matter is fresh in everyone's memory.

Whatever his decision as to the cause, it is recorded in a shop register classified according to causes; that is, it may be recorded against the man, against necessary change of jobs, against breakdowns, etc. With this register always before him, removable causes of unexpected high cost will press themselves on his attention at all times.

WATCHING IDLE MACHINES

The next thing that it is important for the foreman to watch closely is the idleness of machines. From adequate time notes, the working hours of each machine can be obtained by a quick sorting and aggregating. Where machine rates are in use, as they should be, the money value of machine earnings is also easily found. By a simple tabulation on a properly designed blank, a running record is kept of each machine's working time, and by deducting the day's total from standard time and earnings, the day's loss due to idle machinery is made visible to the foreman each morning. This, again, is a kind of information that is particularly useless two or three weeks or a month after the facts have passed into history. What the foreman wants to know is, "How were my machines occupied yesterday?"—not how they were occupied at some past period. He should be able to cast his eye over their earnings or working time day by day for the past few days, so that he can see how things are going.

Next, he wants a good idea of how the work is coming on—whether he is keeping up with it or falling behind. Is work piling up half finished in the shop, or is it being carried through in a steady stream? Closely connected with this information is the total of the payroll from day to day, and its division into productive and nonproductive work.

At the end of each day there will be a certain volume of unfinished jobs (work in progress) in the shop. To this is added today's productive wages, and from it is deducted the wages on jobs finished this day. The resulting amount is the volume of work on hand to be carried forward to tomorrow. This figure, representing the volume of work in the shops each night, is of value to the foreman, provided he gets it day by day. If it is going up while

115

productive wages remain steady, it shows congestion of half-finished work. A little familiarity will make this a highly significant figure to the foreman.

But this does not tell him how he stands in relation to orders in sight. This information cannot always be provided in definite form. It can be furnished only in the case of work that is sufficiently standardized to allow the expected or standard cost to be placed against each job as and when it is handed to the shop. When this can be done, then the total expected cost of each day's jobs will be added to the expected cost of all jobs in hand, and each day's completed jobs will be deducted at cost, leaving a balance of unexecuted orders as at each night. Every morning, therefore, the foreman will have a figure representing orders on hand and will be able to take measures as to overtime, extra help, etc., on a basis of actual figures.

DAILY RECORDS OF SPOILED WORK

Another matter that should be brought to the foreman's attention daily is the "spoiled work." This should receive his attention in the same manner as exceptional jobs, previously mentioned. His opinion as to the cause of each item should be indorsed on the record, and a tabulation by causes posted up against men, bad castings, or other visible causes.

We may now consider other data that will be sufficiently useful if compiled once a week, instead of every day. Chief among these is the record of indirect-expense items. The foreman is not interested in the large question of expense save at the points at which his responsibility is incurred. A very simple return will therefore satisfy all his needs. He is interested, first, in expense items incurred in his own shop and therefore under his own control, and secondly, in expense labor and material charged against his shop by other departments.

A tabular blank should be provided listing all the usual items of expense, including repairs of all kinds, and work done by other departments should be shown separately. Every week the charges against each item should be inserted in the proper column, so that comparison with previous weeks may be easily made. A few minutes' study of this return will suffice to show the foreman how he stands on each item under his control, and whether he is being fairly charged by other departments with work done for him.

The daily returns of exceptional jobs and spoiled work will contain items that go against sundry workmen. A record should therefore be kept for each man, to include reference to all such losses, and also his bonus earnings, late attendance, and other data against him or in his favor. With properly designed methods such a record can be compiled at little expense, and will be first-hand evidence of each man's value.

These are the principal matters with which the foreman is concerned, and which he is entitled to expect from any cost system that pretends to be efficient. He may require more than this in some shops, because the status and duty of a foreman vary a good deal, but in few shops should he be asked to put up with less. We have now to consider the viewpoint of other officials.

The superintendent's viewpoint is quite different from that of the foreman. He is not so much interested in details, but more in broad results. Consequently, he does not require such red-hot and up-to-the-minute information as the foreman. But he wants it frequently.

Just as the foreman is interested in the cost of jobs, so the superintendent is interested in the cost of orders. An order may be defined as a collection of individual jobs, such as a machine, erected, or a thousand fittings which have passed through several departments. It is the superintendent's business to see that orders are turned out at an expected or standard cost and that they are not being delayed in their passage through the plant. A proper system of cost accounts should secure these two kinds of information at one and the same time. As every departmental job is finished, it should appear on the superintendent's record and thus vouch for itself as to expected cost and expected date. Just like the foreman, the superintendent is interested only in the exceptional cases, but he is not interested in the same way. The questions he will ask himself are: Is there any serious delay on any item of this order? Is there any serious or general increase of cost on this order?

CONTROL OF ORDERS

The superintendent's control of orders should be based on a "master schedule" listing all the different components belonging to an order, and against each component all the different processes to be carried out on it. A space will also provide for the weight and cost of castings and forgings and other material against each component. Standard or former costs being stated against each process, the general condition of the order as regards completion and its general standing as regards increase or decrease of cost, will be visible from inspection at any time, provided finished jobs are posted daily to it. He will also see whether components are being hung up for want of material, and whether material has been issued in excess (as for example in the case of a spoiled part). As soon as all the spaces are filled up, the cost of the whole order will be known. This should be the day after completion.

Apart from cost of individual orders, the superintendent is chiefly interested in the efficiency of departments. It is he who should have a close grip on indirect expense, and he requires, therefore, much more detail than the foreman in this respect. Expense will be of two kinds—the ordinary items arising from the payroll, small repairs, regular issues of stores, etc., and specially authorized items such as extensive repairs that are carried out on works orders. All expense will be classified according to the purpose for which expended. For example, all expenses relating to buildings will be classed under buildings, all relating to power, including fuel, wages, repairs, etc., under power. Other classes will be handling of stores and shop transport of materials; supervision; organization; operative machinery.

VARIOUS REPORTS FOR THE SUPERINTENDENT

Each of these classes of expense will be budgeted or forecasted, and actual expense will be placed alongside each item. Any departure from expected cost of an item will be called to the superintendent's attention, just as the wages cost of an exceptional job was called to the foreman's attention. This will be done each week, and the items tabulated on a large sheet carrying a series of weekly columns, so that the tendency of any item to increase will come under constant observation.

Power-house efficiency will be the subject of special technical reports, which, coupled with the above segregation of all expenditure on the power plant for whatever cause, should give a close grip on this item of expense.

Departmental efficiency in various directions will be the principal remaining item to come under the notice of the superintendent. This may be divided into three classes—(1) as to men, (2) as to machines, (3) as to wastes.

Information as to the first class is tabulated from the finished jobs already scrutinized by the foreman with his indorsement of the reasons for increased cost. Jobs will be tabulated under their reasons, so that the loss or gain for each such reason can be reckoned up in a total. Each item will be recorded on a columnar statement, so that the increase or decrease against each reason can be compared. Thus, we may have a constantly increasing amount under the heading of "Job Interrupted for Urgent Work," which would be unfavorable and demand inquiry, or we might have in one department a much higher ratio of increased cost due to breakdowns. Whatever the classification, scrutiny is applied as to increase or decrease of each item in each shop, and also comparison is made as between different shops each week. When this is done whatever unfavorable conditions may develop cannot escape notice very long.

THE MACHINE-HOUR VALUE OF LOST TIME

As regards the second class, the machine-hour value of lost time due to idle machines is tabulated for each shop in weekly columns. Comparison of one shop with another and one week with another is easily made, and any undue increase of this item, not warranted by slackness of business, is kept in view.

In the third class, that of wastes, the superintendent will have a record showing the amount of spoiled work for each shop, classified by reasons. These will also be tabulated in weekly columns, so that different shops can be compared together, and each shop can be observed from week to week.

With these returns made promptly each week, the superintendent will be in a position to turn the searchlight on any point of weakness that may develop, without losing himself in detail or trying to overlook everything at once.

WHAT THE EXECUTIVE WANTS TO KNOW

The higher we mount the official ladder, the more general become the data necessary and the longer the interval at which tabular statements are required. The executive's interest in cost accounts, as such, is comparatively small. His viewpoint is that of the financial outlook. He wants to know what is going into the business and what is coming out. Generally speaking, monthly returns will provide all the information he requires. Of course, all the sources of detail information already described are also open to him.

The most satisfactory plan of control is that of the budget. This is, in effect, a forecast of the main operations of the business, month by month, based on previous experience. All principal outgoings, such as payroll, stores purchases, taxes, insurance and depreciation, are listed, and their expected amount set out in the different monthly columns. Another set of items is expected balances, such as stores in hand, work in process, cash on hand and at bank, accounts owing by the firm and to the firm; while a third set consists of expected sales in each line of goods manufactured, sales expense, including ad-

vertising, etc. The main movements of cash in the business are thus scheduled, and against each item the actual amounts expended, received or in hand will be entered each month for comparison. Value of orders received, executed, and balance on hand is also listed.

Undue and unexpected increases or decreases in any item and their amount and significance are thus immediately seen. Thus, if the balance of stores in hand or of work in process is rising, without a corresponding movement in orders received, something is wrong. It can be seen at a glance if collections are falling behind normal, if sales expense bears a just proportion to results, if any line of product is falling off in orders, or is becoming congested in the shops, if indirect expense is increasing, if repairs are unusually high or low—in short all the significant movements of the business are focused and compared with the experience of previous years.

Under the head of the executive department the question of estimating may be considered. As the records already described under the heads of foreman and superintendent give the ultimate detail possible as to every part manufactured and as to every machine or group of articles made, the basis of estimating will be full and complete. The only thing to be discussed is the influence of idle time, or half-full shops, on the cost of production and therefore on the price which should be quoted to get new business. This, however, is a theoretical matter, or one of policy, and cannot be gone into here. All the necessary data for decision will, on the other hand, be found at hand in the records provided for.

WHAT THE PROPRIETOR WANTS TO KNOW

The proprietor, or whoever represents him in a corporate business, is mainly interested in one thing—profits. He is also interested in the condition of his property, its liabilities and the quick and fixed assets that offset this liability. Both these wants are fully met by the provision each month of a full balance sheet of assets and liabilities, and of a profit and loss account. With a system of accounting designed to give the information described, there is no reason why such a balance and profit and loss account should not be prepared every month, at no more expense than the filling in of the figures on a printed form. This is in fact most desirable, for it is the final test of the general accuracy of the returns. Returns that will not balance do not comply with the dictum of "safety first." If the accounts are arranged in the pyramid form described in this article, each stage should be built up in more and more general terms from detail that was verified at the beginning. The balance sheet should thus be the final coping stone that completes the edifice and makes its correctness visible to the eye.

In a future article some of these arrangements will be described in greater detail than has been possible here.

∎

117

What a Foreman Should Know About Costs

By A. Hamilton Church

SYNOPSIS—A brief outline of what information a foreman should be able to get from machine-shop cost records. A simple method of handling the cost details to give this information is included.

There is probably more than a grain of truth in the suggestion that some of the more highly elaborated modern systems would never have been invented if every foreman had always been provided with what he wanted to know at the time he wanted to know it. By whatever name he is called, there must be somewhere a man who is responsible for operative efficiency, and the more this man is in control of the situation, the more flexible will be the adjustment of the shop to the unexpected. It is not our purpose here to discuss how far "planning" should go. Planning is specifying in advance all that can be specified, but its degree of development must obviously depend entirely on the kind of work that is being done. But specifying in advance is not doing the work, though sometimes spoken of as if it were. Someone has got to see that the work is actually done, has got to nurse and shepherd it, and this man is called, for the purpose of this article, a foreman. Now the question is, What does he want to know, and when?

In a previous article this question was very briefly answered. In the present article the methods necessary to provide the information will be described. There will be no attempt to describe a complete system of manufacturing accounts, but only so much of such a system as the foreman is concerned with.

The first step is to provide for recording the time of men and machines on work. There are literally dozens of methods of doing this, some of them involving complex and expensive appliances. The problem, however, is

Machine Shop No. I	Man's Name	Check No.	Mach. No. P. V.		—		Hrs.	Wages	Mach.
Began	Order No.	Job		Good	P. W.	Man	Hrs.	Wages	Mach.
Fin.	Piece No.			Bad		Mach.			
Began	Order No.	Job		Good	P. W.	Man	Hrs.	Wages	Mach.
Fin.	Piece No.			Bad		Mach.			

FIG. 1. BLANK TIME CARD, USUALLY 5 SECTIONS AND STUB

simple. It is to have accurate record of the time at which each job was changed, and to so arrange, first, that the total hours accounted for check up with the gate time for each man, and then, secondly, that the verified details can be rapidly grouped in any way desired. Further, the original records should be assembled so that they are always available for reference. A simple and effective plan is given here, which has worked well in practice, is easily understood by the men and possesses the advantage of quick results and easy reference to the original record at any time.

Each man is provided with a daily time sheet (Fig. 1). This is usually a thin card, and each department has a

different color appropriated to it. The card is divided by thick rules, the space between each corresponding to the record of one job. Such a division is called a "section," because the card is cut up into sections at a certain stage. The smaller division at the top is called a "stub."

The ruling of each section is a matter depending on the nature of the work. The sample shown was used in a plant making heating apparatus and steam fittings, thus including rather heavy pieces and also small pieces in lots up to a hundred in each. In special cases modified rulings are used, as, for example, in pattern shops, core shops, foundries, etc., and for laborers.

At starting work, each man takes a blank card and writes his name, check number and machine number on the top section, called the "totaling stub," as this ultimately goes to the payroll clerk. Then he enters the time

Machine Shop No. 1	Man's Name A. Williams	Check No. 361	Mach. No. P. W. 26		Hrs.	Wages	Mach.
Began 6.00	Order No. 1061	Job Turn levers		Good 3	Man	Hrs.	Wages	Mach.
Fin. 12.30	Piece No. 7339			Bad 1	Mach.			
Began 12.30	Order No. 1921	Job Turn pin		Good 1	Man	Hrs.	Wages	Mach.
Fin. 6.00	Piece No. 8263			Bad 1	Mach.			

Items in bold-face type are those inserted in the shop

FIG. 2. TIME CARD AS FILLED OUT IN SHOP

of starting his first job in the space "Began," also the order number and piece number, and when necessary (in some shops) a brief description of the work, such as "facing boss" or "drill and tap for setscrew." He then proceeds with his job until finished.

When the job is finished, he enters the time in the "Finished" space and also in the "Began" space of the next section, and also the order and piece number of the next job. This is all he has to do. Only when he proceeds to a new job does he have to make an entry, except that at night, when he finishes work, he enters the time in the "Finished" space on the last section used.

Whoever passes the work, makes an entry of the number of pieces, "good" or "bad," in the space provided, and is also responsible for seeing that the correct order and piece numbers have been entered up for the job so passed. If the job is wholly finished, that is, if no more pieces are to be done on that order, the official passing the work punches the section with a handpunch to signify to the cost clerk that costing of the job may be completed.

Verification of the time of beginning and finishing jobs may be effected either by a perambulating clerk who goes round frequently to observe whether the job on the machine corresponds with the last, or "Open" section on the card, or by inspection at time of passing the work, according to whatever arrangements are most convenient in any given shop. At the end of the day each man drops his time card into a box as he leaves the shop. Fig. 2 shows the card at this stage.

The next morning the shop clerk takes the cards and sorts them into order of the men's numbers. He is provided with two series of small rubber stamps, one giving men's numbers and their wage rates and the other giving machine numbers and their machine rates. These stamps are so made that rates can be changed when necessary without destroying the stamp. Each stamp frame has a pad of different ink, say red for men and green for machines. They give impressions thus:

361—25c   L26—20c.

reading "Man number 361, hourly rate 25 cents" and "Lathe number 26, hourly rate 20 cents." They are so arranged in the holding frame that the figures can be read on the wood tops like lines of print, so that any number can be picked out unhesitatingly.

The clerk takes the first card, picks out the man's stamp corresponding, and stamps the impression, first on the totaling stub and then on all the other sections that have entries on them. This operation is then repeated for the machine concerned. Both these operations take place more quickly than they can be described. Verification is by observing that the impressions on the totaling stub correspond with what the man has written there. We are then sure that all the other sections on that card have proper rates on them.

CHECKING UP WITH THE TOTAL TIME

The next step is to make sure that the tale of work as shown by the time card does really correspond with the time the man has actually been at work as shown by the gate time. Here again there are all kinds of elaborate arrangements that may be used to ascertain gate time. We cannot discuss this question here. Whatever system is used should be able to do one thing, namely, to permit the gatekeeper, as soon as the last man has passed the gate, to prepare without delay a list of men and the total hours they have worked. The list of course may be printed and the time rapidly filled in by the pen. The main thing is to have it done swiftly and accurately the same night, so that a list is ready for each shop clerk early next morning, covering all his men. The same list may be made to last a week or longer, as it is free long before the end of the working day and may be returned to the gateman.

The shop clerk takes his time cards, which are already in order of men's numbers, one at the time, adds the hours shown by the sections, and places the total on the totaling stub. Then he compares the total thus shown, with the gate time as shown by the gateman's list. If there is any discrepancy, he goes into the shop and interviews the offender there and then. On first putting such a system into work, many discrepancies will be found, but patience and perseverance will soon improve matters, and the men will get to be careful about odd quarters, usually due to coming late, that they have missed on their time cards.

When this is all done, we are sure that our job time is correct, and the troubles of that day are behind us, as far as time is concerned.

TOTALING THE STUBS

The next step is to extend the wages and machine earnings on each section and on the totaling stub. This is best done by means of a "ready reckoner," which should be a small book simply giving a separate hourly rate on each page and a series of figures representing the value of any number of hours and quarters up to the highest likely to be worked in one day. If higher rates are paid for overtime, a separate column can contain these figures also.

One reading for each job should be all that is necessary. Such books can be easily made up by the drafting room and blueprinted. I do not know of any really compact or simple book of the kind on the market. There are many full of unnecessary elaboration and of inconvenient dimensions.

Having extended all the sections on a card, the next step is to verify the total by adding up the working sections on an adding machine and seeing that they agree to a cent with the total on the totaling stub. Usually they will be a cent or so out, due to quarter- or half-hours. One of the sections must be altered so that the total of all-job-time agrees with payroll earnings and machine earnings on the totaling stub. This is important, so that absolute balance can be obtained in the accounts later. When this is done we are sure that job time is locked into gate time and into payroll. Fig. 3 shows the completed card.

Before slicing up the time cards into sections it is usually convenient to take off the machine time and tabulate it. A printed list of all machines in the shop, with their normal days work and earnings is provided thus:

Mach. No.   Kind   Rate   Full Hours   Earnings
181   36" Mill   15   10   1.50

Columns are provided for each day, in which the actual

Machine Shop No. 1	Man's Name A. Williams	Check No. 361	Mach. No. 26		361—25c L 26—20c	Hrs. 9	Wages 2.25	Mach. 1:80
Began 8.00	Order No. 1061	Job Turn levers	Good 1	P. W. ✓	Man 361—25c	Hrs.	Wages 1.12	Mach. 90
Fin. 12.30	Piece No. 7330		Bad	✓	Mach. L 26—20c	4½		
Began 12.30	Order No. 1921	Job Turn pin	Good 3	P. W. ✓	Man 361—25c	Hrs.	Wages 1.13	Mach. 90
Fin. 6.00	Piece No. 8363		Bad 1	✓	Mach. L 26—20c	4½		

Items in bold-face type are those inserted in the shop.
Note that the odd cent in wages has been adjusted on the lower job.

FIG. 3. TIME CARD WITH ALL ENTRIES COMPLETE

hours and earnings for each machine are entered. Each day's hours and earnings are totaled and compared with standard hours and earnings, showing loss due to idle machines. The individual machines at fault can be indicated by a tick at the time of making the entry. The figures for entering are taken from the totaling stubs where they are already summarized.

GROUPING THE DETAILS

We are now ready to consider how the details of jobs, which are contained on the sections giving hours, wages and machine charges on each job, shall be most conveniently grouped together, so that all the work on one piece or group of pieces and all the work on various expense jobs or services may meet together. The quickest way of doing this is by dissecting the time cards and sorting the sections according to their order numbers, or standing order numbers in the case of expense work. This is rapidly done by a paper cutter with a suitable guard. The time cards are sliced up into sections, and then these sections are sorted in properly designed trays, first to thousands, then to hundreds and later to tens and units. The totaling stubs are sorted out at the first sort, and handed to the payroll clerk or department, along with the gate time report, which is returned to the gateman after checking with the stubs. We do not need to follow these stubs further.

All yesterday's work of the shop is now sorted into job numbers, or standing-order numbers. Each piece will be represented by from one to four or five sections. Each standing order will be represented in the same way. How shall the information therein contained, which is not only verified information, but also information in the ultimate detail, be made available for reference?

The first step is to add, with a machine, all the sections bearing work-order numbers and enter their total opposite the lines on the blank Fig. 4; namely, productive wages, ordinary and overtime respectively. Sections reporting bonuses earned, which come from another source to be mentioned presently, are also added together and entered. These three items form the total of productive wages for the day.

Next, the sections bearing standing orders are added, each order number separately, and the result is entered opposite the proper line, such as "cleaning buildings," "repairing machines." The examples given will of course be varied according to the actual shop wants. The total of expense items being added, the grand total will represent total payroll for the day.

Watching this simple report daily will give the foreman the closest grip on every cent of expense wages in his shop. Daily familiarity will enable him to tell at a glance whether any increase in any item is legitimate or not. Such expense is thus closely controlled at its source.

THE SHOP ALBUM

The next matter is the disposal of the sections which refer to productive work. We know their total, but not their detail. They are disposed of by being pasted in what may be called "shop albums." These are simply books of blank leaves, one for each order and containing as many leaves as there are components in a given order. Thus, if a machine is being made containing twenty parts, there will be twenty leaves. On the cover of each album is a list of components, and of the processes or operations on each, in the order of their execution. Against each operation is the standard cost or the previous cost. This

D ily Wages Report.................S:io;.   W.E...............

	Mon.	Tu.	Wed.	Th.	Fr.	Sat.	Total
Productive Wages:							
Wages, Ordinary...........							
Wages, Overtime...........							
Bonuses....................							
Total Productive........							
Expense Wages:							
Building Repairs...........							
" Cleaning........							
" Sundry.........							
Power Equipment Re airs...							
" Oiling......							
Cranes, etc., Repairs......							
" Operating......							
Supervision...............							
Organisation (C erks)......							
Machines, Repairs.........							
Total Expenses..........							
Total Payroll...........							

FIG. 4. DAILY PAYROLL REPORT. THE DETAILS OF EXPENSE ITEMS ARE ONLY SUGGESTIVE

schedule should, of course, be blueprinted or manifolded and issued from the drafting or planning department. Each piece will have a job number appropriated to it (Fig. 5). In cases where large lots are going through, each operation may have a separate job number. Numbers cost nothing and blank leaves, little.

Beginning with the earliest order number, the sections are now pasted on the leaves they belong to. Thus the sections referring to turning starting lever on order 1061,

will go on leaf 1 of the album belonging to that order number. All the sections are thus rapidly disposed of by pasting on their proper leaves. Each leaf is thus accumulating the history of the piece exactly as it was actually worked on. Every incident is reflected. If the job was interrupted, if part of it was worked overtime, if men were changed while it was on the machine, if some was done at one time and some at another, if the man failed to earn a bonus, or if, on the contrary, the job went through promptly and smoothly—the whole story can be read from a simple inspection of the pasted sections, without a particle of additional clerical work or any delay. Moreover, it is not only there, but it is there for all time. Ten years hence, if required, it will be easy to refer back and see

Order 1061		Cutting Machine			
		No. 1 Shop			
Piece	Leaf	Stan Cost	This Time	Dif.	
Starting Lever...........	1				
Turn..............		1.12	1.12		
Bore..............		1.00	90	—10	
Slot..............		90	95	+5	
Mill..............		2.00	2.00		
Side Wing Piece..........	2				
Plane.............		2.10	2.00	—10	
Mill..............		1.30			
Drill.............		80			
Front Foot..............	3				
Mill..............		50			
Dri...............		30			
Back Foot...............	4				
Mill..............		45			
Drill.............					

FIG. 5. SCHEDULE FORMING FIRST LEAF OF ALBUM

what man drilled a particular hole and what it cost for him to do it.

Another important feature is that these pasted sections are the original records, made by the men or in their sight. They are not copies or abstracts, they are recognizable authority for their statements. Jack Smith can be called in and shown his own record and will recognize it. All the shop staff will have confidence in the story exhibited by the album. This is a condition not always brought about by highly elaborate systems worked on a centralized plan.

We have shown in considerable detail the steps up to this point, in order to emphasize the fact that the proper place to elaborate detail is at the starting point, in the shop, where alone detail is a matter of daily bread and possesses a live significance wholly missing at either a later stage or at a later date. Detail must be piping-hot, or it is of slender value. The people who make the detail are the people who can use the detail.

BRINGING THE DETAIL INTO LINE

The way in which this detail is brought into line with the rest of the system must now be briefly discussed. As soon as a job is finished, if it is a bonus job, the bonus earned is worked out on the job order given to the man, and summarized on a stub at the foot of the order. This stub is then detached, credited to the man in his book, and passed to the shop clerk to be included among his sections, as mentioned. It thus finds its way both to the payroll and to the album.

When a job is finished, notified by receipt of the bonus stub or, if daywork, by the punched section mentioned, the shop clerk, after all his sections have been pasted in the albums, proceeds to add the sections of all such finished jobs, so as to find their cost. A further development of the stub system comes into play here. The cost of every job is summarized on a stub in duplicate, showing stand-

121

ard cost and actual cost. These stubs have a distinctive color. One of these duplicates is at once forwarded to the superintendent's office for entry on his master schedule (see last article), and the other is pasted on the leaf it refers to. It is also entered at the same time on a blank, showing entries thus:

DAILY RETURN OF FINISHED JOBS .... SHOP

Order No.	Part No.	Process	Stand. Cost	Actual Cost	Reason
1061	7320	Turn	2.90	2.84	.....
1065	8756	Mill√*	3.89	4.24	Overtime

*The mark √ means increased cost, and calls foreman's attention.

A mark is made against all such jobs as have cost more than standard (or more than an agreed percentage of standard), and these are examined by the foreman, who puts his reason against them. An examination of the pasted sections will frequently explain the reason, such as "interrupted job" or "overtime." In other cases the defaulter may be interviewed for an explanation. Anyway, the foreman's attention is called promptly to all cases of increased cost and to these only.

The total of finished jobs at actual cost is used by the accounting department to credit the shop and is also used as explained in the last article to give the foreman daily information as to the balance of work in hand in his shop. This is done by the shop clerk by taking yesterday's balance, adding today's productive wages and deducting finished jobs. This gives the new balance to be carried forward to next day. A columnar sheet makes each day's figures comparable with the preceding days.

SPOILED WORK

Another byproduct of the sections is the matter of spoiled work. The number of parts good and bad being vouched for by the official punching the last section, the total parts spoiled are disclosed by the pasted sections, and when the job is being costed these are summarized on the duplicate stub. They are also listed on a special blank for the foreman's investigation and note as to reasons. These reasons are tabulated as described in the last article.

This is necessarily a very cursory description of the method of costing by sections, stubs and albums, but anyone familiar with cost work will see how it can be modified and extended. It may be mentioned that in some cases the material issues (which are made on suitably ruled sections and cut up and sorted to numbers after they have been priced out and the day's total of issues taken off) are pasted in the shop album on the leaf corresponding to the part which the material is for. In other cases the material sections go to the superintendent, and are entered on the master schedule. This depends on the nature of the work.

The method of advising each foreman of the cost of work done by the repair department or other shops is sufficiently obvious not to need description.

Many details not given here will be filled in readily by those familiar with cost accounts. The control attainable over idle machines, over spoiled work, and over the regular progress of jobs will be easily understood, but that over replacements, urgent lots and delayed work will be understood if the central fact that the whole history of each job as it occurred and as it is occurring appears on the leaves of the album of each order. We have only to pick this up to know all about the order and its present position, and to answer any possible question about it that is within the purview of the shop. I do not know of any other method that answers queries so minutely, and at the same time so authoritatively, as this.

122

What the Superintendent Should Know

By A. Hamilton Church

SYNOPSIS—The viewpoint of the superintendent is broader and more comprehensive than that of the foreman. He is occupied not so much with details as with tendencies. He should have a close grip on the cost of jobs in each of his shops and a good perspective of idle machine time, spoiled work and expense items.

The paramount interest of the superintendent is to insure that the work is carried through the various departments in sequence and with regard to the time schedule. Closely connected with this is the question of material, of new parts that have to be ordered and made to replace those spoiled at some stage of the work. Control over the progress of work is attained by means of master schedules, which are sheets on which are listed all the parts or components in an order, and all the departments working on each component, arranged in the sequence in which the work of the departments is to be carried out.

The arrangement of schedules will differ with the nature of the work. They can be made to control either the sequence of work alone or to keep such matters as variation from standard cost, delays and replacements

A more complete master schedule is shown in Fig. 2. This does not record processes *within* departments, but the complete work of each shop on each component. The information is derived from the finished-job stubs (mentioned in the last article), which are sent in by each shop as soon as it has completed all the work on a component or batch of parts; and from material section sheets recording the issue of material, corresponding in form with the time section sheets already mentioned. These material sections are sorted to order numbers and entered on the schedule so as to record weight and price of each component.

MANIPULATING THE SCHEDULES

The blank schedule contains the names and piece numbers of all components, and against each are given the departments which have to do work on them and also the date at which each stage should be completed. (In small plants the actual operations might be given instead of departments, similar to Fig. 1.) Against each department the standard cost of the labor in that department is also given. Then the labor and material stubs are entered up daily as received, so as to show the weight and cost of material, the actual labor cost, the difference between actual and standard cost, the delay in

ORDER NO-				FOR-										Cost of Order to Date*			
Part No.	Part Name	Material Wt. Cost		Dept.	Labor Cost Stand. Actual		Loss or Gain —	+	Mach. Rates	On	Due Late	No. Good	Replace	Total Cost	Re'd 3.80	Wages 11.35	M. R. 7.80	Total 22.95
370	Exc. rod	00 3 80		Forge	5 00 4 80			0 20	3 00	Jn. 7		1)						
				Tempering	1 00 1 00				70	8	1	1)						
				Milling	2 50 2 75		0 25		1 50	10	1	1}		22.95				
				No. 2 shop	3 00 2 80			0 20	2 80	11	2	1)						

* These totals are cumulative—that is, they show the aggregate of all entries on the schedule to date.

FIG. 2. MASTER SCHEDULE

also in view. Fig. 1 represents a portion of a sequence-control schedule used in an English plant about fifteen years ago. As each operation was reported finished the symbol representing that operation was blotted out by a rubber stamp. A glance at the schedule was sufficient to show whether operations were being carried out regularly. Each schedule represented an order for one machine, and being mounted on separate carriers, the different orders on hand could be arranged according to due dates. In this way a rather good control over time sequence was obtained, especially considering the very simple form of the schedule.

FIG. 1. SCHEDULE USED IN AN ENGLISH PLANT

CYLINDER

Cylinder	P	F	In	Tt	B	T	P	D
Cyl. Cover	P	F	In	T	D			
P. Rod Gland	P	F	In	P	No	T	D	
Exh. Flange	P	F	In	T	Tp			
St. Flange	P	F	In	T	Tp	D		
P. V. Cover	P	F	In	T	D			
P. V. Cover	P	F	In	T	D			
P. V. Tube	P	F	In	H	T	D	St	
S. V. Bush	P	F	In	H	H			

STANDARDS

Quad. Std.	P	F	In	Pf	Pb	Pt	Df	Dt
Plain Std.	P	F	In	Pf	Pb	Pt	Df	Dt
Loose Slides	P	F	In	P				
Footstep	P	F	In	D				

BUSHES

Die. Bushes	P	F	In	T	G		
Quad. Bushes	P	F	In	T	G		
Crank Bushes	P	F	In	B	G	T	

The first three columns refer to patterns and castings. P = pattern ordered. F = sent to foundry. In = casting received. The other symbols refer to machine operation.

days, if any, the number of parts good, the reference to the replacement sheet, if any, and the cumulative cost to date.

Inspection of the schedule at any moment will show the condition of the order as regards completion, the degree of delay already incurred, the extent to which the cost is coming out as expected with reference to standard, and the cost to date of all finished parts on the order.

As far as the superintendent is concerned the principle of exceptions applies to the work of controlling orders. As long as the different shop and material stubs come through without undue delay, and as long as no important increase of actual as compared with standard cost occurs, the superintendent's attention does not need to be called to the schedule. But if anything shows a tendency to go persistently wrong, then he is warned and can make inquiry in the proper quarter. The degree of increase of cost and of delay that needs to be brought to his attention is of course a matter of experience in each plant, and may from time to time vary also according to known conditions. Where all orders are behind, and well known to be so, then only extra-bad delays will be reported. The general idea will be quite clear after a little study of the makeup of the schedule, as shown in Fig. 2.

On completion of all the parts shown on the schedule the order is complete and the figures give the total cost of the order, as well as a detailed record of the cost of each part. Comparison of the totals of the "standard-cost" column with the "labor-cost" column will disclose how far the order as a whole has come up to expectations. If further investigation is desired, the individual departments at fault will be indicated by the loss and

124

ORDER NO———— FOR————

Factory Cost	Memoranda	Cost, Sale Price and Profit
Material	Cost of Patterns	Sale Price
Wages	Material	Factory cost
Mach. rates	Wages	Commissions
Produc. cost	Mach. rates	Shipping
Supp. rate	Total	Foreign duty
Factory Cost	Cost of Tools	Sales exp.
Add (if chargeable)	Material	Total
Patterns	Wages	Profit
Tools	Mach. rates	% on sale pr.
Total	Total	% on prod. cost.
Comparison with	Spoiled Work	% on fac. cost.
Standard Cost	Material	Customer
Standard cost	Wages	Name
Actual cost	Mach. rates	Town
Over %	Total	State
Under %	Ordered Delivered	

FIG. 3. FINISHED-ORDER STUB

gain columns. If then any particular department shows up badly, the fullest detail as to what happened will be found in the shop-cost "album" referred to in the previous article.

When an order is completed the information on it is transferred, by totals, to a finished-order stub (Fig. 3). Though this may be an 8x10 card, it is called a stub, because it bears the same relation to the finished order that the finished-job stub does to the job. Its object is to summarize the information about the order in order to pass it on to the next higher authority, namely, the executive.

Separate master schedules, appropriately ruled, are provided for patterns, tools and replacements in connection with each order. The expenditure on these three heads is summarized on the finished-order stub, the sheets being withdrawn from the current file when the main order is completed. In a few cases patterns and tools are chargeable to customer, but whether they are or not, these costs are always entered as memoranda on the stub, and are charged to their proper accounts at a later

FINISHED ORDERS.   W. E.————   CLASS————

Compared with Stand	Un-Over	Order der No.	La-Mfg.	M. bor	To-tal Rate	S.	To-tal Rate	Spoiled Patts. Tools Work

FIG. 4. FINISHED-ORDER LIST

stage. The importance of recording such cost figures in conjunction with the cost of the order itself will be readily understood.

As each finished order stub is filled out, the data as to cost of the main order, and the patterns, tools and spoiled work in connection with it, are entered on a finished-order list (shown in Fig. 4), which is sent weekly to the executive. It summarizes, of course, by classes the exact value at shop cost of all finished orders, to which is added the supplementary rate representing wasted burden not absorbed by working machines. The difference between expected or standard and actual cost is entered in one of the columns on the left of the blank.

WEEKLY REPORTS ON SHOP EFFICIENCIES

Having thus acquired a close control over the run of orders through the departments and a detailed knowledge of their expected and actual cost, the superintendent will require figures to show him how the shops are

getting on in the matter of certain kinds of efficiencies. These are afforded by what may be termed "reason registers." Their general ruling is shown by Fig. 5.

One of these blanks is devoted to "exceptional jobs" and one to "spoiled work." The information is derived from the weekly totals of the corresponding shop records (see previous articles), so that the comparative performance of each shop from week to week can be seen in regard to each class of reason. Thus it may be found that a particular shop is running high on account of "inter-

Shop	Reason	Week—	Week—
Foundry	1		
	2		
	3		
Shop No. 1	1		
	2		
	3		
	4		
Shop No. 2	1		
	2		
	3		
Shop No. 4	1		
	2		
etc.			

FIG. 5. SPOILED-WORK REGISTER

rupted jobs," or "man's fault," or a general tendency to attribute spoilage to "bad castings" may be visible, or, similarly, exceptional cost may show a tendency to blame "too much metal" as a reason. If carefully selected, the different reasons to which inefficient operation is attributed will disclose very interesting matters, and the effect of attempted remedies will be easily followed up.

PRODUCTION AND EXPENSE REPORTS

The daily statements of productive and expense wages and machine earnings made in each shop are also summarized weekly on a blank similar to that used by the

Dept.	Standard Week— Hrs.	Earn-ings	Hrs.	Earn-ings	%	4-Week Average Hrs.	Earn-ings	%
Forge								
Foundry								
Milling Dept.								
Mach. Shop A								
Mach. Shop B								
Total Earnings								
Total of Lost time, etc.								

FIG. 6. LIST OF MACHINE EARNINGS

shop, and sent to the superintendent. He will enter the weekly figures on appropriate blanks, so that a comparison is set up for each shop, covering production (including labor and bonus and machine earnings), expense in one's own shop, expense chargeable to other shops, and total of production and expense. These figures signify nothing for one week, but when placed side by side with a series of previous weeks they give a good rough idea whether the normal proportion between production and expense is being maintained.

The weekly statement of machine earnings, which is part of the foregoing report, is also posted to another

Shop	Week	Week	Week	Week
Foundry				
Forge				
Machine Shop A				
Milling				
Machine Shop B				
Total in shops				

FINISHED JOBS PER SCHEDULE

Including material				
Total work in process				

FIG. 7. UNFINISHED JOBS IN SHOPS

comparative blank, which records, shop by shop, the actual and the standard machine earnings. This is a very important return, as it enables the superintendent to see how far machines are being kept at work. If any shop seems at fault, reference is made to the shop record of machine earnings (see Fig. 6), where the actual duty of each machine is recorded.

WEEKLY BALANCES OF WORK IN PROGRESS

The value of unfinished work in the different shops and the value of finished jobs not yet closed out into finished orders are figures that give a good idea of the smoothness or congestion obtaining in the plant. Fig. 7 shows the weekly balances of work in each shop, and

FIG. 8. BURDEN SCHEDULE————DEPT.

also of finished jobs, the total of each weekly column indicating the total unfinished orders in the whole plant. The value of the return is, of course, the facility it affords for comparing the weekly totals over a series of periods. These figures are abstracted from the balances remaining in the shop and finished-job ledger accounts after all finished work for the week has been credited.

FIG. 9. WAGES REPORT

Even in a large plant this involves only a few minutes' work a week, and the information—particularly if compared with the current balance of orders in hand—gives a useful view of the way in which each shop is keeping up with its work.

THE CONTROL OF EXPENSE

In the previous article the record of expense as far as it affects the foreman was dealt with. The superintendent has of course to review the same figures, and

FIG. 10. STORES REPORT

he also has to control the economics of the non-productive departments, such as the power plant, the repair department, the stores, and any others that minister to production only indirectly. Thus in some big plants

there may be departments for fuel oil, for powdered coal, for oxy-hydrogen gas, etc. The expenses of these have not only to be watched, but their output has to be costed and then allocated to the productive departments in proper proportion.

The power plant is a good type of these special departments. The returns should deal with it as a separate business. Space does not permit of describing a comprehensive power report, but in a plant of any size the

FIG. 11. FACTORY BURDEN REPORT

cost should be expressed as a rate per horsepower hour, and a charge made to each shop on the basis of its actual consumption of power, for lighting, for crane work, and for machinery. Steam for heating should also be made the subject of a similar charge.

The first step in control of burden in the productive departments is to arrange all expense in "production factors"; that is to say, all expense pertaining to the upkeep, repair, lighting, heating and cleaning of buildings is segregated in one group. Other groups deal

FIG. 12. ADMINISTRATION EXPENSE DISTRIBUTION

with the similar segregation of expense relating to stores and material and transport, including craneage; to supervision, to organization (clerks, stationery, messengers, watchmen, etc.), and to the upkeep, repair, cleaning, oiling, etc., of productive machinery. All the normal ex-

FIG. 13. PRODUCTION REPORT

penses of a plant can be reduced to one or other of these groups. Then for each shop a very close forecast is possible of what that shop will expend in each of these ways when it is working at normal full time.

125

A schedule (Fig. 8) is prepared for each shop, in which the expected figures are set out in alternate columns, each column representing one month. Then in the alternate columns left blank the actual figures as given weekly by the foreman's reports are summarized monthly and filled in. In slack times some of these figures will tend to fall, and experience will show which of them should fall as work diminishes. But they should

	Jan.	Feb.
Burden not absorbed by M. rate		
Supplementary rate, %		

FIG. 14. UNABSORBED BURDEN REPORT

never be higher than the expected amount, which therefore acts precisely as a standard cost does in the case of productive work. A little experience will serve to indicate which items should diminish as work falls off, and vice versa.

On the other hand, only those items within the control of the superintendent are included in the burden sched-

	Jan.	Feb.
Balance at last month		
* Work on additions this month		
* Stores per stores report		
* Wages per wages report		
* Burden transferred from prod. report		
Total this month		
Total in		
Finished additions this month		
Balance unfinished forwarded		
Total out		

FIG. 15. ADDITIONS TO EQUIPMENT REPORT

ule. Thus depreciation, insurance, taxes and the proportion of administrative expense chargeable to factory have no place in it, because the superintendent is not responsible for them, and cannot reduce them if they seem disproportionate.

SUMMARY OF SUPERINTENDENT'S INFORMATION

The information provided for the superintendent will now be seen to be divided into three main groups: First,

	Jan.	Feb.
Total value as last month		
Finished additions this month		
Total in		
Depreciation per adm. report		
Value forward to next month		
Total out		

FIG. 16. EQUIPMENT REPORT

daily information as to the progress of orders is furnished, leading to a complete schedule of weights and costs of each component of an order and to a summary of the cost of the entire order, together with the subsidiary expense for patterns, special tools and jigs, and

	Jan.	Feb.
Adm. expense per ad. report		
Salaries		
Advertising this month		
Traveling expense		
Printed matter used		
Shipping expense		
Total in		
Expense on:		
* Product A		
* Product B		
*Product C		
Total expense on product		
Expense held up:		
* Product A		
* Product B		
* Product C		
Total held up		
Total out		

FIG. 17. SALES BURDEN REPORT

spoiled work, which latter items may or may not be ultimately chargeable to the order itself. Secondly, information is supplied as to certain kinds of shop or department efficiencies, namely, the average loss due to idle time, spoiled work, and exceptional jobs, shop by shop. The balances of work in hand at the end of each week in each shop, and in the shape of finished parts and material, are also provided, and can be compared with the total of finished orders, and of orders received. Thirdly,

	Jan.	Feb.
Factory cost of finished product per production report		
Selling expense per sales, burden report		
Profit on Product A		
Sales of product A as charged to customer		

FIG. 18. TRADING REPORT: PRODUCT A

a current comparison of actual expense, classified by production factors, is maintained, comparable with the budgeted or expected figures for such expense. This enables the superintendent to observe, at once, any in-

	Jan.	Feb.
Balance last month:		
* Due		
* Not due		
* Overdue		
Total from last month		
Sales this month		
Total in		
Discounts allowed		
Balance forward:		
* Due		
* Not due		
* Overdue		
Total forward to next month		
Total out		

FIG. 19. COLLECTABLE ACCOUNTS REPORT

crease in expense items in any part of the plant, and if illegitimate, to curb it before it assumes either large or permanent form.

126

What the Executive Wants to Know About Costs

By A. Hamilton Church

SYNOPSIS—In this article the kind of information wanted by the executive and the proprietor is discussed. While the executive requires a wide range of information, the proprietor (as, for instance, the shareholders in a corporation) is interested mainly in profits and assets. These are generally disclosed by a balance sheet and a profit and loss account, in which, however, the executive is also interested. No harm will be done, therefore, by ignoring any division of interests in this case.

The ordinary profit and loss accounts and balance sheet are derived from mercantile practice, and are much older than modern manufacturing. For this reason they do not commonly present the facts in a strictly logical order, having reference to the actual occurrences which have taken place in a plant during a given period. For the executive's use we require to serve this information in a series of groups, each of which corresponds to the practical distinctions between production, selling, credit and cash. A short discussion as to these natural groupings will be of service.

The operations of a plant have four main features—money has been expended, and product (finished and partly finished) is a result. That is one clearly defined group. Next, a certain portion of this product has been sold, by the aid of additional expenditure for salesmen, advertising, etc., and from such sales a profit has resulted. This is also a clearly defined group. If all transactions were

	Jan.	Feb.
Wages on production		
Wages on equipment, additions		
Wages on burden		
.Total Wages		

FIG. 1. WAGES REPORT

for cash, these two groups would only need to be supplemented by an account of cash received, expended and on hand to complete the story of the period. Actually, however, we extend credit to our customers, and the status of this credit—whether our outstandings are increasing or diminishing—must also be recorded. Frequently we take credit ourselves, and if so, the amount of our liabilities must be recorded. These transactions form a third clearly defined group. Finally, our disbursements and collections must be tabulated so that the amount of cash we possess is known. This is the fourth and final group in which we are interested.

It will be seen that as regards each of these groups the executive asks the same series of questions, namely: What went in? What came out? What is left in, and in what form is it left?

In all these groups there are not only ingoings and outgoings, but there is also commonly a remainder or balance of something. In the first group we have balances of unused material and of work in process. In the second group we have, in most cases, a balance of goods unsold. In the third group we have a balance of collectible accounts, and perhaps of accounts payable by ourselves when we can spare the money to do so. In the fourth group we have the balance of cash in the safe or at the bank.

Though all these transactions and their resulting balances can be read in an ordinary mercantile profit and loss and balance sheet, their essential independence is not brought out clearly. The fact that they are all entirely separate groups of transactions, however, is most important to emphasize, if the executive is to form a clear mental picture of the result of the operations of the period. Further, it assists to a clear grasp of the situation if certain groups of transactions, such as, for example, those relating to stores, to burden and to administration expenses, are presented separately, so that their individual movements can be seen more distinctly and the main story more easily read by their separation from it.

There is also the important consideration, in many plants, that several different lines of product are made,

	Jan.	Feb.
Balance in hand last month		
Purchased last month		
Total in		
Purchases returned		
Stores issued:		
For production		
For equipment, addition		
For burden		
Balance on hand		
Total out		

FIG. 2. STORES REPORT

and we may desire to ascertain just how we stand with regard to each of them. The latter information rarely if ever reaches the final profit and balance sheets which go to the shareholders of a corporation; but it is of prime importance to the executive.

If we imagine an executive who has just taken charge of a business and wants to be put into possession of its salient features, we shall have a viewpoint that lends itself to demonstration. But though the first thought of such an executive would be directed to the month's trading results—the profit that had been made—his second thought would be for the general position of the business as regards production; and as profits logically arise from production, and not vice versa, I will develop the series of reports presented to him from the viewpoint of the factory first.

Preliminary to the actual story of production will come the reports on the expenditure that makes production possible. First, there will be provided a summary of wages paid, showing its distribution to burden, production and equipment (that is, to additions to equipment values, which in many shops are a regular feature of each month's work). Next in order is a summary of stores, showing purchases, issues to burden, production or equipment, and balance of stores left on hand.

The next step is to present the various items of expenditure that go into burden, both factory and sales, and this is presented in three divisions, namely, administration expense (which is all distributed either to factory or sales burden), factory burden and lastly sales burden. Consideration of the latter is postponed until the whole question of production has been disposed of.

The main story of production is now ready to be told. The wages, stores and burden that have gone into product are set against the cost of the finished product, arranged in classes, that has been delivered to the selling depart-

127

ment. The burden which has not been taken up by machine rates is reduced to a supplementary rate and in that form appears as part of cost of finished product, and the balance represents work unfinished and still in the factory, thus showing, as in the other cases, what has gone in, what has come out and what still remains in.

A similar return is made for additions to equipment, buildings and to other capital accounts. The wages, stores and machine rates that have gone to the production

	Jan.	Feb.
Balance last month		
Stores as per stores report		
Wages as per wages report		
Adm. expense as per report		
Sundries		
Total in		
To production		
Balance held over		
Total out		

FIG. 3. ADMINISTRATION-EXPENSE DISTRIBUTION

of new equipment items are placed on one side of the account and the cost of finished items on the other. The balance left is the value locked up in unfinished additions to equipment still in the shops.

The equipment itself is then similarly reported on. Finished additions from the foregoing report appear on one side. Depreciation written off into burden appear on the other, and the balance represents the present value of equipment, buildings and other capital items.

This finishes the story of production. It has been told step by step, from the separate statements of what has gone in to the statement of what has come out in the form of finished goods and of additions to plant. Also the balances of stores, of work in shops on orders, and of work in shops on additions to equipment are clearly set out. Finished additions to equipment are also shown in their relation to capital accounts.

DEALING WITH THE FINISHED GOODS

We have now to deal with finished goods and their sale, and of course also with the selling expense. If we have, say, three lines of product, each of these is reported on

	Jan.	Feb.
Salaries		
Stationery		
Office expenses		
Rents, taxes		
Depreciation		
Insurance, etc.		
Total in		
To factory burden		
To selling burden		
Total out		

FIG. 4. FACTORY-BURDEN REPORT

separately from this stage onward. In most cases finished goods will not be sold straight from the factory to the consumer, but will be kept in stock ready for delivery. This necessitates intermediate reports, to keep track of the balance of goods on hand. Otherwise finished goods from the production report and selling expense from the sales-burden report would go direct to the trading report. In the present instance, to simplify explanation, we shall assume that this is so, and that all production is on customer's order and goes direct from the factory to the customer.

A separate trading report is provided for each line of product. The ingoings are finished goods and selling expense. On the other side is sale price, the balance between each being profit on that line of goods.

The goods having now been sold and the profit ascertained, we have to consider the question of collecting what is due to us. For this purpose a ledger-balances report is provided. On one side is placed sales for the month

and balance brought forward from last month, graded into three classes, namely, accounts due, not due and overdue. On the other side is placed the amount actually collected during the month, also the discounts allowed, and the balance in accounts outstanding, graded, as before, into due, not due and overdue.

Where we do not pay prompt cash for purchases a similar report is made for accounts owing by us. This shows the amount of our liability outstanding at the end of the month.

Finally, the disposal of the cash so collected is reported on. Cash received is set on one side, cash paid on the other, and the balance is cash on hand in safe or bank.

This general scheme is applicable to any manufacturing business, subject to extension in a few cases to cover special circumstances. It will have been seen that it covers all the operations of the plant in distinct stages. In regard to each stage the three questions stated previously have been asked and answered. Certain of the reports, such as administrative expense, serve to show the collec-

	Jan.	Feb.
Work in hand last month:		
*Stores		
*Wages		
*M. rates		
*Supp. rates		
Total work on hand last month		
*Stores as per stores report		
*Wages as per wages report		
*Burden per factory burden report		
Total production this month		
Total in		
Finished product, Class A:		
*Stores		
*Wages		
*M. rates		
*Supp. rates		
Total for Class A		
Finished product, Class B:		
*Stores		
*Wages		
*M. rates		
*Supp. rates		
Total for Class B		
Work in hand at month end:		
*Stores		
*Wages		
*M. rates		
*Supp. rates		
Total work on hand		
M. rates on equipment, additions		
Transferred to F. A. account		
Total out		

*Items with star are details of totals that follow, and should be filled out with colored ink.

FIG. 5. PRODUCTION REPORT

tion of items and the distribution of their total to other reports. Others contain balances. If all is correctly stated, these balances when brought together, and the capital stock of the business added, will *balance*. In other words, they are verified by a balance sheet of the usual kind. Having thus outlined the system of reports, and explained the scope of each, some specimen blanks will be shown. It may be pointed out here that an important feature of the control that such reports give is their arrangement in such shape that each month can be compared with previous months, with regard to each item appearing on the reports.

More than this is also possible. In a business of an established character we can, by using alternate columns on the blank for that purpose, forecast the expected value of each item; or, in other words, we can *budget* all the information, thus setting up a standard, variations from which may be cause for inquiry. In some businesses the value of budgeting is considerable, and in every case it fosters the habit of looking ahead.

The wages report (Fig. 1)[1] explains itself. As wages are necessarily spent, and cannot be stored, there is no balance

[1] Through error the forms in this article were also given in that published on page 675.

in this report. Wages are all distributed to one or other of the following reports:

We begin with a balance of stores in hand (Fig. 2). To these is added the value of purchases during the month. Against this total is placed the issues of stores, and also any purchases that may have been sent back to the supplier. The amounts entered as issues are distributed to one or other of the following reports. But in this case there is left a balance, namely, of materials still in stores and not yet issued. This is carried forward to next month. If desired, this report can be made more detailed by division into classes of stores, such as brass, steel, or castings, wire, etc.

The distribution of administrative expense (Fig. 3) collects all such items as have to be divided on some determined basis between factory and selling departments.

	Jan.	Feb.
Burden not absorbed by M. rate		
Supplementary rate., +		

FIG. 6. UNABSORBED-BURDEN REPORT

The basis of such distribution does not appear here. It depends on the nature of the business, and is a matter of careful inquiry. When determined it should be applied uniformly each month. As all administrative expense is distributed to one or other of the following reports, no balance remains in this report.

FACTORY-BURDEN REPORT

The executive is probably not interested in the technical details of burden expenditure, which are matters for the superintendent. The factory-burden report (Fig. 4) therefore gives him merely the total chargeable to the factory, and against this the amount actually charged. The balance "held over" represents the equalization of expense, such as the holding over of part of the cost of heavy repairs. This is the really significant figure of the report. It keeps uncharged expense prominently in view.

The production report (Fig. 5) brings forward the balance of work in hand at the beginning of month, adds

	Jan.	Feb.
Balance at last month		
*Work on additions this month		
*Stores per stores report		
*Wages per wages report		
Total this month		
Total in		
Finished additions this month		
Balance unfinished forwarded		
Total out		

FIG. 7. ADDITIONS TO EQUIPMENT REPORT

to it the wages, stores and burden from previous reports expended during the month, and against the total of these two items places the work finished during the month, leaving a balance of work unfinished to go forward. The finished is classified by products, such as superheaters, steam fittings, condensers, or whatever kinds there may be. As regards each class, there is also shown how the cost is made up, namely, how much of it is material, how much wages, how much machine rates, and how much consists of unabsorbed burden or "supplementary rate." A credit is also made here for machine earnings expended on additions to equipment. This is usually a small item, and appears here to avoid complexity in the accounts. As shown, the balances of work in hand are not divided into classes of product, but this could be done without much extra work if desired. This work is a very important one, especially if we consider that the vertical columns represent months. The monthly variations in all the facts of production are therefore disclosed by this report, which lends itself particularly to the budgeting principle as already explained.

Burden charged to the shops and not absorbed by machine rates represents, of course, wasted opportunities. If all the machines had been working to the full there would have been none unabsorbed. In order to get rid of it, one of two plans may be followed: It may be charged off at once to profit and loss, since it is simply waste and does not really represent the cost of anything made. But a safer way is to prorate it over the work that has been done. It increases the cost of this, and in that way reaches profit and loss account after all. The unabsorbed-

	Jan.	Feb.
Total value as last month		
Finished additions this month		
Total in		
Depreciation per adm. report		
Value forwarded to next month		
Total out		

FIG. 8. EQUIPMENT REPORT

burden report (Fig. 6) keeps in view, month by month, its amount, and the per cent. rate that has been found necessary to get rid of it by prorating. Each month's waste is not prorated over that month's finished work. That would produce too violent fluctuations. The balance of work in hand, including the finished work, is taken into account. Thus work in hand always includes a percentage of supplementary rate, as shown in Fig. 5. This unabsorbed burden must not be confused with the "held-over" burden in Fig. 4. The latter has already been explained. The significant figure in this report is the percentage of supplementary rate. It is an index to the degree in which the machinery of the plant is being kept at work. In slack times, of course, it tends to rise.

The additions to equipment report (Fig. 7) is practically a production report confined to plant additions. It is not included in the production report—first, because it is a class of activity that merits being viewed separately, and, secondly, because it does not take a supplementary rate. It would be quite illegitimate to charge plant additions with unabsorbed burden due to idle machines. In fact, it would be absurd to do so, since that would mean that such work would cost more in slack times than in busy times. Yet it is in slack times that as much as possible should be put in hand.

EQUIPMENT REPORT AND SALES REPORT

All equipment is shown in one item in the equipment report (Fig. 8). Subdivision into buildings, machinery, tools, etc., would be desirable in most cases. The general

	Jan.	Feb.
Adm. expense per ad. report		
Salaries		
Advertising this month		
Traveling expense		
Printed matter used		
Shipping expense		
Total in		
Expense on:		
*Product A		
*Product B		
*Product C		
Total expense on product		
Expense held up:		
*Product A		
*Product B		
*Product C		
Total held up		
Total out		

FIG. 9. SALES-BURDEN REPORT

idea would remain the same, namely, to provide a means of showing the present value of the equipment from month to month, after new finished additions have been charged up and depreciation taken off.

The sales-burden report (Fig. 9) collects all the items of selling expense and shows its allocation between the various classes of products. This being determined, some

129

portion of it may be held up, as, for instance, when heavy expense for a particular campaign has just been incurred. If so held up, it must of course be carried forward to the next month. The *basis* of distributing expense to the various classes of product is not disclosed by the report. It must, as in the case of administrative expense in the foregoing, be decided on after careful consideration of all the facts. Once this basis is fixed the allocation of the different items of selling expense to the different products is a routine matter, so that all that is needed here is a statement of the fact that they have been so allocated.

	Jan.	Feb.
Factory cost of finished product per production report.....		
Selling expense per sales, burden report..................		
Profit on Product A......................		
Sales on Product A as charged to customer...............		

FIG. 10.   TRADING REPORT: PRODUCT A

The "held-up" balance is the most significant figure of this report.

One of these trading reports (Fig. 10) is made for each class of product. Also a summary, consolidating all the separate product reports in one set of figures, is desirable if there are more than two products. The factory cost of the finished product for the month (including its proportion of supplementary rate) is added to the selling expense for that class of product for the month. Against these items is placed the price of the goods as billed, the difference or balance being the profit on that class of product.

The collectible-accounts report (Fig. 11) shows the status of credit. It collects the total collectible and deducts the amounts collected and the discounts, leaving the amount still outstanding at the month end, classified into accounts due, not yet due and overdue.

Where a firm makes subsidiary lines for its own use, such as nuts, bolts, screws, etc., which are transferred to stores on completion, a report like Fig. 7 should be used, and such work separated from ordinary production. The reason is that such work does not take supplementary rate. To charge it with such rate means that the cost of making things for oneself is higher in slack times than in busy times, which is obviously untrue. This is one of the absurdities that have been promoted by the usual percentage burden systems, and many firms have lost and

	Jan.	Feb.
Balance last month..............................		
*Due..		
*Not due....................................		
*Overdue...................................		
Total from last month.................		
Sales this month................................		
Total in....................................		
Discounts allowed..............................		
Balance forward:..............................		
*Due..		
*Not Due...................................		
*Overdue...................................		
Total forward to next month..................		
Total out..................................		

FIG. 11.   COLLECTIBLE-ACCOUNTS REPORT

are losing money because they suppose that work for themselves is costing them much more than it really is. The real truth of the situation is that in slack times they *are losing less* by such work than would be the case if they purchased outside, since such work absorbs machine rates which would otherwise go into unabsorbed burden and be wasted.

Nothing has been said as to the cash report, nor as to the ordinary profit and loss accounts and balance sheet, which will be familiar to everyone. But the method of carrying the items in vertical columns month by month should be extended to the executive's copies of these documents.

Paper No. 238

INDUSTRIAL MANAGEMENT.

By

A. HAMILTON CHURCH
Consulting Industrial Engineer
New York, N. Y., U. S. A.

132

During the past fifteen or twenty years, owing in great part to the increasing complexity and scale of manufacturing operations, it has been obvious that the older traditions and practices of what is termed "management" were beginning to prove inadequate to modern needs. In a few words the change may be described as a movement away from rule-of-thumb towards quantitative treatment of management problems.

Management is, of course, a very comprehensive term. It extends all the way from the large questions of business policy and finance down to the detail specification of the daily duties of particular men. It includes, therefore, what may be termed the "determinative" element, and the "administrative" element —the former concerned with the general shaping of the course of affairs, and the latter occupied with the making of arrangements whereby the policy thus originated is carried out in practice. Improvements in the art of management lie almost wholly within the latter sphere.

As far as dealt with in this paper, Industrial Management may be defined as the organization and administration of industrial plants in accordance with some previously determined aim or policy. It comprises the purchase, storage, handling and transportation of materials; the engagement and organization of all kinds of labor, both mental and physical; the provision and upkeep of suitable premises, machinery and equipment; the design of product; control of the technical processes of manufacture; and the storage and marketing of product.

The history of the development of management cannot be considered in this paper, first, because it is a somewhat controversial question, and it would be a thankless task to try to distinguish between rival claims to originality in the various improvements that have been contributed by a number of individuals over a considerable period of years; and, secondly, because such an attempt would occupy too much time, and even then would be of little practical value. To properly undertake such a task, we must wait until modern management methods have taken a somewhat more settled form, and have secured a somewhat more uniform and general recognition, so that a general perspective of the whole movement may be secured.

This attitude is the more necessary inasmuch as what has taken place is not so much revolution as evolution. The new elements that have been brought into prominence are in few cases wholly new. I do not mean merely that they have in many cases been of the nature of re-discoveries of practices that were at one time known and then passed out of use, though this appears, unquestionably, the case as regards "time-study" and some other modern practices. Every art is full of instances of inventions that were born before their time, and this in no way diminishes the importance of their re-discovery and fresh application under wholly new conditions. The point I wish to make is that progress has been evolutionary in the sense that most of the new devices have existed in more or less rudimentary form in the past, but the development of industry has so altered their relations to the general process of manufacturing that they had, perforce, to be developed, improved and given greater precision.

The general tendency under which management has been evolving is that of acquiring a more precise and exhaustive knowledge: (1) of what is to be undertaken, (2) of the forces and materials by and through which work is to be done, and (3) of the methods by which the forces are to be applied to the materials so as to produce the required effect in the shortest time and with the least expenditure of effort. The peculiar character of the management problem is indicated if we realize that, for the most part, the forces to be organized by the administrator are human forces. For this reason management

133

involves much more subtle elements than are commonly found in any art, such as electrical engineering, that deals with physical forces alone.

It is very important to understand that Industrial Management as a specific art, based on some approach to scientific principles, is a wholly different matter from the technical art of manufacture. If this were not so, then obviously there would be as many different kinds of management as there are separate industries, one might almost say, as there are separate plants. The art of dyeing has very little similarity to the art of producing steel ingots, and the manufacture of locomotives little in common with the manufacture of cotton yarn. The technical processes in each of these cases have no application at all to any other. Great experience in spinning yarn would be no qualification for setting up a manufacture of shrapnel. Nevertheless, all these industries, so diverse as regards the technical knowledge required, are subject to common principles when it comes to a question of administration, and it is precisely these common principles that it is the task of industrial management to discover and perfect.

This distinction must be insisted on, because it is frequently supposed that because, historically speaking, the more recent development of modern management methods was carried on side by side with, and to some slight extent might be considered to have grown out of, the introduction of high-speed steel into engineering industry, therefore such matters as "cutting speeds" and "feeds" are matters of industrial management. Such an idea is quite erroneous. They belong wholly to the technical practice of machine shops. It was the more strenuous conditions set up in machine shops by the introduction of high-speed steel that made the necessity of reform of management methods more visible. That certain management necessities, disclosed by the introduction of high-speed steel, set going a whole chain of development is purely accidental, and the same might have happened in any other industry which was being subjected to sudden change in technical methods which had the effect of intensifying the movement which it is the business of management to maintain.

In the same way, industrial management has nothing to do with the perfection of technical equipment, or of technical design. These matters have to do with the technics of manufacture but not with the technics of management. In discussing management, therefore, we must begin by assuming that the design of the proposed product and the equipment that has been gathered together to make this product are already the best that technical experience demands, since improvement in management will not remedy any technical defect, any more than a technical improvement will directly increase the efficiency of management.

These remarks apply to the operative equipment—to the machines, tools, looms, vats, presses, mixers, ovens, and so forth, by which technical work is done on material. On the other hand, all other equipment comes under the notice of management in as far as its intelligent functioning is concerned. Of such equipment may be mentioned buildings and their heating and ventilating appliances, conveying and transportation equipment of every kind, power equipment, and so forth. It will be noticed that whereas the former class of machinery has to do with a particular industry, and can rarely or never be imagined as transferable to another industry, the latter class of equipment is that which is common to nearly all forms of manufacturing, and is therefore properly considered as being within the scope of management—the science or art which is concerned with those problems that are common to industry in general.

Having thus roughly defined what Industrial Management is, the nature of the improvements that have been made in its practice in the last decade or so may be generally touched on. The great development has been in the much greater use of Analysis as a tool or instrument of management. Formerly, people were content with merely approximate knowledge. "We are nearly out of tool steel"; "Order some", might be considered a typical instance of the older method. Today we are beginning to find that vagueness of this kind is no longer possible. We begin by studying the precise kind of steel that we want for our work. We decide how much of this should

135

always be kept in stock. We also decide how much shall be ordered at a time, whenever our stock has fallen below a set limit. In other words we analyse all the steps of the problem of tool-steel consumption. We examine all its stages, we follow out in detail its history, and when we have done this we place quantitative values on all the transactions that can be foreseen.

Today this principle of analysing all the elements of each problem has become very prominent. The careful manner in which routing is considered and arranged is a case in point. But though this process of analysis is carried much farther than would have been considered "practical" a generation ago, it is necessary at the same time to remember that it was always more or less considered, and compliance with its demands was always implied in the rule-of-thumb days. The function was rudimentary then; it is fully developed today; but the lines of gradual expansion could still be traced by anyone who cared to go into the history of the matter.

When we consider that manufacturing is, in fact, made up of an almost infinite number of separate, disconnected acts; that it consists of thousands of independently made steps by, frequently, hundreds of individuals, and that the operation as a whole may continue to progress even though a considerable number of these steps are taken out of their proper order, and made at inconvenient times, we can understand why the application of analysis to management details has had so wide a field, and so sudden a success.

Most of the progress in management that has been made in the last twenty years has been due to the introduction and use of analysis. It would be perhaps more proper to say the re-introduction of analysis, for it is a curious but well ascertained fact that very critical and detailed methods of analysis were in use, particularly in the way of process- and time-study, in the early stages of factory development, though these methods seem afterwards to have been entirely disused and forgotten.

In attributing much of modern progress in management to the skilful and discriminating use of analysis as applied to

the innumerable acts that go to make up the routine of manufacture, we must not forget that Analysis is not a constructive
instrument. It distinguishes, differentiates, enables us to find
out which are the important and salient and which the unimportant and negligible steps in any series. But it does not
make anything. It helps to settle relative values, but it does
not build. It is not a constructive instrument.

To complement analysis, synthesis is necessary. While
analysis is an instrument for dissecting, synthesis is an instrument for combining. It is by far, from the viewpoint of management, the older of the two. It represents the selective
power. In the early stages of any art it is exercised in a way
that depends on instinct or judgment for the elements of a
decision. Frequently it makes mistakes, because its judgments
are not based on a true appreciation of the elements that enter
into the problem. When industry is still in a primitive stage,
the elements entering into management are few, and though erroneous judgments are not difficult to make, the mind is able to a
large extent to analyse these elements almost unconsciously. But
as soon as conditions become really complex, this unconscious
analysis must be superseded by conscious and very exact analysis,
in order that a true and complete synthesis may be reached.

The general distinction between synthesis and analysis
may be defined by stating that synthesis selects means to effect
large ends, while analysis determines the exact relations of the
different elements of means. The one is general and constructive, the other local and observing. Synthesis keeps its
attention fixed on some predetermined end and seeks to shape
forces accordingly. Analysis does not concern itself with ends
at all, but merely with a correct presentation of minute relations and minute facts. Analysis can be, and too frequently
is, applied to work of which the ultimate value may prove to
be very small, but synthesis always has an end of definite value
in view.

This distinction is not merely an academic one. It has a
practical bearing on successful management. A successful
organization for manufacturing may be regarded as a collection of small separate aims—a combination of grouped activi-

137

ties, each devoted to a special end. These groups must be
coördinated and synthesized so that these minor and immediate
ends are merged in the larger aim, namely, the efficient production of some specific article.

Industrial synthesis is not merely a grouping of men.' It
is essentially a grouping of activities or functions. Any individual man may be working today as a stoker, and tomorrow
as a time-keeper, but the significant point about this would not
be that the man has been transferred from one department to
another; it is that the direction of his activity has been
changed—he is now fulfilling a different function. Management, therefore, is a synthesis of separate functions. The interior arrangements and mechanism of each function can be studied
by the aid of analysis, but analysis will not aid us to organize
and coördinate these functions for a common end.

138

This essential difference in the part played by the two
intellectual instruments of management—analysis and synthesis—has been enlarged upon because the more recent advances
in the art have been brought about by the development to a
degree before unheard of, of the powerful lever of analytical
study of conditions. But the synthetic side of management has
not been correspondingly developed beyond its former stage.
Thus there has arisen an idea that analysis is a method of management, whereas it is only one of the instruments of management, and indeed the less essential of the two. That it is the
less essential is proven by the fact that it is only recently that
it has been highly developed, and all the not inconsiderable
triumphs of industry in the past were attained without its aid.
I believe it to be true that the failures of the new methods,
where they have failed, have been due to inability to perceive
that synthetic mastery has not by any means been displaced, or
rendered less vitally important to industry, but simply that it
has been supplemented by a new and powerful instrument of
research. Analysis discusses and reveals, but synthesis chooses
and combines. It is evident that neither of these processes can
be henceforth dispensed with.

Management being a synthesis of functions, it follows that
a very clear idea of these functions is necessary. In the course

of my own studies of this question, published last year*, I have found that these functions are few and capable of rigid definition. They form, in fact, water-tight compartments, since the efficiency of any one function is wholly independent of the efficiency of the others. Briefly stated, these functions are:

1. Design
2. Equipment
3. Control
4. Comparison
5. Operation

No form of activity exists in a plant <u>for the purposes of production</u> that cannot be included in one or other of these five functional divisions. Consequently we can say that production is a synthesis of Design, Equipment, Control, Comparison and Operation. Not only is this so, but it has been found possible to trace the gradual separating out or "devolution" of each of these functions from the early beginnings of industry to the modern highly organized plants. It should be mentioned, however, that only the administrative side of management is included in this classification. The determinative side, which is responsible for "policy", stands outside and above these administrative functions, which, indeed, only exist for the purpose of carrying out such policy as and when determined.

In attempting to describe the present development of modern management, it will be convenient to treat the subject according to the classifications of functions just mentioned. To begin with, therefore, we may consider the function of "design", by which the mental picture of product is physically reproduced. The product so pictured is afterwards made tangible and actual by the aid of the remaining functions. It will be obvious that the function of design does not assume equal dimensions in all industries. It is always present, but often quite rudimentary, as for example in cotton spinning. But in other industries, and particularly in the great group of engineering industries, it takes on an enormous extension. Very elaborate preliminary arrangements are necessary before a

---

* See "The Science and Practice of Management". 1914. New York, The Engineering Magazine Co.

machine can be constructed and put together, and the modern
ideas are very well illustrated by the increasing precision given
to designs, and even to the greater extension given to the idea
of what is comprised by design than formerly.

Engineering design for manufacture frequently includes
today (1) the usual specification of the shape, size and dimensions of components, and these components are made frequently to conform to what is called "standardization" or the
principle of "fewest things"; (2) specification of certain auxiliary appliances, such as jigs and templets to be used in producing each component; (3) specification of what machines are to
be used in the manufacture of each component; (4) specification of the tools, reamers, drills, and other dimension-giving
appliances that are to be used; (5) specification of the order
in which the step in manufacture of the component is to be
made; (6) specification of the standard time that is to be consumed in carrying out these steps on each component.

It may not be recognized at first sight that all these specifications are true "designs". But what else are they? They
obviously belong to specific pieces and are the forecast of what
should be performed in regard to each. The proof comes when
we consider that after all these elaborate specifications have
been prepared, the piece may never be made at all. They are
clearly therefore steps taken antecedent to manufacture to indicate its path, and consequently are matters of "design" and
"design" only. Design is a specification of intention, and all
the steps just enumerated were specifications of intention, even
though it might happen that the intention was never realized,
and the machine never made.

Now in the preparation of such designs, the modern instrument of analysis sometimes plays a great part. Not in all
industries, for it frequently happens that machines will only
do one thing, at one speed, and in one way. But in proportion
as machines are universal, and most machine tools are of this
kind, there arises the possibility of endless combinations of
feeds and speeds, of methods of supporting or "jigging" the
piece, of doing this before that, and of using some hole or
groove already made as the datum line for a new operation.

140

Under such circumstances an exact analysis of these elements, and even of the physical handling of the tools and levers by which work is performed, becomes desirable. Thus we have what is called "time-study" with its further extension into "motion-study" by which we map out the shortest way to perform operations, and this analysis is embodied in elaborate (sometimes too elaborate) written instructions, which then become part of the design of the particular piece. They do not apply to any other piece.

Thus, we see that "design", under advanced modern methods in those industries where the necessity exists, really is made up of four distinct parts: (1) The "piece" or component, its shape and dimensions, finish, etc.; (2) the accessories peculiar to the manufacture of the piece; (3) the method of operating on the piece; (4) the time to be consumed in operating on the piece.

There is also a technical aspect of design that is wholly separate from its aspect as above described. This may be termed "design for use". The component or machine when designed, and made, may prove unsatisfactory or even worthless for the purpose intended. Management as such—as a special science or art—has nothing to do with this. The technical efficiency of a particular design is obviously a matter pertaining to the special industry, and poor designing for "use" may exist alongside the best type of organized management. Conversely, we may have excellent technical designs and very poor management. The technical efficiency of "design" is not a part of the science or art of administration. In discussing management problems, we must always assume that technical efficiency is at a maximum; otherwise we complicate the problem so that its true bearings can no longer be perceived.

Before proceeding to discuss the remaining functions of management, the exact significance of the application of analysis to the details of design must be ascertained. What is it we do when we make a design, when we specify requirements under any of the four heads just mentioned? What we do is to establish "standards". A large amount of the progress in management is due to the recognition of the value of carefully

141

ascertained standards in regard to the various acts of production. It must of course be understood that no standard used in production is anything like a final or last word on the subject with which it deals. If, after analysis of the elements of a problem, we decide that a certain result is attainable, we make this result a standard by which to measure actual attainment. A "standard" is thus a datum line; but it is not often a fixed datum like a mile-post, because industry has as yet reached no condition anywhere of which it may be said "this is the uttermost possible". We set up a standard as a convenient measure or reference, but we may either fail to reach it in practice, or we may surpass it. In the latter case we have made a new "standard", which in its turn will endure until superseded.

The use of standards is not of course entirely new. Always there has been a more or less conscious use of them, but they were embodied in that vague and mysterious region, the instinct of the practical man, and were not for the most part quantitatively expressed. A certain operation, for example, coming under scrutiny of the practical man, would be assigned a period of duration within vague limits. It might take "from a day to a day-and-a-half". That is, the variation might be fifty percent. This approximation, though not very scientific, is still a standard. The modern tendency, however, is to limit such variations to 5%, to 1%, or some finer degree, according to the nature of the matter investigated. But the only way to do this is by careful analysis of the elements—you cannot pump accurate approximations out of merely instinctive judgments made by looking over the field generally.

The modern use of standards, though increasing, is probably only at the beginning of its career. In fact as soon as we begin to collect standards of general application, we are at once confronted with a realization of how little has yet been reduced to positive and exact knowledge, in regard to management. Such standards as we have are as yet mostly confined to specific instances, such as the time study of particular processes. Few of these can as yet be expressed in general form, such as the standard time or cost of removing a pound of chips by planing, milling or turning. The problem has indeed, hardly been attacked as yet from that view-point.

Generally speaking, however, the use of analysis is closely connected with either the establishment of prospective standards, or the attainment of already existing standards. Not all standards can be quantitatively expressed. In "routing", for example, that is, analysing the path of product with a view to reducing its travel to a minimum, it would be hard to put the result into any significant figures. But in these and similar instances, there is an implied standard. In this case the implied standard is the "path of least effort".

The next function to claim attention is that of "equipment". This is a double-barrelled function, inasmuch as it has both a static and an active aspect. The first represents the equipment installed, but not working. The second represents its actual functioning. In other words we have to regard "equipment" from the viewpoints of its "installation" and also of its use. In regard to equipment, modern analytical methods have wide application.

Before setting up a plant, the nature of the product will naturally have been determined. The first step in deciding the nature and form of our equipment will be an analysis of the components of this product, so that an estimate can be made of the varieties of equipment that will be required. Next the quantitative treatment of these varieties will be made, so that the relative importance of operative machinery, power plant, storage, handling and transporting equipment, offices, etc., can be determined. This will lead to a systematic allotment of the quantity of space required for each type of equipment. The arrangement of the equipment is, however, not yet provided for. This is based on a careful analysis of the sequence of processes, both within and between departments. Then the best arrangement of buildings, yards, offices and machinery in regard to the space available can be made.

Some of these successive analyses have perhaps always been made to a greater or less degree in setting up a new plant. But they are carried today to a much greater degree of refinement than was formerly customary—some were perhaps

absent altogether. It would almost seem, to judge by many
instances, that the idea of economy in the direct handling of
material along the shortest possible path hardly ever occurred
to manufacturers a generation or two ago. It was probably
regarded as a mere "theory" unworthy of the notice of strong
practical common-sense. Otherwise, it is hard to understand
the degree to which this almost obvious principle was violated
when there seemed to be no necessity for it.

"Equipment in use" presents of course a wholly different
series of problems from its "installation". This implies, of
course, a wholly different set of "standards" to be observed.
The simplest illustration will be that of the power plant. This
is a very clearly marked group of equipment, with its own
standards of economy and of performance. On this side, analysis is directed to ascertaining the working conditions and demands, such as the amount of power called for in each hour of
the day, or the amount of fuel and ash to be handled per hour.
Such analyses enable working conditions to be adjusted with
much greater accuracy than would otherwise be possible. In
the same way a study of the transport equipment performance,
as in the case where goods are accumulated at a receiving point,
and cleared from there at stated hours, may show the way to
distribution of the labor force so as to eliminate waiting about
and idleness.

A close study of the standards possible to observe in the
operation of equipment is frequently of great importance, because the inefficiencies of equipment are difficult to discover.
They are easily left unperceived, since they only affect production indirectly, and the cost of this inefficiency is generally
merged in a vague total of "burden", and so escapes scrutiny.

The general aim to be observed in the operation of equipment is that of even, uniform service. It is just the occurrence
of uneven, broken conditions of equipment service that pull
down the efficiency of a plant almost unnoticed. Analysis of
all conditions tending to interrupt service should therefore be
made and sufficient inspection assigned, or other measures
taken that will prevent such interruptions. The time to remedy a breakdown is before it happens.

"Design" and "equipment" are both, in one sense, preliminary "functions". The one specifies the intention, the other provides the physical means. We must now consider the plant in action; and the "coördinating function" that sets it in motion, and keeps it going is that of "control". This is also a double-barrelled function, inasmuch as it has to be planned and established (installation) and also observed in action, or from its administrative side. It is the function concerned with duties and responsibilities, and the exercise and limitation of initiative. It thus deals with the living factors of management.

The installation of "control" begins by the mapping out of spheres of duties. It therefore plans the interior structure of the various departments that exercise functions. Beyond this it settles the relations between departments and arranges the specially administrative duties, such as ordering, receiving and storing material, receiving customers' orders and dissecting them or passing them to the departments concerned, and arranges for the supervision and coördination of all departments. It does this by planning duties, including the organization of expert advice and assistance where needed.

Analysis will play a large part in settling the details of "control" installation. A quantitative examination of the flow of material and of product will be made, and of customers' orders, and on this the schedule of duties, or spheres of duty, will be determined. Then in regard to the spheres of duty thus set up, there may be a further analysis to determine what particular qualifications are required for each, and the wage or salary that would be appropriate. Then the method of paying for work will be considered, and what duties will arise in connection—such as rate fixers, time-study men, time and pay clerks, etc. In some complex industries, a regular coördinating mechanism is set up, controlling the meeting of orders, designs, instructions, and the movement of material and product correspondingly. This involves a careful analysis of the working capacity of productive plant, and the settlement of a range of spheres of duty to operate this mechanism, or as it is sometimes called "planning department".

On the administrative side, "control" sets everything in motion. The various spheres of duty set up, begin to function. Designs are issued, complete with all their auxiliary instructions as to method. Material is ordered, held in stock, issued and worked on. Product is gathered up, transported from point to point, inspected, perhaps assembled into units, and passed into warehouse, or packed for shipment and shipped. The function of "control" has to do with the performance of these innumerable acts in the right quantity at the right moment. In advanced plants such acts take place in accordance with a pre-determined time-schedule. This implies an ascertained relation between the times of operation as determined by design (see above) and the possible output of the operative or productive equipment. Means must therefore be provided to keep record of each machine (or it may be only of each department) and the amount of work done by it in a given period, and this must be continuously checked with the amount of work coming forward, so the time that a given piece of work will pass through a machine or department can be forecasted with a near approach to accuracy. On this, in turn, hinges the possibility of being sure that material, orders and instructions can meet together at the right moment, so that there is no unnecessary delay owing to the absence of one of these. It also implies a close control over the purchase, storage and issue of material, to the end that nothing may be overlooked so as not to be forthcoming when wanted.

Control at every stage depends for its success on an accurate knowledge of conditions, and these conditions can only be fully grasped, to the degree that makes prevision possible, by the aid of quantitative analysis of every movement taking place in regard to product. The subdivision of duties following on such analysis is sometimes carried very far, as in the case of what is called "functional foremanship". Subdivision of duties is however limited by the necessity for subsequent coördination, and especially by the importance of conserving a point of application of great definiteness for responsibility. While, therefore, the tendency to subdivide duties, if based on a thorough analysis, is a good one, it is not desirable to carry it too far; and of course there is no super-eminent virtue in any special subdivision, which obviously may fit one plant and class of industry and be wholly inapplicable to others.

The main end of control is to maintain a steady stream of production. Organized control prevents annoying delays and untimely discoveries of forgotten things. It regulates and limits the amount of money locked up in material and in product in process, and particularly it enables promises of delivery to be made with a fair prospect of their being kept—a matter in which the older type of management, in the absence of analytical examination of the field of production, was frequently at fault.

Closely connected with the function of control is that of "comparison". This function has two sides or divisions, one dealing with numbers and values (this is "accounting"), the other with the examination of physical properties (this is "inspection").

147

Comparison is the great instrument by which control steers its path. Both inspection and accounting depend for their value on standards, actual or implied. For the former, the specifications of design as to size, shape, dimensions and material, form a standard, and in metal manufacturing some of these standards are frequently expressed as "limits and fits". In accounting, a different series of standards is used for comparing with actual results. Thus, the time actually occupied on jobs, as compared with specified or expected time; cost and quantity of material, as compared with specified cost and quantity; actual output, as compared with specified and expected output—all these are examples of the accounting division of comparison.

Comparison is usually associated with the making of "records". No record is of value unless it can be compared with a similar past record, or will be used sometime for comparing with a future record. In large establishments it not infrequently happens that records are prepared month after month that are not compared with anything. In nearly all such cases they may be suppressed, and their cost saved.

The development of comparison as a distinct function is

almost a growth of the past twenty or thirty years. It is only in some industries, and in select plants of even those industries, that it is properly developed even today. This is natural if we regard the modern progress of management as largely a tendency towards quantitative treatment and examination of problems. But, historically speaking, there is another good reason. It will be found in the keener competition that exists today, and is continually increasing. In former times, strict accounting was confined to actual money transactions, mainly because money can be so easily stolen. The progress of a business and the degree to which it was making profits was judged by the bank balance. Indeed, there was no other way to judge it, except at long intervals, since the books could not be closed until after the long and costly process of the annual "stock-taking" had been carried out. And stocktaking was too great a disturbance to be undertaken any more often than could be possibly helped.

One of the important uses of comparison is in connection with "wastes". Careful analysis of the different sources of waste is necessary, and then records are set up to compare the fluctuations between one period and another, and compare these fluctuations again with other figures which may explain them, or indicate causes of fresh loss.

Some accounting records do not, at first sight, seem to give rise to comparison. Ordinary ledger accounts obviously do, since they maintain a continuous record of what has gone in, compared with what has come out, in regard to any class of transaction. Accounting, in its broadest sense, is the practical application of the science of measurement of quantities and values. But in manufacturing operations the units with which accounting has to deal are, for the most part, complex units. Thus the cost of a job is built up of a number of units, each of which contains several elements. The first is time; the second is a wage rate multiplied by this time; the third is a "burden" distribution, generally also based on time, though it may also be based on the amount of wages. There may be, in advanced accounting, another element, not based on time, but based on the amount of "burden" appropriated to the job. (Supplementary rate.) Not all of these elements are required for comparison in themselves; but they have to be collected and worked up for the sake of being incorporated in a result that is the subject of a comparison.

Analytical methods play a large part in determining the appropriate distribution of burden or expense in many cases. There is no subject more neglected by practical manufacturers than this, principally because the methods that have been employed in the past are very easy to apply, though frequently they give most erroneous results. They continue to be used because the erroneous nature of the results cannot be detected and isolated, save by substituting a more accurate method. They exert, of course, a strong influence on profit, because prices are very often fixed by them, without anyone being cognisant of the error. The error may be on the right side or on the wrong side, but unless something happens to demonstrate the fact, the resulting loss or gain is hidden in the general result of the business operations. Analytical methods of burden distribution would sometimes disclose that particular lines, thought to be money-makers, were being carried on at a small margin of profit, or even at a loss, while other lines supposed to be of small value were really the staple of the business.

149

The final function is that of "operation". Operation is the act of applying labor and machinery to material so as to transform it in accordance with the dictates of design. But the two functions are obviously distinct. Design, as defined above, effects no transformation. It alters nothing. It merely specifies intention, and nothing beyond. On the other hand "operation" is the function that transforms material. It effects changes in its status—either in form, dimension or composition—but it does not give rise to new intention; that is, it does not design anything.

It is true that, as we have seen, design sometimes specifies with great minuteness every step that operation is to take. It tells "which way". But telling "which way" is not doing the work. Operation does the work—and it may do it well or ill, however minutely the steps have been specified. This distinction is important, because there is a tendency in some quarters

to confuse the sphere of the two functions. That portion of
design which concerns itself with the method of operation has
been in some cases rather overdone. The idea of giving the
operative copious "written instructions" has been made into a
fetish, without its true bearing being altogether clearly perceived. The necessity for "written instructions" (which was
first discovered in the engineering industries) arises chiefly
from one of two causes: Either the machines used are "universal", that is, have endless combinations of ways in which
they can be set up and used (machine tools are of this class);
or, the degree of operative skill—the operative tradition—is
not very high. In a few cases both these causes may be at
work.

In the former case, the thinking out of the details of operation in advance is a most important act of design. It enables
operation to proceed with assured swiftness, and keeps the machines busy, instead of their being held up while experiments
are being tried out. It is no reflection on the skill of the operative, so long as the instructions do not descend to trifling
and unimportant details. The excuse for and value of "written
instructions" under such circumstances are that, as has been
contended in this paper, such instructions are a part of the
complete design of the individual piece. They cannot be reduced to any new practice, they cannot form or assist in forming any new operative tradition, because they are essentially
confined to one piece, which may or may not ever be made
again.

In the other case, namely, where such instructions are
necessary from the defective experience or skill of the operative, no such value belongs to "written instructions". In this
case, they are not part of design, but an attempt at educating
and training operatives. Under such circumstances "written
instructions", if necessary at all, are obviously a merely temporary measure. As soon as the standard practice they incul-
cate has been absorbed by the operatives and has become habit,
then "written instructions" become mere red tape.

This distinction would not have arisen had it not been for
the fact that most of the modern ideas of management have

been developed in engineering works and machine shops, which form the most complex kind of industry, dealing as they do with machines of very universal application, and with a great variety of operations amounting, in many cases, to distinct trades. Hence, as the new analytical instruments of time- and motion-study came to be applied, wholly new practice was found advisable in many directions. Some of the new practice was intimately connected with individual pieces, and some with general operative practice. Under the circumstances, it is not surprising that "written instructions" were considered to be the method applicable to both these conditions, whereas, had the development taken place in an industry where machines had fixed duty, it would have been obvious that what was wanted was to train operatives in the newly discovered practice, and this would probably have been done with a very small development of written instructions.

151

This brief review of the five functions and the extent to which modern methods of analysis have penetrated them may be summarized as follows:

1. Design originates.
2. Equipment provides physical conditions.
3. Control specifies duties and gives orders.
4. Comparison measures, records and compares.
5. Operation makes.

The importance of this classification of functions is that each of them has a separate efficiency of its own. In this respect each forms a water-tight compartment. If design is inefficient all the operative efficiency in the world will not help. Excellent equipment service may exist alongside poor operation. All three of these functions may be excellently run, and yet inefficiency in control will not thereby be remedied. If comparison be undeveloped, speeding up operation or modifying equipment will not help to throw light on what is going on. The practical importance of this is very great. In a failing business, diagnosis must first be applied to decide in which function the fault lies; and if in more than one, then the remedies to be applied must be taken in a certain order, or more harm than good will result. For example, where control is already undeveloped and strained to the breaking point, the speeding up of operation might easily be the last straw which would break down the entire organization and throw it into hopeless confusion. Some of the failures that have been met with in applying the new ideas have in all probability been due to applying them to the wrong function at the outset.

In addition to these five functions, there are certain fundamental laws of action or "effort" that lie behind all management. Space does not permit of their being discussed on this occasion, but they may be briefly enumerated as follows:

First law of effort

Experience must be systematically accumulated, standardized and applied.

Second law of effort

Effort must be economically regulated in four ways

1. It must be divided.
2. It must be coördinated.
3. It must be conserved.
4. It must be remunerated.

Third law of effort

Personal effectiveness must be promoted (six ways)—

1. Good physical conditions and environment must be maintained.
2. The vocation, task or duty should be analyzed to determine the special human faculty concerned.
3. Tests should be applied to determine in what degree candidates possess this faculty.
4. Habit should be formed on standardized bases, old or new.
5. *Esprit de corps* must be fostered.
6. Incentive must be proportioned to effort expected.

In regard to these laws of effort, it may be said that while they have always been implied in manufacturing activity of every kind, most of them have only recently become revealed to the consciousness of managers. Taking the first law: it is obvious that experience has always been, more or less, the basis of action, but the <u>systematic</u> gathering of all experience available, and its standardization, must be regarded as a very modern development. In former times, indeed, the practice was all the other way about. Men refused to exchange experience and guarded jealously every little advance they made, as a trade secret of the direst importance. This attitude is not yet dead; but in proportion as industry takes on a scientific character, it is rapidly fading. It is beginning to be realized that the exchange of experience and data of all kinds is far more important to both the individual and the industry than any private cornering of ideas can possibly be.

The <u>division</u> of effort has, at least since the days of Adam Smith, been recognized as the foundation of the industrial system. But in proportion as the division is carried further and further, the necessity for <u>coördination</u> of the divided threads becomes more pressing. Coördination may be defined as the avoidance of "gap and overlap". In modern factory organization it has assumed immense importance. The <u>conservation</u> of effort as an end to be consciously sought out is both an old practice and a new departure. At the outset of the factory system it was studied in a fashion that was both minute and far-reaching. The famous mathematician, Charles Babbage, described some of the methods and their results as far back as 1832. But in the intervening years the vast development of industry and the necessity to produce quickly, rather than with minute economy, apparently led to the abandonment of these analytical methods until their re-discovery and re-application by the late Frederick W. Taylor. Modern practice demands that every stage of effort, not only as regards operation, but also in other functions, be conserved to the utmost, so that the maximum effect may be forthcoming from a given expenditure of energy. The <u>remuneration</u> of effort, in this connection (that of the second law), has reference to the discovery by analytical methods of the special type of efficiency that must be rewarded in each class of work. Thus, in some work exactness, in other, punctuality, inventive faculty, or initiative may be the proper basis for special remuneration. This division of the second law is as yet not very far advanced in application.

153

The two laws of effort just described have to do with effort in the abstract; the third law has to do with the individuals who put forth the effort. The general tendency of the law is much like the attitude of a good gardener, inasmuch as it deals with the cultivation of individual effectiveness, as the gardener deals with the conditions efficient for the raising of fine plants.

This also is largely of modern development. In the beginning of the factory system it was not only wholly ignored, but would have been looked on almost as a heresy. The days of *laisser faire* and unbridled individualism had no place for any such "sentimental" doctrines. It was strictly up to the individual to make the best of the situation. If conditions were bad, so much the worse for the individual.

This doctrine is now exploded—not for, or not only for, sentimental reasons. Neglect to promote personal effectiveness of those he employs is found to be bad business by the employer. Hence the third law of effort is now firmly established.

The first subdivision of the law indicates the necessity for good physical conditions and environment for all workers. This implies that light, air, quiet, safety, and wholesomeness in reasonable degree, according to the nature of the work to be performed, are to be looked on as essential to efficiency. In reasonable, rather than absolute, degree, because necessarily the standard for one occupation is not that for another. But all avoidable departures from these standards are to be eliminated. The principle regards the human organism in relation to its reaction to the environment, and no psychological principle is better established both theoretically and practically. Hence arises the necessity for ensuring that the environment is as satisfactory as it can possibly be made, having in view the nature of the work to be done.

The second and third subdivisions of this law are very new indeed. The idea of vocational fitness is hardly yet familiar. Its general idea may be found in the application of tests to determine color-blindness in the case of mariners and locomotive engineers. This is, of course, a very elementary case, but application of the law is in course of expansion at the present time. Certain occupations are found to call for certain physical and psychical qualifications, such as memory, calculation, self-reliance, personal strength, quick reaction, inflexibility, etc. The desirability of determining these qualifications for any post, and then of selecting the candidates by tests that demonstrate their possession of these qualities is obviously very desirable, in as far as it can be done in practice. It would prevent misfits and exclude the square pegs from the round holes, without the humiliating experience of failure. It would, conversely, steer the candidates towards the occupations for which they were best fitted. Not a great deal has been accomplished in this direction as yet, though the field is a promising one. Unfortunately in a region so subtle and uncharted as human faculty, the opportunity of the quack occurs. Some of the theories put forward in this field are as preposterous as the claims of the old-time phrenologists, which indeed they are based upon. Much time must elapse, and much examination of the subject by competent and trained investigators working with a scientific and not a money-making end immediately in view is necessary, before any practical assistance can be obtained from these new tendencies.

155

The fourth subdivision of the third law of effort suggests the importance of correct habit. This is a very promising field. Habit should be formed, that is, consciously formed, on standardized bases. These bases are not necessarily new. Thus, punctuality is such a standard, but of course has always been recognized as important. We may consider, however, the case of industrial and, particularly, operative habit which is being disturbed and reformed by the application of time- and motion-study to existing practice. Habit cannot be changed in a moment. As Mr. James Hartness has pointed out "habit possesses inertia". Therefore, in introducing new practice it must be done gradually, that is, by instalments, allowing time for each successive instalment to overcome inertia, to displace old habit and finally to become established as new habit.

The fifth subdivision deals with the formation of *esprit de corps*. This is not the same thing as team work, though it sometimes includes it. The nearest English equivalent to the phrase may be found in "group pride". The man who believes in his group will exert himself for its welfare beyond the strict letter of his bond. Belief in the purpose for which the group exists is the first essential, and in industrial affairs this means belief in the firm, in its product, in its superiority to other firms in the same line. Naturally, this condition of mind cannot be brought about by any mechanism. It must grow out of the environment, out of a sense of confidence in the justice meted out to all and sundry, out of fairness and pleasant relations with all the individuals to be associated with. Some attempt is made by firms with large selling staffs to furnish such information as will create enthusiasm for the product and for the work of selling it, but very little progress has been made to extend this idea to the manufacturing force also. In some cases it could be done with excellent results, and whatever lends interest to the daily work, and reveals that it has an importance in the world at large, will certainly assist in developing group pride. Neither can coöperation be considered as an equivalent to *esprit de corps*. It is sometimes claimed that this or that system of management gives rise to a spirit of coöperation. But to speak of a spirit of co-öperation is something of a misnomer. Coöperation is not an end of itself; it is a result of something. Men will not coöperate for the sake of coöperating, or because they are told it is a fine thing to do. They will coöperate if their attention is focussed on a definite end, and this end may be an indefinite and intangible one, like the honor of the regiment or the credit of the plant. In fact, the more intangible the end, so long as it contains a definite principle, the better. This, however, is *esprit de corps*—a larger issue that controls the will of men unconsciously. Wherever it can be developed it is an asset of the highest value.

The final subdivision of the third law of effort states that incentive must be proportioned to effort expected. This is a vast subject and would take another paper to do it justice. The various rival systems of management that have been put forward in recent years have for the most part some special method of payment by results as their foundation. The different methods are generally divided into piecework, premium and bonus. Among all these various systems there is a strong family likeness, and the difference between them is not so great as many per-

156

sons have been disposed to think. They attain closely related
results by rather similar paths. The difference between them re-
solves itself for the most part into the shifting backward and
forward of time-limits, allowances and tasks, and the greater or
less share that is retained by the employer or given to the man
at various degrees of attainment. It must not be forgotten that
the modern systems have been accompanied by a large use of
analysis (time- and motion-study) which gives them precision
far beyond what was attainable under any system a decade or
so ago. But the use of such analysis need not be confined to
bonus systems; it could equally well be applied to setting piece-
work rates. Under such circumstances, I do not believe that any
one system would be found to have great advantage over another. Probably each of them might be applied to certain
special conditions with greater success than another, but that
is a different matter from a universal superiority.

157

The present condition of the science or art of management
is one of assimilation and digestion rather than of active change.
After a period of discovery and invention has come a period of
application and modification. This is likely to continue for some
time. The high tide of excitement and enthusiasm caused by the
introduction of analytical methods has receded, and a more dispassionate view of the situation is being taken generally. It is
beginning to be realized that, just as a study of military science
does not produce great generals, so a knowledge of the science
of management, inasfar as it can be called a science at the present stage of its development, will not produce great managers.
The man has to bring something to the study in each case. A
knowledge of mechanisms and of principles is of the greatest
value, but the competent manager, like the great general, is born
and not made. In all cases where men are associated together
for a common end, the influence of personality is enormous, and
there is no mechanical substitute for it. The elusive element,
"capacity", yields to no analysis, and the synthetic influence of
a strong personality must remain, as in the past, the great indis-
pensible factor in industrial management.

DISCUSSION

Mr. Holaday.   **Mr. Fred M. Holaday*** said he would like to have some discussion of the measurement of the human element and to know if the science of phrenology is of any use.

Mr. Duncan.   **Mr. L. Duncan,†** Mem. Am. Soc. M. E., said that in connection with the question of workingmen's psychology, many firms are establishing employment bureaus, endeavoring to fit men to the job. It is an economic crime to put a man in a place he is not fit to fill. Phrenology will indicate what class of work a man is best suited for. A lady, Dr. Blackford, has done much in this line and conducts a correspondence school, teaching how to select the right people for a given job.

Mr. Dickie.   **Mr. Geo. W. Dickie,‡** Vice-Pres., Am. Soc. M. E., remarked that the human element is a very large factor in all management. Its control has never been figured out by any known process. There is no place for so-called scientific management. The introduction of a new line of men who make cards for workmen to fill out, places a barrier between the designer and the workman.

158

Mr. Church.   **Mr. A. Hamilton Church,** in closing, said that attempts to resuscitate the so-called science of phrenology should be viewed with the gravest reserve. The judgment of scientific men in the matter is well represented by the following words of Professor Alexander Macalister, F. R. S., in the latest edition of the Encyclopaedia Britannica (Art. Phrenology). "Psychology, physiology and experience alike contribute to discredit the practical working of the system, and to show how worthless such diagnoses of character really are . . . it is capable of doing positive social harm, as in its proposed application to the discrimination or selection of subordinate officials".

The pioneer in applied psychology (which must be carefully distinguished from phrenology), Professor Muensterberg, of Harvard, has also issued warnings as to the danger of premature attempts to apply cut and dried rules and formulas for the determination of vocational fitness. Only exhaustive research by trained psychologists applied to particular and definite problems can delimit either the qualifications required for any task or the data on which candidates for such work can be accepted or rejected. The whole subject is in its infancy, and though of great promise, the most intolerable injustice would result from premature and unintelligent attempts to apply it practically at the present time.

---

* Mechanical Engineer, Oakland, Calif.
† Mech. Engr., Nevada Cons. Copper Co., McGill, Nev.
‡ Naval Arch., San Francisco, Calif.

THE FUTURE OF INDUSTRY

I. Movements Beneath the Surface

IN attempting to pierce the veil that separates us from a vision of the future, even of the immediate future, it is necessary to remember that all such attempts must be purely speculative. We should therefore at all costs avoid the temptation to be dogmatic, and not take our attempt too seriously. It is in this spirit that the suggestions to be made in the present article are offered. They are guesses, founded on observation of certain new tendencies that are abroad. But how far they are correct guesses, only time can show. Their best justification lies in the absorbing interest which the future possesses for every progressive mind.

It is the opinion of many people, and this opinion is sometimes met in somewhat unexpected quarters, that our present economic system has passed its zenith of usefulness, and is becoming less and less adapted to modern needs with every passing year. That it often gives rise to undue concentration of such wealth as is produced is too obvious to need argument, but there is also good reason to suppose that as a wealth-producing mechanism, it is not far from being abreast of the possibilities engendered by the enormous development of man's control over nature during the past century and a half.

If, as some suppose, the economic machine is becoming unworkable, one of three things must happen. It may be altered in direction and aim, gradually and without convulsion or breakdown. It may end in catastrophe of the most alarming kind. It may be gradually superseded by a new system that will grow up alongside it, and draw the life out of it by degrees, precisely as commercialism grew up alongside the later feudal system, and gradually drew the life out of it until it decayed.

It is not very difficult to guess the direction from which this new system will come. The nineteenth century saw the highest development of political democracy that the world has ever known. The twentieth century will see the development of economic democracy.

This will not be reached, as far as one can judge, by any vast *bouleversement* of existing things. The socialist dream of waking up one morning in a socialized world, brought into being by decree of a committee of Public Welfare, self-appointed, is not likely to mature. When the feudal world was superseded it was not taken over bodily as a running concern by the commercial world. On the contrary, the latter rose gradually into power from many centres, and its rise was accompanied by many failures and setbacks, so that the substitution of "contract" for "status" — the great legal distinction between the two forms of social organization — was so gradual that neither its beginning nor its end can be marked with certainty. It does not seem any more likely that a new social order, if such is immanent in present movements, will come into being by taking over the social or industrial mechanism of the present day, if only because such mechanism is utterly unsuited for the expression of new social relations. It may be, indeed, that the vast complexity of the modern industrial world is only a temporary phase, just as the commercial system that succeeded the feudal was, organically, a far simpler and looser one. This of course looks unlikely *now*, but not more so than the other change must have looked *then*.

It is not impossible to suppose that the germs of a new order of economic relationship are already sown. That, of course, is not practically important now, unless we can also perceive something of the path which is likely to lead from the old to the new. It must be confessed that something of the eye of faith is necessary to make the connection, more particularly as it is not in this country, but in Europe, that the most promising beginnings are to be observed. Yet it also seems probable that it must be in America, still the land of endless possibility and opportunity, that the most energetic experimental development must take place.

It is a curious fact that it is in democratic America that the organization of industry has developed along the lines of absolutism. In Europe on the contrary, such organization has reached out toward democratic forms and in certain instances has already developed them to a wonderful degree. To discuss the reason for this would lead us outside our present subject, which is to discuss the new ferments already working, and endeavor to appraise their value in the future.

161

Industry is based on three main elements. First, the possession of natural resources. Without these it cannot exist. The Eskimo has developed his civilization on snow as a building material, blubber and fish as diet, skins as clothing, and the bones of fish and bears as raw material for manufacture. Considering his material, he has done reasonably well. Modern civilization is built on coal and iron, and it is the possession of these resources that determines its whole course, and makes it so different from anything that has gone before.

The next element of industry is the productive unit. Formerly a large part of the industry of the world was carried out by very small groups of men, even by single workers. To-day, the tendency is to enlarge the size of the productive unit, until its organization has become a science in itself. Within the productive unit, order reigns. Each function to be performed is determined in advance, both qualitatively and quantitatively. There is no scramble, no uncertainty as to who is to do this work and who that. Men compete with each other to get into the productive unit, and they rival each other in qualifying for more responsible work, but within the unit neither gap

nor overlap is permitted, and the work of everyone is co-
ordinated most carefully; each is engaged on a complete
engineering proposition — the application of forces to
materials on a definite basis to a definite end.

If that were all the problem that industry affords, our
troubles would be very much fewer than they are. Trial
and error would in the long run work out a plan for the
just distribution of the fruits of work among those that
participate in it, and those that provide the sinews of war.

But unfortunately there is a third element in industry
that is not yet brought under the reign of scientific law.
While each productive unit in its internal structure is
an example of coördinated activity, industry as a whole
is still in the stage of being wholly uncoördinated, and is
in fact a veritable scramble, very much as if in a factory,
each new job were to be thrown on the floor and the whole
body of workers invited to fight for its possession.

From this want of adjustment arise some of the most
bitter struggles, and many of the greatest distresses of
the modern world. Unemployment is largely due to it.
And so little is the matter understood that the fiercest
invective and the strongest opposition are applied to anyone who attempts, as regards any particular trade, to
set up a more or less approximate coördination of the
industry by consolidating productive units, and cutting
out superfluous energies in the production and distribution of goods. The moment this is attempted, the cry
is raised that "competition" is imperilled, whereas the
power of competition depends on quite other conditions
that have little to do with consolidation.

It is impossible to discuss matters like these without
coming at once into the presence of the idea of "competition" and its obverse, "combination," about which
the foggiest notions generally prevail. In speaking of
"competition," as the life-blood of progress, it is entirely
forgotten that there are no more changeable things than
the *forms* of competition, and that they are by no means

confined to the strife of the spear and the strife of the market. What we term competition is in general a very crude form of measurement of capacity, and though it is quite certain that capacity will always differ as among individuals, and will always find its own level, it is equally certain that the particular form suitable for one age will be unsuitable for another. In a barbaric military age, thews and sinews and physical courage will be the elements of competition; in a mercantile age, shrewdness and cunning. In a scientific age, such as we are now entering on, still higher faculties than to prod one's competitor with a spear, or delude him in a bargain, will be called on, with necessarily a more marked shifting of the play of competition to another arena.

163

While therefore it is quite reasonable to say that competition must be maintained, it is quite another matter to assert that *some particular variety* of competition of the moment should be maintained. To say that it is for the public advantage that ten firms in the same industry, with a total capacity exceeding any possible demand for their goods, should be compelled to maintain expensive individual selling organizations, and scramble for each order that comes into the market, instead of dividing them up on a pro-rating basis, seems illogical. It means the diversion of attention from the prime work of production. It means unnecessary fluctuations in the amount of work handled by each firm. It means unemployment here, and over-employment there. It means plant idle in one place, and overburdened in another. And who benefits?

It is evident that if these productive units combine, either on the Trust plan, which means centralized control, or on the Cartel plan, which means a kind of parliament for that industry, the stream of production is steadied, and, *provided that a market monopoly is not used to raise prices*, no one is harmed. It is evident, therefore, that the evil of combination lies not in the fact of combination, but in the improper use of the power of monopoly that such consolidation may make possible. The evil does not arise from the elimination of a certain kind of competition among the firms themselves, but in the possibility of their using their combination to raise prices.

In the ordinary course, such conduct would bring its own penalty. High prices would invite new competition outside the combine, and force prices down. In a perfectly free and open market, no combination could afford to run that risk. But if they can succeed in some method of cornering the market, and driving out new competition before it has time to gather head, then we have an illustration of the successful but wholly illegitimate use of the advantages of combination. It should be noted, however, that a new variety of competition is concerned here, namely, competition between the combine as a whole and a new comer. *That* is the competition that it is to the public interest to see maintained.

How can an open market be maintained? Feebly and uncertainly by legislation, because there are as clever minds on the side of the combine as on the side of the state. And while the state can only legislate for particular conditions as it discovers them, the combine can shift its ground very rapidly, and so evade the law. But there is one way of doing it that will put the strongest combine on its good behavior at once and for ever, and that is by an answering combine of *consumers*. Is such a thing possible? Let the facts answer. In England, the cooperative societies maintained by the working people are now estimated to embrace one-fifth of the population, and the turnover of their transactions is already some $550,000,000 yearly. The most powerful trust would hesitate to play tricks with an organized body of consumers like that. Except by a monopoly of raw material (perhaps the easiest form of monopoly to reach by the regulation of the law), there is no possible answer to the demand for competitive price when consumers as a whole insist on it.

All this has been introduced for the purpose of showing that what appears to be the most portentous industrial phenomena of our day, tending to overwhelm the people in the grip of an industrial autocracy, are really not what they seem. No form of wealth is more fragile and evanescent than that engaged in production. Nothing is more timid than capital when it finds itself in presence of superior forces intelligently applied. There is only one form of ownership that confers lordship, and that is ownership of land. The largest and best organized plant, capitalized in millions, rapidly falls to the value of scrap-iron, once the fertilizing stream of "orders" is diverted from it. And as a speculative fantasy one might imagine a time when people will come to gaze on the vast decaying ruins of the twentieth century trust plants, as they now go to gaze on the ruins of the feudal castles of Europe. But let us hope that it will not come to that.

We observe, then, a tendency to consolidation and to the elimination of unnecessary competition, but this tendency is itself but the expression of a need imperatively felt, namely, for *a form of coördination between the productive units themselves and the entire output of the industry*. It is this that really gives strength to the combining movement. It is this that is both its impulse and its justification. To expect to roll it back is like ordering the advancing tide to recede. We may expect to prevent its abuse, but the only way in which this can be done permanently is by an answering coördination, that of consumers. But if we once assume that the whole body of consumers can be organized and their wants coördinated, we step at once into a wholly new economic world, that will have very little real relation to the present system. It is evident, however, that this must be a slow development, and cannot take place overnight.

This principle of coöperation has made enormous strides already. In addition to the British coöperative societies and those of other countries, the movement has spread to the most individual of all callings — agriculture. Here it has had a double development, association for purchase, and association for common manufacture and common sale. On the one hand, groups of agriculturalists combine to standardize, purchase, and test the qualities of seeds, fertilizers, and other supplies, thus rescuing the individual from greedy exploitation, and what is worse, deception as to the quality of goods, which had reached enormous proportions. On the other hand, groups are formed to receive, standardize, and distribute products on a wholesale scale, thus again rescuing the individual from exploitation by those who received a large reward for a very poor and inefficient distribution or marketing service. Further, the organization of associated producers has led to proper grading of product, associated with definite brands, so that the buyer knows in advance what he is ordering and paying for, without the necessity of close inspection of each consignment.

In particular may be cited the great work done by the Irish Agricultural Organization Society founded by Sir Horace Plunkett in 1894. In 1911 this organization had grown to a membership of 100,000, in 900 branches, and an annual turnover of $15,000,000. Combined with its regular activities is a department advancing funds to credit societies, and it was recently reported that out of loan transactions aggregating $90,000, only $500 had been irrecoverable.

In Denmark the dairy industry has been transformed by the introduction of coöperative creameries, which now handle four-fifths of all the milk of the country, and produce butter to the value of $45,000,000 annually. Danish agriculture may be said to be almost entirely conducted on coöperative plans, — purchasing societies, egg societies, bacon-curing societies and so forth being universal. It is said that a Danish farmer frequently has membership in as many as ten such societies, each dealing with a different branch of his business. In Germany the movement has also made good progress though only of recent introduction. The *syndicats agricoles* of France number thousands, and their principal trading function is the purchase of farm requisites, especially fertilizers, for their members on a large scale, and with the guarantees which large transactions are able to command. In the United States some noteworthy producers' societies, both for purchase and marketing, also exist and have exhibited strong vitality and growth.

Such coöperative associations are examples of organic forms of productive units not dependent on single ownership, or on stockholding ownership. They represent the principle of *voluntary* association, and may be likened more to a college team for baseball or football than to an ordinary commercial firm. They perform all the functions of the latter with an entirely different fundamental idea at their base. Here, then, is one new influence creeping into our present-day economic system, that is in it, but not of it, and may be considered to represent a type of organization of which more will be heard in the future.

Closely allied with the question of such voluntary productive units, with their coöperative buying function, and their coöperative selling function, is the development of a new variety of finance, of which again the most widespread examples are to be found in agricultural industry. The so-called "Mutual Credit" movement has made enormous strides in European countries, and has in many cases wholly transformed the economic position of those who operate under it.

The general idea is a very simple one. Suppose a neighborhood group of twenty or thirty farmers associating themselves to borrow money for reproductive improvements, — the money being borrowed on the liability of all the members, and loaned to an individual member on

167

his personal responsibility. No profits are sought. All debts of the association are backed by the mutual liability, unlimited. Loans may be in cash, if necessary, but are frequently in kind, the association purchasing at wholesale, and selling on credit to their members. For convenience the local associations are grouped in larger district and national associations, forming banks, — one German example of a central bank does business with some 5000 local associations. Here we have a considerable financial system, throughout which no private profit is sought, yet which by the peculiar principle of its fundamental idea exercises a continuous pressure towards efficiency that no privately exploited financial system can exert.

The fundamental idea is simply that the granting of loans is based on the responsibility of the borrower, not in a property sense, but in a moral and efficiency sense. The whole idea rests on the fact that the local groups are small enough for each member to be thoroughly known to his fellow members. Theirs is the responsibility for the loan, and consequently they take good care to investigate the borrower and his projects from every point of view that affects the question of repayment. He must be a capable man in every sense. He must be reliable, a man of his word. The purpose for which he asks the money must be an approved one, and likely in the judgment of his fellow members to produce the results he claims for it. And they are not likely to fail in their scrutiny, since in that case they have to bear the loss that may ensue. It will be seen that this system supplies capital to capacity on the sanest and safest terms, and without any fuss or feathers.

Another influence that is making itself felt in the modern world is that of Insurance.

The modern tendency is to make Insurance compulsory. This is as it should be. As the idea develops, and it is only as yet in its infancy, it will be extended to every kind of mishap that is unforeseeable as far as the indi-

168

vidual is concerned, but calculable as far as the mass is concerned.   When.this has been done a tremendous burden of misery will have been lifted from the shoulders of humanity.   Instead of great organizations to pick people up after they have fallen down, they will be prevented from falling down at all, and in that respect our present system will seem extraordinarily barbaric in comparison. Insurance will be to the social process like a flywheel to a reciprocating steam engine.   It will continue prosperity between the strokes — between the life happenings tending to progress — and convert a spasmodic motion into a smooth and regular one.

These three new principles — coöperation, mutual credit, and insurance — have come into operation in the modern world so gradually and so silently that their significance has been to a large extent over-looked.   They represent ideas wholly foreign to our forefathers, and the proof is that many worthy persons look uneasily on their progress even now.   Sub-consciously, perhaps, they are perceived to be likely to undermine the structure of economic society as we know it, for they all tend to the democratization of industry, and to the restoration of the individual to his place in the sun of which the so-called "industrial revolution" deprived him.

Is this so?   Do these movements represent a force tending to form new economic organisms, and to disintegrate the present forms?   I do not think it can be denied that this must be their effect.   Whatever tends to free the individual and enchance his powers and his responsibility must, unless democracy is the sham that its opponents claim it to be, prove in the end attractive to the stronger individuals, and be adopted by them.   It is, I venture to say, a very hopeful outlook, against which a continuance of the present system has very little to offer.   The *coördination* of industry by the association of consumers, the free *association* of producers with free *access* to capital in proportion to capacity, the *averaging*

169

out of the largest portion of human calamity by the agency of insurance, make a picture that is as yet far off from realization, but is at least commenced and sketched out.

Now let us attempt to connect these elements of a new economic age with the present position of manufacturing industry.

II. *The Promise of the Future*

Social forces, in their inception, are nearly always blind forces. They arise no one knows how, and they operate along the line of least resistance long before their presence is recognized. The village community grew into the manor, and the manor into the complex organization of feudalism, so imperceptibly that no clear dividing line can be found. In the same way modern "capitalist" industry rose by such slow degrees, and from such very small beginnings, that even half-way in its career the most gifted seer could not have predicted its future dominion. Factory industry has enormously developed within the memory of men still living. None of these evolutions was brought about by conscious planning of statesmen or social reformers. They simply happened, — our way of saying that the causes are deeper than our ken.

Before we can guess at the proximate developments likely to take place in the evolution of industry, it will be necessary to try to understand the general tendency — the shape and direction of the curve — of the new movement. We must begin with the most general terms and then narrow down the problem until it comes, however slightly, within the grasp of practical endeavor.

The most general statement that seems likely to be true is that already indicated — that the direction of evolution is towards the democratization of industry. And secondly that this process will be accompanied by a rise in the importance of the individual, *based on an increased capacity for voluntary coöperation in organized work*.

This, of course, is a very vague statement. We can

however proceed to give it a little more definiteness. To do this we must consider the citizen from the point of view of his function of consumer apart from his function as producer. And we must also glance at his position simply as a living being.

The latter may be dismissed in a few words. It has to do with the applied law of Average, in the form of Insurance, as already referred to. Unquestionably, as statistical science extends its dominion, very few of the mishaps of life will be left outside the operation of this principle. The process of civilization upward from primitive savagery is, in fact, a continual increase of safeguarding of the individual from mishap. The savage is at the mercy of nature to a degree infinitely greater than the civilized man. He cannot control the flood, nor fight the fire. Disease to him is the act of a hostile power. His cattle die, or his crops are blighted by the anger of the gods, where the civilized man sees only microbes. And this process of collective action on the ills, and collective bearing of the burden of mishap, obviously must develop until men may walk with little fear, and much confidence that whatever befalls them beyond their individual power to prevent, the whole power of society will *automatically remedy*, not by way of charity, but by way of mutual protection and organization.

There remains the position of the individual as consumer and as producer. With the former we have but little concern here, although it is precisely in this field that the most momentous developments may be expected in the future. For on the organization of the consumer depends the successful coördination of the productive power of society, and its rescue from the arena of hap-hazard struggle in which it now exists. Upon this organization also depends the substitution of a sane and ordered finance for our present method, which suggests the collection of eggs by a farmer from under haystacks and barns and from all manner of odd corners wherever the hens hap-

171

pened to lay them, and then the assembly of the collected eggs in enormous masses, whereby breakages on a
great scale are in frequent danger of happening. This,
however, is beyond our present field of inquiry, though
the new development of "Mutual Credit" shows that
in this field also new ferments are working.

We are thus left face to face with the question of the
individual in his function as producer. Now the most
general term in which we can express the tendency that
seems in the air with regard to him is unquestionably
the transformation of the productive unit from an organization of master and servant to an organization, such
as we have seen has already been developed widely in
agriculture, of voluntary and independent associates.
Of course, this culmination is a long way off, as yet.
Industry requires an infinitely more complex organization than does agriculture, though probably, as time
goes on, some of its present complexity will be lost, and
simplification ensue.

We cannot avoid the issue once we get it squarely
presented to our minds. Are we to assist in the transformation of men into "hands" or the development of
"hands" into men? And if we believe that it is our duty
to assist and not hinder the coming of economic democracy,
what is it in our power to do, consistently with present
responsibilities, to foster the coming of the change?

Again we must have resource to very general terms in
an attempt to solve this problem. For what we are alone
able to do is to encourage a social force that is working
out its own ends. We may hinder it, or we may remove
obstacles from its path. But we do not know enough
about its working (or that of any social force) to control
it actively. We are not called on at this stage to consider
the type of the future organizations that it will bring
forth, although we might guess at these, too, if necessary.

Nor can we consider problems arising out of the present
uncoördinated condition of industry. At present whole

172

productive units may be swept away, bought up, forced out of the running, subjected to operations much like those of predatory warfare. It is obvious that such a fate for any productive unit does not depend at all on its internal organization. It happens because industry as a whole is not organized in the same way as each productive unit is organized within itself. The answer to part of the problem will be found, as already suggested, in the coördination of industry by the association of consumers, and the application of searching statistical methods so that productive energy will not be applied where it is not wanted, but precisely where it is wanted.

173

The great English coöperative consumers' movement, with its annual turnover of $500,000,000 in household and domestic supplies is, of course, an example confined to a particular field. The agricultural societies that purchase seeds, fertilizers, and machinery for their constituent members are an example in another field. It is not unthinkable that such organizations may be extended, area by area until the principal fields of consumption are covered. This would bring about an immense steadying of industry and a great decrease of speculative entry into any productive field in which there was really no need for additional productive facilities.

Our problem is, here, confined to the relations of men associated for production within a productive unit, and the encouragement of whatever social force is at work to transform such units from the present type to a true democratic type of free associates. *Not actually to transform them,* be it understood, *but to give free play to the forces that seem to be acting in the direction of so transforming them* at some future time. There is a difference between these two aims. The first is Utopian; the second within the bounds of practical possibility.

To begin with, it is necessary to distinguish between the opportunity to rise and the opportunity to develop. While it is, of course, most important that the avenue to higher positions shall be kept open and made available as far as possible to members of the rank and file, it must be recognized that this alone is no solution of the problem. Though every private may carry a marshal's baton in his knapsack, it is obvious that very few can ever attain possession of that baton. The law of average in Human Faculty shows that the possession of capacity is comparatively rare, and no amount of education, especially of the book-learning kind, can change the bearing of this law. The important part of the problem is the provision of opportunity for the rank and file to develop, quite apart from the rise of certain units out of it. It is action on the mass of ordinary men that is required, rather than the cultivation of exceptional men, for the latter are able to take care of themselves under any social or economic system. In the closest autocracies men have always risen from the ranks to high position, while the condition of the bulk of the people has remained wretched enough.

They must in some way be brought into the system, while remaining relatively speaking, just a mass of ordinary men. I wish to emphasize this point, because it is not always clearly perceived. Many persons suppose that some equilibrium can be reached by arranging that the ordinary man shall have an opportunity of *rising above his fellows*. They lay stress on night schools, educational facilities, libraries, and so forth, and believe that these agencies are really all that are necessary to give contentment. These are excellent institutions of course, particularly if they effect a general rising of the level of education throughout the mass. But they no more affect the main question than one can affect the level of a reservoir by pouring in a few buckets of water.

In the same way, no permanent equilibrium can be expected from the introduction of special forms of wage remuneration. The tendency of organized labor is to oppose these, just because organized labor has a very clear view of what it is after, and that is not the cultivation of exceptional men. In as far as injudicious employers yield to the temptation to force the pace by setting up standards of performance based on the work of the most skilful and energetic men, organized labor is found, naturally enough, in bitter opposition to these special forms of remuneration. The meaning of this attitude should be dispassionately examined by employers. It is not due to a desire to prevent its own members from reaping the fullest reward of their capacity, but to a fear that their general class solidarity will be to some extent disrupted by the separation of the interests of the more capable men from those of the less capable.

175

As no such individual jealousy is exhibited towards those members who pass out of the ranks of the class into the higher organization, it is evident that we have here an attitude that is dictated by some very strong perception of consequences. What these are there can be no manner of doubt. Men who pass into the higher organization are lost to the rank and file, it is true, but they are in no sense competing with the internal interests of the rank and file. They may acquire different and even to some extent antagonistic interests, but they are not doing the same work as those who remain. Now the man of special capacity who earns large bonuses is doing the same work as his fellows. He is getting a larger share of the wage fund than they. They regard him as taking away from his fellows work that they would otherwise have an opportunity to do. In the long run this is always a fallacy. Demand tends to rise in proportion as cost falls, and the superior man's larger wages come from product that would not exist but for his superior capacity; but from the peculiar and personal point of view of the employee it is difficult to attain this perspective. Organized labor clings to the doctrine, however often it may be exploded, and more particularly dreads the possibility of cleavage in its own ranks that might sometime arise therefrom.

We may take it, then, that, however valuable it might be economically, organized labor will not accept the proffer of opportunity for the individual to rise, as any substitute for opportunity to develop *as a class*. Unfortunately at that point its contribution to the problem generally ends. It can bring forward no constructive plans, save a general attitude of watchful waiting for opportunity to force wages up. But as a general rise of wages has no other effect than to induce a general rise of prices, it is evident that this process is simply a vicious circle, and that not only can labor never gain on the higher organization of industry by such means, but that the contest is one that must continue for ever, with all its attendant loss, bitterness, and misery.

A little consideration of this problem shows that it has many solutions, or at least partial solutions. These may vary all the way from modest attempts at group remuneration — such as for example a dividend on wages to all the members of a specific function, *e. g.*, the power plant, dependent on the general efficiency reached in any period — up to general profit-sharing schemes in which dividends are set aside in such a way that the workers gradually acquire a share in the ownership of the business. To begin with, such a form of organization is obviously but little removed from present forms, and that in fact is its chief point of interest. But that it affords a bridge over which industry may pass by steady development from master-and-servant to more coöperative forms is more than probable. Its hopefulness lies in the educative influence brought to bear on the ordinary man, and in the intensified economic value his services thus acquire, without separating him from his class.

Such an outcome is not a mere figment of the imagination. Apart from the classic examples of the Godin Ironworks and other well-known French coöperative establishments, a great deal of experiment along the lines of coöperative production has taken place in England.

This has taken two forms, one a type of organization permitting the workers to acquire an interest in the business — a type that has been introduced with considerable success in the United States also — and another a type which may be described as purely democratic, in which the workers themselves are voluntarily associated, elect their own "bosses," and carry on business for themselves. Over 100 of these latter societies exist in England and Scotland at the present time, with an aggregate turnover of some $21,000,000. Many of them have existed for years, and have always exhibited healthy growth. It is a significant fact that those most successful are more or less closely affiliated with the great coöperative consumers' movement spoken of above.

177

The subject cannot be fully considered without taking into account the presence in the field of the systematic organization of Labor in Trade Unions. The trade union is the outgrowth of the general dissociation of interests between the mass of the workers and the higher organization of industry. It is based on the idea that while the individual is very weak and helpless as compared with this higher organization, a sufficiently strong combination of workers is able to establish and maintain standards of wages and hours beyond what would otherwise be conceded. Though their way of doing this is commonly based on the procedure of "trial and error," and is consequently very disturbing to industry and in fact is not infrequently unjust to individual employers, there seems no reason why, by degrees, they should not bring themselves to coöperate with employers in a veritable industrial parliament, based on the principle of opportunity to develop, rather than on opportunity to rise.

A platform of greater confidence, and interchange of views between organized labor and the higher organizations of particular industries, would give rise to a higher type of Unionism, and also to a more uniformly higher view on the part of employers. Mr. Carroll D. Wright has observed that the larger and better organized Unions are more disposed to be reasonable than the smaller and weaker ones. In the same way regular coöperation and discussion between workers and employers would bring to the front men on both sides of large caliber, and assist in relegating to the background the hot-heads and irreconcilables who can never see reason.

The foregoing discussion may now be summed up, and a general view taken of the influences at work in the modern world. In the first place the difficulty of the position of the American manufacturer must be recognized. His is not an easy task. Compared with his contemporaries in European countries, where the mass of workers have a common tradition, a common standard of life, and a common language, the material on which he has to work is not at first sight a promising one. But on the other hand he has some advantages that the others have not. The pace is faster, the atmosphere more electric, the desire to progress more intense. The mistakes and even the bitternesses of yesterday are more quickly passed by and forgotten in the aspirations towards the future — though this may work in two directions, producing a more constant tension and expectation of disturbance as well. Nevertheless, on the whole his advantages are perhaps greater than those of his European confrères. And he himself is less bound by tradition, less certain that he is of other clay than those he employs. Perhaps on the whole, he is far more sympathetic with the idea that opportunity to develop as well as opportunity to rise shall be provided as rapidly as possible.

Next we observe that the movement toward consolidation of industry, whatever the evils that arise from the present form of that consolidation, is due to the steady pressure of an impulse that cannot be denied or turned back — the necessity for coördinating the external relation of productive units just as their interior mechanism has already been coördinated. The answer to the abuses of this tendency will probably be found, not in legislative attempts to turn back the tide, but in a corresponding coördination of consumers' demands in the future, perhaps no very distant future in some cases. Such coördination will probably be piece-meal, and by no means nation-wide, at any rate to begin with. The example of what has been done in England in this connection was introduced as a proof that the tendency exists, and is not merely an academic possibility.

It was also noticed that the principle of coöperation has passed in the case of agriculture into three streams of influence — common purchase; common manufacture, as in creameries and bacon factories; and common marketing. The progress made in some cases can only be described as truly revolutionary. It has also been introduced into that most tangled of all modern problems — finance. Mutual credit, as yet largely, though not wholly, confined to agricultural operations, is the germ of a force that cannot fail to transform industrial relations also when the time arrives for its application in that direction.

179

Finally, the relations between the higher organization of industry, and the mass of workers as producers were considered. The difference between opportunity to rise and opportunity to develop is an important one. The latter is the crucial question at the present time. The desire to preserve solidarity of interests within the ranks of the workers was noted as a phenomenon that must be reckoned with and allowed for in any attempt to develop higher forms of industrial organization. The organized workers feel no interest in, but sometimes considerable jealousy of, the work of their more skilful members, in the fear that a dividing line of interests will thus be brought about in their own ranks. Thus we have organized labor arrayed in more or less active opposition to efficiency, and the dividing line between its ranks and the higher industrial organization is to some extent widened instead of closed. It asks for opportunity to develop as a class, rather than for opportunity to become differentiated within the class, and thus disintegrate its present solidarity.

In the past twenty years, during which the present writer has been closely in touch with the higher organization of divers industries, a great change in the spirit of the piece has become manifest. The more progressive employers are awake to the fact that the basic relation on which factory production was originally founded during the so-called industrial revolution, needs alteration. It is unfortunately true that the Trade Unions have not advanced in equal degree. They have very little constructive theory — there is even a tendency in some quarters to revert to earlier types of obstruction, not merely by strikes, but by *sabotage* and wilful damage. No progress can be made that way: for the theory on which such action is based is an anti-social one, and therefore foredoomed to failure.

The true line of development is therefore seen to be some form of organization capable of being applied to existing productive units — since the form of organization obviously controls the *direction* of development — that will not merely allow, but foster, an increasing solidarity of interest between the workers as workers and the higher organization of industry. In this way alone can the eventual democratization of the economic relation be brought about. Such organization can only be developed by experiment, and in its experimental working out, it is important that both organized labor and the higher organization of industry shall be more mutually helpful and less mutually suspicious. That such a development can be successfully attained only by mutual coöperation, and not by paternalism, seems essentially true.

By A. HAMILTON CHURCH
Consulting Industrial Engineer
Taunton, Mass.

OVERHEAD-

182

Every new use of automatic equipment increases the importance of a correct distribution of overhead. Yet industry keeps on striking a meaningless ratio between burden and cost which clouds the picture of the effectiveness of overhead expenditures or their impingement upon processes. Legitimate overhead is no part of the cost of the product. It is the cost of production preparedness.

Mr. Church, in this article, outlines the more modern conception of the true nature of overhead

IF 19 out of 20 executives were to be suddenly asked, "Overhead is the cost of — what?" they would probably frame the definition in terms of product, thus: "Overhead is that part of the cost of product which is neither direct wages nor direct material."

A definition of this kind does not explain the nature of overhead, nor does it give a true picture of the natural relation of overhead to the cost of a product. Under the popular methods of overhead distribution there is, in fact, no real relation between burden and cost. Although a ratio has been struck, it is both accidental and temporary. Nothing has resulted but an arbitrary and misleading mathematical trick. No clear picture is forthcoming as to the effectiveness of overhead expenditures or their impingement on processes. Yet the importance of a correct distribution increases with every gain in the utilization of automatic equipment.

In two books,* published some years ago, I developed the principle that overhead is merely a collective term for several distinct and separate services, each of which has its separate incidence on production, and that it is possible to waste these services as well as to utilize them for actual production. Although this separation of factors which had formerly been lumped into a total was put forward as a practical method of cost-finding rather than as a formal theory, it was a forward step. It has led to the further inference, not then developed, that overhead is not the cost of product, but of something else. *That something is preparedness.*

* "The Proper Distribution of Expense Burden" and "Production Factors." A new and more comprehensive work on "Overhead Expense" has recently been added to the list.

38

If overhead is the collective term for a variety of separate services to production, and if nothing can be included legitimately in overhead that does not so serve production, then it follows that overhead is the sum of expenses incurred to maintain the plant in a condition of preparedness to do process work. Legitimate overhead is the definite cost of a definite amount of standard processing capacity. This cost can be expressed in dollars per hour.

A picture of the nature of overhead is given in Figure 1, which shows a plant with nine processes arranged in four departments. Two of these (B and D) are single-process departments; the others (A and C) have more than one process. If, in a 200-hour month, the aggregate and legitimate cost of services throughout the plant is $5,400, then the cost of maintaining the manufacturing capacity is $27 per hour, though this figure is of no use for cost purposes. Subdivision of this amount by suitable accounting shows that departments B and D have process rates of $4 and $6 per hour respectively, while rates in the other departments range from $1.50 to $4 per hour. Whether working or idle, the cost of the processing capacity remains the same. We may, therefore, picture process dollars dripping from the delivery point of process B at the rate of $4 every hour, and similarly for the others.

Figure 2 exhibits the same facts from another viewpoint. The clock dials show the intervals at which one whole process dollar drips from the delivery points. For process B, this occurs every 15 minutes, for processes 1 and 3 of department A, only every 40 minutes and so on. The drip continues at these rates whether it falls

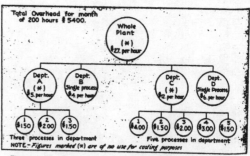

Figure 1. On paper, overhead expenditure looks something like this. Here the total cost of preparedness—in this plant $27 an hour—is split up among departments and processes.

the cost
of production preparedness

onto jobs or not. If no jobs are absorbing the drip, it may be asked, what becomes of it?

Figure 3 shows what happens. One production center or process is figured, which may be any of those in the diagrams. The process is represented by a hopper into which the various services (collectively termed overhead) are flowing evenly for the purpose of maintaining the process in a state of preparedness. From the delivery point, one whole process dollar drips at certain intervals (every 15 minutes if process B is considered). Beneath the delivery point, jobs are pictured as passing at a uniform rate, but these jobs are of different sizes and do not take the same time to pass. Job 1 passes in 30 minutes and therefore absorbs two process dollars; job 2 takes 45 minutes and absorbs three process dollars. But in between jobs 2 and 3 an interval occurs during which the process is idle. During this time, two process dollars will drip into the pool of waste.

This analogy pictures accurately what happens to the money expended for overhead, and indicates graphically the four points whose efficiency we must measure.

Regarding overhead in its true light, these four measures of efficiency are:

(1) The cost of preparedness, or the efficiency of the actual as compared with the possible cost of maintaining a required capacity; (2) the efficiency of utilization, or ratio of the actual to the expected or possible use of this capacity; (3) the efficiency of process time, or of the actual as compared with the possible speed with which any job is done; (4) the efficiency of direct labor, as expressed in earnings.

When processing time is a variable quantity, (3) and (4) are interconnected. These efficiencies will now be considered in more detail.

In the example given, the cost of preparedness, which was $4 per hour, may have been too high. More may be expended by a business for costly equipment or for upkeep of its capacity than is justified by the resultant product. This is the first efficiency. But we cannot measure it so long as the

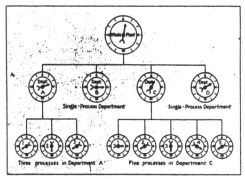

Figure 2. Another view of the true nature of overhead—but from a different angle. The clock dials show the intervals at which process dollars drip from the delivery points.

cost of preparedness is jumbled with other efficiencies into a meaningless total, as is the usual practice.

All calculations of efficiencies are based, necessarily, on some form of standardization. In general a standardized cost, or time, or rate is a *minimum*. It represents the minimum effort, in whatever units it may be reckoned, by which some objective can be attained. Standardization of the cost of preparedness is effected by setting:

(a) Carefully budgeted cost of the various services (factors) which comprise legitimate overhead against

(b) Normal or standard capacity of each department process, measured in actual working hours.

The result will be standard cost of process capacity in standard working hours —that is, a standard process rate. This cost remains standard as long as it is a reproducible efficiency—that is, until permanent alterations in wage rates or material prices which enter overhead take place. Close control over the legitimacy of overhead items is obtained by budgeting factor by factor, and any departure from normal is traced at once.

The effect of variation in (b), the normal capacity, must also be briefly considered. It can be shown that when production is curtailed, as in slack times, standard cost of capacity is unaltered. A sufficient flow of orders restores normal conditions automatically. Though econo-

FOUR EFFICIENCIES OF PRODUCTION

1. The efficiency of preparedness— how does the actual compare with the necessary cost of maintaining a capacity?

2. The efficiency of utilization— how much of the normal capacity is utilized?

3. The efficiency of processing time —is each job done in the shortest possible time?

4. The efficiency of direct labor— are wage costs too high relatively to process cost?

183

mies in overhead may be effected, these are made from that portion which would fall into the pool of waste. It is never possible for them to be carried far enough to reduce process rates. The cost of maintaining what process capacity is actually utilized remains unaltered.

Overtime presents a more complex problem. Here, both budgeted costs, (a), and standard capacity, (b), vary from normal. The variation in (b) is simple. More capacity comes into possible utilization. But with (a) three possible situations arise. The cost of preparedness under overtime conditions may be (1) higher, (2) similar or (3) lower than under normal conditions. This cost depends on the manner in which certain elements of overhead interact.

Long spells of overtime, if unforeseen and therefore not allowed for in the original standardization, require special standardization—that is, special overtime process rates. But if overtime is only a temporary measure, it may be regarded as giving rise to a small net credit or charge to "loss and gain," leaving standard rates unchanged. Ordinarily, no substantial injustice is done by this procedure.

The *second efficiency* is the use of the capacity provided. If the normal capacity is 200 hours per month and only 180 of the hours are utilized, no juggling with figures will recover the $80 which has dripped into the pool of waste in the 20 idle hours. No customer can be persuaded to pay one cent more for the job because of this loss.

Whatever falls into the pool of waste—and it will be seen that not only process dollars but other items do so fall—is no part of the true cost of product. The amount collected in this pool represents a failure to attain 100 per cent efficiency. It is a loss that should not have happened. To attempt to include it in costs is only to deceive oneself and narrow the real margin of profit on the jobs that happen to be going through, to falsify the information on which sales prices are calculated. The only way to deal with this loss is to charge it off to the loss-and-gain account.

Immediately any process stops, not merely does absence of profit appear, but actual out-of-pocket losses begin. It is not idle equipment so much as *wasted preparedness* that is the chief element in these losses. If a department is completely closed down, a number of items of expenditure will still be incurred, but, compared with the items present when the department is being maintained in a condition of full preparedness for work, they will be few and small. On the other hand, in a department which is being maintained in full preparedness for work, the stoppage of any process means inevitably that some of the cost of this preparedness is being expended to no useful purpose. The deliberate curtailment of production and also its extension under overtime conditions are special cases which have been referred to above.

The *third efficiency* of production is that of time of

processing. It is here that costing of the ordinary types usually begins, because the two efficiencies hitherto considered are jumbled together, and some kind of arbitrary ratio struck between their total and that of time on jobs. An imperfect picture of the productive process is obtained in this way. While much attention has been given to the question of incentive, it is doubtful whether the true action of incentive can be perceived until the two first efficiencies are placed on their own bases, so that the cost of preparedness, the utilization of capacity and the actual processing time are all separately known.

Since the cost of process capacity is measured in dollars per hour, the amount absorbed by a job will be strictly proportional to time occupied in passing the delivery point. In some industries, especially machine shops, processing time depends on skill and also on the length of time taken to get the material into place ready for processing. In other industries, these variables are absent. Operation becomes mere feeding of material into machines, and the process is also invariable in speed.

Preparation time and actual processing time are equally chargeable with the cost of maintaining the process in a condition of capacity to do work. If 15 minutes are taken up in setting up the job and 30 minutes in actual processing, then 45 minutes of cost of capacity have been absorbed on the job. The setting up must be regarded as part of the time of processing, because it prevents the utilization of the process for any other purpose.

Shortening the time during which a job takes advantage of the preparedness maintained, has two results. First, less process rate is charged to the job. Second, processing capacity is freed for other jobs. If a process has an hourly rate of $2, and a certain job is worked at 60 minutes, then the process cost of that job will be $2, and 8 jobs will be turned out daily. Now if 12 minutes are saved from processing time, each job will cost only $1.60 for process or burden cost, and 10 such jobs will be put out in an 8-hour day. But if it should happen that, owing to the speeding up of the work, only 8 such jobs could be found, the resulting idleness would wipe out the gain. The jobs would have been done at a lower true cost, but the accompanying waste would cancel the profit made thereby. This result would not be known under any of the more ordinary methods of burden distribution.

We now come to the *fourth efficiency*, that of direct-wage costs. Day wages are based on hours, just as is the cost of processing capacity. Essentially they are two elements of the same cost, namely that of processing time, but they are to be reckoned separately because one is terminable along with the job and the other is not. Piecework, premium and bonus introduce variables that cannot be discussed here.

The point to be noted here is that the cost or efficiency

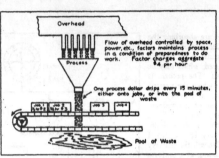

Figure 3. See what happens. Two jobs have passed safely by, each absorbing its share of the dripping dollars. Then an interval and two dollars plunk into the pool of waste!

184

40

is simply the price paid to the operator for a given amount of skill and energy. Consequently, costs will be at a minimum when incentive is sufficient to bring out maximum skill and energy, as measured in minimum time of processing, at as low a price as possible.

The reason why high wages are frequently more economical than lower rates may be inferred if we examine the interplay of processing time, process-rate cost and direct-wage cost. The higher the process rate, the more we can afford to pay out for incentive to reduce processing time. Even though the cost of direct wages per unit of product does not diminish, there will often be an important saving in process-rate cost and therefore in total cost.

Provided that the cost of incentive does not overtake the saving effected in process-rate cost, the operator's earnings are immaterial. Under modern conditions the cost of process capacity, as expressed in a process rate, is often far higher than any operator's wages, but for any given process rate there will be a maximum wage payment, whether this takes the form of day wages,

premium or piecework, beyond which extra incentive is not profitable. But only by properly segregating the first two efficiencies here discussed can this maximum be known with any certainty.

Where work is plentiful, the advantages of quick processing are, as before remarked, not confined to a lowered job or unit cost. Capacity is set free, and this capacity can earn profits. Then, even where the use of incentive did not result in any lower unit cost, it might pay to employ it. The advantage would come from the extra earning power thus set free. But unless the cost of preparedness or process capacity, the efficiency of utilization and the actual hourly rate for each process are known, an attempt to push matters thus far might result in a loss. No percentage or hourly burden method could be trusted for the necessary basic information.

The whole question of what wages may be legitimately paid for specific work can be studied free from all ratios, percentages or other mathematical devices as soon as overhead is recognized to be the cost of manufacturing preparedness—of process capacity and of nothing else.

185